Introduction to Embedded Systems

Introduction to Embedded Systems

Charlie Thomas

STATES
ACADEMIC PRESS
www.statesacademicpress.com

Introduction to Embedded Systems
Charlie Thomas
ISBN: 978-1-63989-304-1 (Hardback)

Published by States Academic Press,
109 South 5th Street,
Brooklyn, NY 11249, USA

Cataloging-in-Publication Data

Introduction to embedded systems / Charlie Thomas.
    p. cm.
Includes bibliographical references and index.
ISBN 978-1-63989-304-1
1. Embedded computer systems. 2. Computer systems.
3. Embedded Internet devices. I. Thomas, Charlie.
TK7895.E42 I58 2022
004.16--dc23

For more information regarding States Academic Press and its products, please visit the publisher's website www.statesacademicpress.com

Table of Contents

Preface

Any combination of a computer processor, computer memory and input/output devices which plays a dedicated role in a much larger electrical or mechanical system is defined as an embedded system. These systems often have real time computing constraints. Embedded systems can range from small and portable devices like digital watches to large and stationary installations such as programmable logic controllers and traffic light controllers. Some of the factors which affect their design and usability include the user interface, processor design and peripherals. Embedded software architectures can be broadly classified into interrupts controlled systems, simple control loop, cooperative multitasking, multithreading, microkernels and monolithic kernels. The various sub-fields of embedded systems along with the technological progress that have future implications are glanced at in this book. It is an essential guide for both academicians and those who wish to pursue this discipline further.

A foreword of all Chapters of the book is provided below:

Chapter 1 - The computer system which is a combination of a computer processor, computer memory, and input/output peripheral devices and which has a dedicated function within a larger mechanical or electrical system is termed as an embedded system. This is an introductory chapter which will introduce briefly all the significant concepts of embedded systems such as number system, logic gates and microcontrollers; Chapter 2 - 8051 microcontroller is an 8-bit microcontroller. Some of the aspects of 8051 microcontroller discussed in this chapter are pin diagram, memory, port configuration, interrupts, etc. This chapter has been carefully written to provide an easy understanding of these facets of 8051 microcontroller; Chapter 3 - The electronic devices used by a computer to perform its work are known as microprocessors. Microprocessors are used to perform the various arithmatic and logic operations of a computer. The topics elaborated in this chapter will help in gaining a better perspective about the different types of microprocessors such as Intel 8085 and Intel 8086; Chapter 4 - An operating system that is made to serve real-time applications, and which processes data without any buffer delays is defined as a real time operating system. This chapter discusses in detail the concepts related to real time operating system such as RTOS design, scheduling and multi-tasking in RTOS, and Windows as RTOS; Chapter 5 - The set of language extensions for the C programming language for addressing the commonality issues between different embedded systems is termed as embedded C. All the diverse concepts of embedded systems in C have been carefully discussed in this chapter.

I would like to thank the entire editorial team who made sincere efforts for this book and my family who supported me in my efforts of working on this book. I take this opportunity to thank all those who have been a guiding force throughout my life.

Charlie Thomas

Understanding Embedded Systems

The computer system which is a combination of a computer processor, computer memory, and input/output peripheral devices and which has a dedicated function within a larger mechanical or electrical system is termed as an embedded system. This is an introductory chapter which will introduce briefly all the significant concepts of embedded systems such as number system, logic gates and microcontrollers.

Number System

There are several number systems which we normally use, such as decimal, binary, octal, hexadecimal, etc. Amongst them we are most familiar with the decimal number system. These systems are classified according to the values of the base of the number system. The number system having the value of the base as 10 is called a decimal number system, whereas that with a base of 2 is called a binary number system. Likewise, the number systems having base 8 and 16 are called octal and hexadecimal number systems respectively. With a decimal system we have 10 different digits, which are 0, 1, 2, 3, 4, 5, 6, 7, 8, and 9. But a binary system has only 2 different digits: 0 and 1. Hence, a binary number cannot have any digit other than 0 or 1. So to deal with a binary number system is quite easier than a decimal system. Now, in a digital world, we can think in binary nature, e.g., a light can be either off or on. There is no state in between these two. So we generally use the binary system when we deal with the digital world. Here comes the utility of a binary system. We can express everything in the world with the help of only two digits i.e., 0 and 1. For example, if we want to express 2510 in binary we may write 11001_2. The right most digit in a number system is called the 'Least Significant Bit' (LSB) or 'Least Significant Digit' (LSD). And the left most digit in a number system is called the 'Most Significant Bit' (MSB) or 'Most Significant Digit' (MSD). Now normally when we deal with different number systems we specify the base as the subscript to make it clear which number system is being used.

In an octal number system there are 8 digits 0, 1, 2, 3, 4, 5, 6, and 7. Hence, any octal number cannot have any digit greater than 7. Similarly, a hexadecimal number system has 16 digits 0 to 9 and the rest of the six digits are specified by letter symbols as A, B, C, D, E, and F. Here A, B, C, D, E, and F represent decimal 10, 11, 12, 13, 14, and 15 respectively. Octal and hexadecimal codes are useful to write assembly level language. In general, we can express any number in any base or radix "X." Any number with base X, having n digits to the left and m digits to the right of the decimal point, can be expressed as:

$$a_n X^{n-1} + a_{n-1} X^{n-2} + a_{n-2} X^{n-3} + \ldots + a_2 X^1 + a_1 X^0 + b_1 X^{-1} + b_2 X^{-2} + \ldots + b_m X^{-m}$$

where a_n is the digit in the nth position. The coefficient a_n is termed as the MSD or Most Significant Digit and b_m is termed as the LSD or the Least Significant Digit.

Conversion between Number Systems

It is often required to convert a number in a particular number system to any other number system, e.g., it may be required to convert a decimal number to binary or octal or hexadecimal. The reverse is also true, i.e., a binary number may be converted into decimal and so on.

1. Decimal-to-binary Conversion: Now to convert a number in decimal to a number in binary we have to divide the decimal number by 2 repeatedly, until the quotient of zero is obtained. This method of repeated division by 2 is called the 'double-dabble' method. The remainders are noted down for each of the division steps. Then the column of the remainder is read in reverse order i.e., from bottom to top order.

Example: Convert $(26)_{10}$ into a binary number.

Solution:

Division	Quotient	Generated remainder
$\dfrac{26}{2}$	13	0
$\dfrac{13}{2}$	6	1
$\dfrac{6}{2}$	3	0
$\dfrac{3}{2}$	1	1
$\dfrac{1}{2}$	0	1

Hence the converted binary number is $(11010)_2$.

2. Decimal-to-octal Conversion: Similarly, to convert a number in decimal to a number in octal we have to divide the decimal number by 8 repeatedly, until the quotient of zero is obtained. This method of repeated division by 8 is called 'octal-dabble.' The remainders are noted down for each of the division steps. Then the column of the remainder is read from bottom to top order, just as in the case of the double-dabble method.

Example: Convert $(426)_{10}$ into an octal number.

Solution:

Division	Quotient	Generated remainder
$\dfrac{426}{8}$	53	2

$\dfrac{53}{8}$	6	5
$\dfrac{6}{8}$	0	6

Hence the converted octal number is $(652)_8$.

3. Decimal-to-hexadecimal Conversion: The same steps are repeated to convert a number in decimal to a number in hexadecimal. Only here we have to divide the decimal number by 16 repeatedly, until the quotient of zero is obtained. This method of repeated division by 16 is called 'hexdabble.' The remainders are noted down for each of the division steps. Then the column of the remainder is read from bottom to top order as in the two previous cases.

Example: Convert $(348)_{10}$ into a hexadecimal number.

Solution:

Division	Quotient	Generated remainder
$\dfrac{348}{16}$	21	12
$\dfrac{21}{16}$	1	5
$\dfrac{1}{16}$	0	1

Hence the converted hexadecimal number is $(15C)_{16}$.

4. Binary-to-decimal Conversion: Now we discuss the reverse method, i.e., the method of conversion of binary, octal, or hexadecimal numbers to decimal numbers. Now we have to keep in mind that each of the binary, octal, or hexadecimal number system is a positional number system, i.e., each of the digits in the number systems discussed above has a positional weight as in the case of the decimal system.

Example: Convert $(10110)_2$ into a decimal number.

Solution: The binary number given is   1 0 1 1 0

        Positional weights   4 3 2 1 0

The positional weights for each of the digits are written in italics below each digit. Hence the decimal equivalent number is given as:

$1 \times 2^4 + 0 \times 2^3 + 1 \times 2^2 + 1 \times 2^1 + 0 \times 2^0$

$= 16 + 0 + 4 + 2 + 0$

$= (22)_{10}.$

Hence we find that here, for the sake of conversion, we have to multiply each bit with its positional weights depending on the base of the number system.

5. Octal-to-decimal Conversion:

Example: Convert 3462_8 into a decimal number.

Solution: The octal number given is   3 4 6 2

$\qquad\qquad$ Positional weights $\qquad$ 3 2 1 0

The positional weights for each of the digits are written in italics below each digit. Hence the decimal equivalent number is given as:

$$3 \times 8^3 + 4 \times 8^2 + 6 \times 8^1 + 2 \times 8^0$$

$$= 1536 + 256 + 48 + 2$$

$$= (1842)_{10}.$$

6. Hexadecimal-to-decimal Conversion:

Example: Convert $42AD_{16}$ into a decimal number.

Solution: The hexadecimal number given is   4 2 A D

$\qquad\qquad$ Positional weights $\qquad\qquad$ 3 2 1 0

The positional weights for each of the digits are written in italics below each digit. Hence the decimal equivalent number is given as:

$$4 \times 16^3 + 2 \times 16^2 + 10 \times 16^1 + 13 \times 16^0$$

$$= 16384 + 512 + 160 + 13$$

$$= (17069)_{10}.$$

7. Fractional Conversion: So far we have dealt with the conversion of integer numbers only. Now if the number contains the fractional part we have to deal in a different way when converting the number from a different number system (i.e., binary, octal, or hexadecimal) to a decimal number system or vice versa. We illustrate this with examples.

Example: Convert 1010.011_2 into a decimal number.

Solution: The binary number given is 1 0 1 0 . 0 1 1

$\qquad\qquad$ Positional weights $\qquad$ 3 2 1 0 -1 -2 -3

The positional weights for each of the digits are written in italics below each digit. Hence the decimal equivalent number is given as:

$$1 \times 2^3 + 0 \times 2^2 + 1 \times 2^1 + 0 \times 2^0 + 0 \times 2^{-1} + 1 \times 2^{-2} + 1 \times 2^{-3}$$

$$= 8 + 0 + 2 + 0 + 0 + 0.25 + 0.125$$

$$= (10.375)_{10}.$$

Example: Convert 362.35_8 into a decimal number.

Solution: The octal number given is 3 6 2. 3 5

        Positional weights   2 1 0 -1 -2

The positional weights for each of the digits are written in italics below each digit. Hence the decimal equivalent number is given as:

$3 \times 8^2 + 6 \times 8^1 + 2 \times 8^0 + 3 \times 8^{-1} + 5 \times 8^{-2}$

$= 192 + 48 + 2 + 0.375 + 0.078125$

$= (242.453125)_{10}.$

Example: Convert $42A.12_{16}$ into a decimal number.

Solution: The hexadecimal number given is 4 2 A. 1 2

        Positional weights   2 1 0 -1 -2

The positional weights for each of the digits are written in italics below each digit. Hence the decimal equivalent number is given as:

$4 \times 16^2 + 2 \times 16^1 + 10 \times 16^0 + 1 \times 16^{-1} + 1 \times 16^{-2}$

$= 1024 + 32 + 10 + 0.0625 + 0.00390625$

$= (1066.06640625)_{10}.$

Example: Convert 25.625_{10} into a binary number.

Solution:

Division	Quotient	Generated remainder
$\dfrac{25}{2}$	12	1
$\dfrac{12}{2}$	6	0
$\dfrac{6}{2}$	3	0
$\dfrac{3}{2}$	1	1
$\dfrac{1}{2}$	0	1

Therefore, $(25)_{10} = (11001)_2.$

Fractional Part:

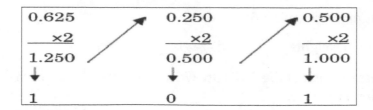

i.e., $(0.625)_{10} = (0.101)_2$

Therefore, $(25.625)_{10} = (11001.101)_2$

8. Conversion from a Binary to Octal Number and Vice Versa: The maximum digit in an octal number system is 7, which can be represented as 111_2 in a binary system. Hence, starting from the LSB, we group three digits at a time and replace them by the decimal equivalent of those groups and we get the final octal number.

Example: Convert 101101010_2 into an equivalent octal number.

Solution: The binary number given is 101101010

Starting with LSB and grouping 3 bits 101 101 010

Octal equivalent   5   5   2

hence the octal equivalent number is $(552)_8$.

Example: Convert 1011110_2 into an equivalent octal number.

Solution: The binary number given is 1011110

Starting with LSB and grouping 3 bits 001 011 110

Octal equivalent   1   3   6

hence the octal equivalent number is $(136)_8$.

Since at the time of grouping the three digits in Example 1.14 starting from the LSB, we find that the third group cannot be completed, since only one 1 is left out in the third group, so we complete the group by adding two 0s in the MSB side. This is called left padding of the number with 0. Now if the number has a fractional part then there will be two different classes of groups—one for the integer part starting from the left of the decimal point and proceeding toward the left and the second one starting from the right of the decimal point and proceeding toward the right. If, for the second class, any 1 is left out, we complete the group by adding two 0s on the right side. This is called right-padding.

Example: Convert 1101.0111_2 into an equivalent octal number.

Solution: The binary number given is 1101.0111

Grouping 3 bits   001   101   011   100

Octal equivalent: 1   5   3   4

hence the octal number is $(15.34)_8$.

Now if the octal number is given and you're asked to convert it into its binary equivalent, then each octal digit is converted into a 3-bit-equivalent binary number and combining all those digits we get the final binary equivalent.

Example: Convert 235_8 into an equivalent binary number.

Solution: The octal number given is   2   3   5

3-bit binary equivalent   010 011 101

hence the binary number is $(010011101)_2$.

Example: Convert 47.321_8 into an equivalent binary number.

Solution: The octal number given is   4   7   3   2   1

3-bit binary equivalent   100 111 011 010 001

hence the binary number is $(100111.011010001)_2$.

9. Conversion from a Binary to Hexadecimal Number and Vice Versa: The maximum digit in a hexadecimal system is 15, which can be represented by 1111_2 in a binary system. Hence, starting from the LSB, we group four digits at a time and replace them with the hexadecimal equivalent of those groups and we get the final hexadecimal number.

Example: Convert 11010110_2 into an equivalent hexadecimal number.

Solution: The binary number given is 11010110

Starting with LSB and grouping 4 bits 1101 0110

Hexadecimal equivalent   D   6

hence the hexadecimal equivalent number is $(D6)_{16}$.

Example: Convert 110011110_2 into an equivalent hexadecimal number.

Solution: The binary number given is 110011110

Starting with LSB and grouping 4 bits 0001 1001 1110

Hexadecimal equivalent   1   9   E

hence the hexadecimal equivalent number is $(19E)_{16}$.

Since at the time of grouping of four digits starting from the LSB, in Example 1.19 we find that the third group cannot be completed, since only one 1 is left out, so we complete the group by adding three 0s to the MSB side. Now if the number has a fractional part, as in the case of octal numbers, then there will be two different classes of groups—one for the integer part starting from the left of the decimal point and proceeding toward the left and the second one starting from the right of the decimal point and proceeding toward the right. If, for the second class, any uncompleted group is left out, we complete the group by adding 0s on the right side.

Example: Convert 111011.011_2 into an equivalent hexadecimal number.

Solution: The binary number given is 111011.011

Grouping 4 bits 0011 1011. 0110

Hexadecimal equivalent   3   B   6

Hence the hexadecimal equivalent number is $(3B.6)_{16}$.

Now if the hexadecimal number is given and you're asked to convert it into its binary equivalent, then each hexadecimal digit is converted into a 4-bit-equivalent binary number and by combining all those digits we get the final binary equivalent.

Example: Convert $29C_{16}$ into an equivalent binary number.

Solution: The hexadecimal number given is 2 9 C

4-bit binary equivalent 0010 1001 1100

Hence the equivalent binary number is $(001010011100)_2$.

Example: Convert $9E.AF2_{16}$ into an equivalent binary number.

Solution: The hexadecimal number given is 9 E A F 2

4-bit binary equivalent 1001 1110 1010 1111 0010

Hence the equivalent binary number is $(10011110.101011110010)_2$.

10. Conversion from an Octal to Hexadecimal Number and Vice Versa: Conversion from octal to hexadecimal and vice versa is sometimes required. To convert an octal number into a hexadecimal number the following steps are to be followed:

- First convert the octal number to its binary equivalent.

- Then form groups of 4 bits, starting from the LSB.

- Then write the equivalent hexadecimal number for each group of 4 bits.

Similarly, for converting a hexadecimal number into an octal number the following steps are to be followed:

- First convert the hexadecimal number to its binary equivalent.

- Then form groups of 3 bits, starting from the LSB.

- Then write the equivalent octal number for each group of 3 bits.

Example: Convert the following hexadecimal numbers into equivalent octal numbers.

(a) A72E (b) 4.BF85

Solution:

(a) Given hexadecimal number is A 7 2 E

Binary equivalent is 1010 0111 0010 1110 = 1010011100101110

Forming groups of 3 bits from the LSB 001 010 011 100 101 110

Octal equivalent   1   2   3   4   5   6

hence the octal equivalent of $(A72E)_{16}$ is $(123456)_8$.

(b) Given hexadecimal number is 4 B F 8 5

    Binary equivalent is 0100 1011 1111 1000 0101 = 0100.1011111110000101

Forming groups of 3 bits 100 101 111 111 000 010 100

Octal equivalent   4   5   7   7   0   2   4

hence the octal equivalent of $(4.BF85)_{16}$ is $(4.577024)_8$.

Example: Convert $(247)_8$ into an equivalent hexadecimal number.

Solution: Given octal number is 2   4   7

      Binary equivalent is   010 100 111 = 010100111

Forming groups of 4 bits from the LSB 1010 0111

Hexadecimal equivalent   A   7

hence the hexadecimal equivalent of $(247)_8$ is $(A7)_{16}$.

Example: Convert $(36.532)_8$ into an equivalent hexadecimal number.

Solution: Given octal number is 3   6   5   3   2

       Binary equivalent is   011 110 101 011 010=011110.101011010

Forming groups of 4 bits 0001 1110. 1010 1101

Hexadecimal equivalent   1   E.   A   D

hence the hexadecimal equivalent of $(36.532)_8$ is $(1E.AD)_{16}$.

Binary Arithmetic

Binary Addition: The four basic rules for adding binary digits (bits) are as follows:

       0 + 0 = 0 Sum of 0 with a carry 0

       0 + 1 = 1 Sum of 1 with a carry 0

1 + 0 = 1 Sum of 1 with a carry 0

1 + 1 = 1 0 Sum of 0 with a carry 1

Examples:

110	6	111	7	1111	15
+ 100	+ 4	+ 011	+ 3	+ 1100	+ 12
1010	10	1010	10	11011	27

Binary Subtraction: The four basic rules for subtracting are as follows:

0 − 0 = 0

1 − 1 = 0

1 − 0 = 1

0 − 1 = 1 0 − 1 with a borrow of 1

Examples:

11	3	11	3	101
− 01	− 1	− 10	− 2	− 011
10	2	01	1	010

5	110	6	101101	45
− 3	− 101	− 5	− 001110	− 14
2	001	1	011111	31

1's And 2's Complement of Binary Number: The 1's complement and the 2's complement of binary number are important because they permit the representation of negative numbers.

Binary Number 1 0 1 1 0 0 1 0
             ↓ ↓ ↓ ↓ ↓ ↓ ↓ ↓
1'sComplement 0 1 0 0 1 1 0 1

2's Complement of a binary number is found by adding 1 to the LSB of the 1's Complement. 2's Complement= (1's Complement) + 1

Binary number	10110010
1'scomplement	01001101
Add 1	+ 1
2's complement	01001110

Logic Gates

All digital electronic circuits and microprocessor based systems contain hardware elements called Digital Logic Gates that perform the logical operations of AND, OR and NOT on binary numbers. In digital logic only two voltage levels or states are allowed and these states are generally referred to as Logic "1" or Logic "0", High or Low, True or False and which are represented in Boolean Algebra and Truth Tables by the numbers "1" and "0" respectively. A good example of a digital logic level is a simple light as it is "ON" or "OFF". Logic operations can be performed using any non-linear device that has at least two distinct regions of operation. Obvious choices for the electrical engineer are the semiconductor diode and the bipolar junction transistor. Particular voltage levels are assigned to logic levels 0 and 1. While many voltage level assignments are possible, one common assignment is:

logic 1 (HIGH)---- ~ 5 V

logic 0 (LOW) ---- ~ 0 V.

This is known as "Positive logic" system. There is also a complementary "Negative Logic" system in which the values and the rules of a logic "0" and a logic "1" are reversed. But, unless stated otherwise, we shall only refer to the Positive Logic convention for all the experiments. It is important to note that noise, power source fluctuations, loading by other circuits, and other factors will cause the logic level voltages to vary over some range.

Simple Basic Digital Logic Gates

Simple digital logic gates can be made by combining transistors, diodes and resistors as discrete components. Let us investigate some of such circuits using Diode-Resistor Logic (DRL), Diode-Transistor Logic (DTL) and Transistor-Transistor Logic (TTL).

Diode-Resistor Logic (DRL)

Diode logic gates use diodes to perform OR and AND logic functions as shown in the circuit diagram. Connection of the LED at the output is optional which simply displays the logical state of the output, i.e. the logic state of output is 0 or 1, if LED is off or on, respectively. Diodes have the property of easily passing an electrical current in one direction, but not the other. Thus, diodes can act as a logical switch. Diode logic gates are very simple and inexpensive, and can be used effectively in limited space. However, they cannot be used extensively due to the obvious logic level shift when gates are connected in series. In addition, they cannot perform a NOT function, so their usefulness is quite limited. This type of logic circuit is rarely found in integrated form.

Circuit Components/Equipments

- Resistors (1KΩ, 3 Nos; 10KΩ, 1 No.),
- 1N914 diodes or equivalent (2 Nos.),
- A Surface mount dip switch,

- D.C. Power supply (5V),
- A Red/Green LED,
- Connecting wires,
- Breadboard.

Circuit Diagram

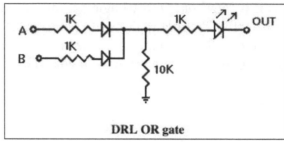

DRL OR gate

Figure: DRL OR gate.

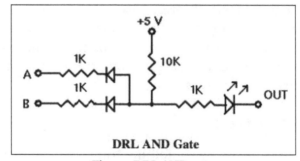

DRL AND Gate

Figure: DRL AND gate.

Procedure

- Assemble the circuit on your breadboard for OR/AND operation.
- Turn on power to your experimental circuit.
- Apply all four possible combinations of inputs at A and B from the power supply using dip switch.
- For each input combination, note the logic state of the output, Q, as indicated by the LED (ON = 1; OFF = 0), and record that result in the table.
- Compare your results with the truth table of a logic "OR"/ "AND" operation.
- When you have completed your observations, turn off the power to your experimental circuit.

Truth Tables

Logic "OR" operation			Logic "AND" operation		
A	B	Q = A + B	A	B	Q = A.B
0	0	0	0	0	0

0	1	1	0	1	0
1	0	1	1	0	0
1	1	1	1	1	1

(I) DRL OR gate:

Input		Output
A	B	Q = A+B
0	0	
0	1	
1	0	
1	1	

(II) DRL AND gate:

Input		Output
A	B	Q = A.B
0	0	
0	1	
1	0	
1	1	

Diode-Transistor Logic (DTL)

The simple 2-input Diode-Resistor gate can be converted into a NAND/NOR universal gate by the addition of a single transistor inverting (NOT) stage employing DTL. Diode Transistor Logic, or DTL, refers to the technology for designing and fabricating digital circuits wherein logic gates employ diodes in the input stage and bipolar junction transistors at the output stage. The output BJT switches between its cut-off and saturation regions to create logic 1 and 0, respectively. The logic level shift problem of DRL gates is not present in DTL and TTL gates so that gates may be connected in series indefinitely. If a gate drives several similar gates in parallel problems may occur: the maximum number of gates that can be driven in parallel is identified as the "fanout" of a gate. DTL offers better noise margins and greater fan-outs than RTL (Resistor- Transistor Logic), but suffers from low speed, especially in comparison to TTL. Diodes take up far less room than resistors, and can be constructed easily. In addition, the internal resistance of a diode is small when the diode is forward biased, thus allowing for faster switching action. As a result, gates built with diodes in place of most resistors can operate at higher frequencies. Because of this diode-transistor logic (DTL) rapidly replaced RTL in most digital applications.

DTL Inverter Circuit

The DTL inverter uses a transistor and a collector load resistor as shown in the circuit diagram. The input is connected through a pair of diodes in series with the base of the transistor. The diode connected directly to the transistor base serves to raise the input voltage required to turn the transistor on to about 1.3 to 1.4 volts. Any input voltage below this threshold will hold the transistor off. The base resistor is also connected which should be sufficient to turn the transistor on and off quickly thus enabling higher switching speeds.

Circuit Components/Equipments

- Resistors (1K 2 Nos., 4.7K; 1 No.),
- 1N914/1N4148 silicon diodes (2 Nos.),
- 2N4124 NPN silicon transistor (1 No.),
- A Surface mount dip switch,
- D.C. Power supply (5V),
- A Red/Green LED,
- Connecting wires,
- Breadboard.

Circuit Diagram

DTL NAND Circuit

The DTL NAND gate combines the DTL inverter with a simple Diode-Resistor Logic (DRL) AND gate as shown in its circuit diagram. Thus, any number of inputs can be added simply by adding input diodes to the circuit. The problem of signal degradation caused by Diode Logic is overcome by the transistor, which amplifies the signal while inverting it. This means DTL gates can be cascaded to any required extent, without losing the digital signal.

Circuit Components

- All the components from the DTL Inverter circuit.
- 1N914/1N4148 silicon diodes (1No.,in addition to the previous two).

Circuit Diagram

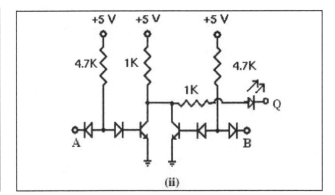

DTL NOR Circuit

Similar to DTL NAND circuit one can construct the NOR gate by using a DRL OR gate followed by a transistor inverter, as shown in circuit diagram (1) One can also construct a DTL NOR more elegantly by combining multiple DTL inverters with a common output as shown in the schematic diagram (ii) Any number of inverters may be combined in this fashion to allow the required number of inputs to the NOR gate.

Circuit Components

- All the components from the DTL Inverter circuit, except power supply and 4.7 K resistor.

- 1N914/1N4148 silicon diodes (1No., in addition to the previous two) or All the components from the DTL Inverter circuit.

- 1N914/1N4148 silicon diodes (2Nos., in addition to the previous two).

- 2N4124 NPN silicon transistor (1No., in addition to the previous one).

Circuit Diagram

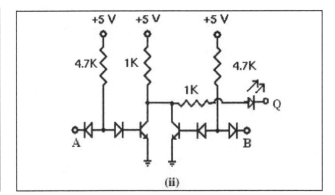

Procedure

- Assemble the circuit on your breadboard for NOT/NAND/NOR operation. First, start with the inverter circuit. Keep this circuit in tact after finishing the inverter experiment. The rest two circuits can be constructed by just adding extra components to the inverter circuit.

- Turn on power to your experimental circuit.

- Apply all four possible combinations of inputs at A and B from the power supply using dip switch.

- For each input combination, note the logic state of the output, Q, as indicated by the LED (ON = 1; OFF = 0), and record that result in the table.

- Compare your results with the truth table of a logic NOT/NAND/NOR operation.

- When you have completed your observations, turn off the power supply.

Truth Tables

Logic "NOT" operation		Logic "NOR" operation			Logic "NAND" operation		
A	Q = A'	A	B	Q = (A+B)'	A	B	Q = (A.B)'
0	1	0	0	1	0	0	1
1	0	0	1	0	0	1	1
		1	0	0	1	0	1
		1	1	0	1	1	0

(I) DTL NOT gate:

Input A	Output Q = A'
0	
1	

(II) DTL NOR gate:

Input		Output
A	B	Q = (A + B)'
0	0	
0	1	
1	0	
1	1	

(III) DTL NAND gate:

Input		Output
A	B	Q = (A.B)'
0	0	
0	1	
1	0	
1	1	

Transistor-Transistor Logic (TTL)

Transistor-transistor logic uses bipolar transistors in the input and output stages. TTL is commonly found in relatively low speed applications. Thus before using commercial ICs that uses TTL, let's first understand the circuit in discrete form.

TTL Inverter Circuit

Looking at the DTL inverter circuit, one can note that the two diodes are opposed to each other in direction. That is, their P-type anodes are connected together and to the pull-up resistor, while one cathode is the signal input and the other is connected to the transistor's base. Thus, one can replace these two diodes with a single NPN transistor as shown in the circuit diagram. This makes lot of sense owing to the fact that the amount of space required by a transistor in an IC is essentially the same as the space required by a diode and by eliminating the space required by one diode at the same time.

Circuit Components/Equipments

- 2N4124 NPN silicon transistors (2 Nos.),
- Resistors (1K, 2 Nos.; 4.7K 1 No.),
- A Surface mount dip switch,
- D.C. Power supply (5V),
- A Red/Green LED,
- Connecting wires,
- Breadboard.

Circuit Diagram

TTL NOR Circuit

TTL integrated circuits provide multiple inputs to NAND gates by designing transistors with multiple emitters on the chip. Unfortunately, we can't very well simulate that on a breadboard socket. However, a NOR gate can be designed using an extra inverter transistors just as in the case of DTL NOR gate.

Circuit Components/Equipments

- All the components of TTL inverter circuit,
- 2N4124 NPN silicon transistors (2Nos),
- 4.7K resistor (1 No.).

Circuit Diagram

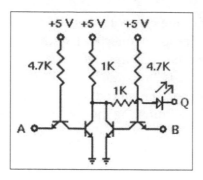

Procedure

- Assemble the circuit on your breadboard for TTL NOT/NOR operation. First, start with the inverter circuit. Keep this circuit in tact to use it further in NOR circuit.

- Turn on power to your experimental circuit. Apply all four possible combinations of inputs at A and B from the power supply using dip switch.

- For each input combination, note the logic state of the output, Q, as indicated by the LED (ON = 1; OFF = 0), and record that result in the table.

- Compare your results with the truth table of a logic NOT/NOR operation.

- When you have completed your observations, turn off the power supply.

Truth Tables

Logic "NOT" operation:

A	Q = A'
0	1
1	0

Logic "NOR" operation:

A	B	Q = (A + B)'
0	0	1
0	1	0
1	0	0
1	1	0

(I) TTL NOT gate:

Input A	Output Q = A'
0	
1	

(II) TTL NOR gate:

Input		Output
A	B	Q = (A + B)'
0	0	
0	1	
1	0	
1	1	

Boolean Logic Operations using Digital ICs

Standard commercially available Digital Logic Gates are available in two basic forms, TTL which stands for Transistor-Transistor Logic such as the 7400 series, and CMOS which stands for Complementary Metal-Oxide-Silicon which is the 4000 series of Integrated Circuits, (IC) or "chips" as it is commonly called. Generally speaking, TTL IC's use NPN type Bipolar Junction Transistors while CMOS IC's use Field Effect Transistors or FET's for both their input and output circuitry. There are a large variety of logic gate types in both the Bipolar and CMOS families of digital logic gates such as 74L, 74LS, 74ALS, 74HC, 74HCT, 74ACT etc, with each one having its own distinct advantages and disadvantages and the exact voltages required to produce a logic "0" or logic "1" depends upon the specific logic group or family. However, when using a standard +5 volt supply any TTL voltage input between 2.0V and 5V is considered to be a logic "1" or "HIGH" while any voltage input below 0.8v is recognized as a logic "0" or "LOW". TTL outputs are typically restricted to narrower limits of between 0 V and 0.4 V for a "low" and between 2.7 V and 5 V. The voltage region between the maximum voltage of logic "0" and minimum voltage of logic "1" of either input or output is called the Indeterminate Region. CMOS logic uses a different level of voltages with a logic "1" level operating between 3 and 15 volts.

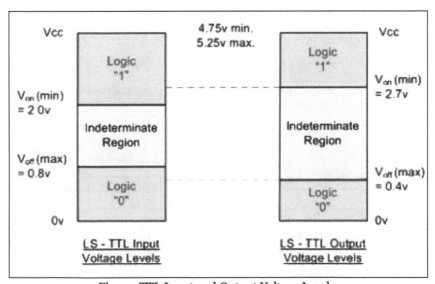

Figure: TTL Input and Output Voltage Levels.

There are several simple gates that you need to learn about. With these simple gates you can build combinations that will implement any digital component you can imagine.

- The simplest possible gate is called an "inverter," or a NOT gate. It takes one bit as input and produces output as its opposite. The logic table for NOT gate and its symbol are shown below:

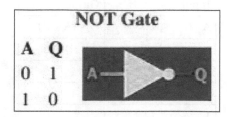

- The AND gate performs a logical "and" operation on two inputs, A and B:

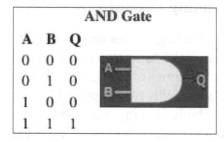

- The OR gate performs a logical "or" operation on two inputs, A and B:

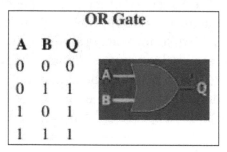

- It is quite common to recognize two others as well: the NAND and the NOR gate. These two gates are simply combinations of an AND or an OR gate with a NOT gate.

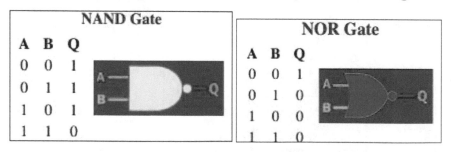

- The final two gates that are sometimes added to the list are the XOR and XNOR gates, also known as "exclusive or" and "exclusive nor" gates, respectively.

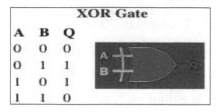

XNOR Gate		
A	**B**	**Q**
0	0	1
0	1	0
1	0	0
1	1	1

Circuit Components/Equipments

- Digital ICs,
- Resistors,
- DIP switch,
- D.C. Power supply (5V),
- LEDs,
- Breadboard,
- Connecting wires.

Circuit Diagrams

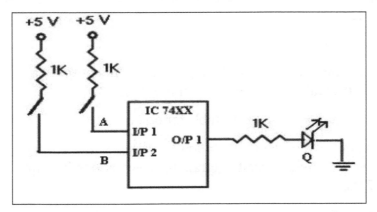

De morgan's law:

$$\overline{(A + B)} = \overline{A} \cdot \overline{B}$$

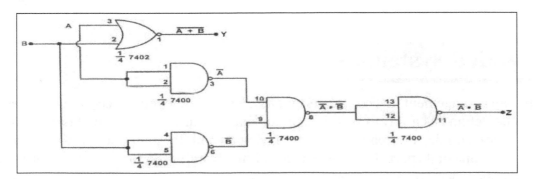

De morgan's law:

$$\overline{(A \cdot B)} = \overline{A} + \overline{B}$$

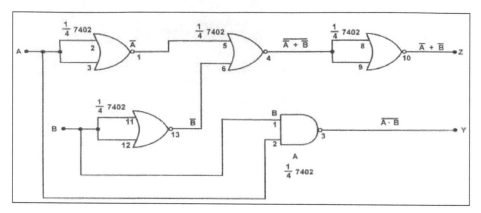

Procedure

- Place the IC on the breadboard.

- Connect pin 14 (VCC) to 5V and pin 7 (ground) to 0V terminal of the power supply.

- Following the general circuit diagram facilitate all possible combinations of inputs from the power supply, using dip switch and resistors. Connect the output pin to ground through a resistor and LED.

- Turn on power to your experimental circuit.

- For each input combination, note the logic state of the outputs as indicated by the LEDs (ON = 1; OFF = 0), and record the result in the table.

- Compare your results with the truth table for operation.

- For verification of De Morgan's laws, follow the respective circuit diagrams using appropriate ICs. Follow the general circuit diagram for connections for input and output using dip switch and LEDs.

- Monitor the outputs Y and Z using LEDs and confirm that Y and Z are the same for any states of A and B.

- When you are done, turn off the power to your experimental circuit.

Embedded Systems

A system is an arrangement in which all its unit assemble work together according to a set of rules. It can also be defined as a way of working, organizing or doing one or many tasks according to a fixed plan. For example, a watch is a time displaying system. Its components follow a set of rules to show time. If one of its parts fails, the watch will stop working. So we can say, in a system, all its subcomponents depend on each other.

As its name suggests, Embedded means something that is attached to another thing. An embedded system can be thought of as a computer hardware system having software embedded in it. An embedded system can be an independent system or it can be a part of a large system. An embedded system is a microcontroller or microprocessor based system which is designed to perform a specific task. For example, a fire alarm is an embedded system; it will sense only smoke. An embedded system has three components:

- It has hardware.

- It has application software.

- It has Real Time Operating system (RTOS) that supervises the application software and provide mechanism to let the processor run a process as per scheduling by following a plan to control the latencies. RTOS defines the way the system works. It sets the rules during the execution of application program. A small scale embedded system may not have RTOS.

So we can define an embedded system as a microcontroller based, software driven, reliable, real-time control system.

Characteristics of an Embedded System

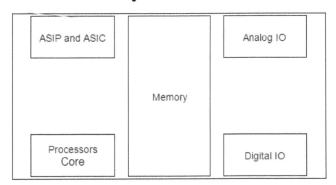

- Single-functioned: An embedded system usually performs a specialized operation and does the same repeatedly. For example: A pager always functions as a pager.

- Tightly constrained: All computing systems have constraints on design metrics, but those on an embedded system can be especially tight. Design metrics is a measure of an implementation's features such as its cost, size, power, and performance. It must be of a size to fit on a single chip, must perform fast enough to process data in real time and consume minimum power to extend battery life.

- Reactive and Real time: Many embedded systems must continually react to changes in the system's environment and must compute certain results in real time without any delay. Consider an example of a car cruise controller; it continually monitors and reacts to speed and brake sensors. It must compute acceleration or deaccelerations repeatedly within a limited time; a delayed computation can result in failure to control of the car.

- Microprocessors based: It must be microprocessor or microcontroller based.

- Memory: It must have a memory, as its software usually embeds in ROM. It does not need any secondary memories in the computer.

- Connected: It must have connected peripherals to connect input and output devices.
- HW-SW systems: Software is used for more features and flexibility. Hardware is used for performance and security.

Advantages

- Easily Customizable,
- Low power consumption,
- Low cost,
- Enhanced performance.

Disadvantages

- High development effort,
- Larger time to market.

Basic Structure of an Embedded System

The following illustration shows the basic structure of an embedded system:

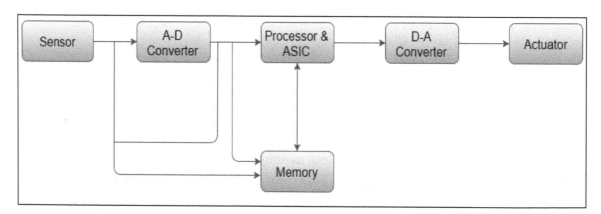

- Sensor: It measures the physical quantity and converts it to an electrical signal which can be read by an observer or by any electronic instrument like an A2D converter. A sensor stores the measured quantity to the memory.

- A-D Converter: An analog-to-digital converter converts the analog signal sent by the sensor into a digital signal.

- Processor & ASICs: Processors process the data to measure the output and store it to the memory.

- D-A Converter: A digital-to-analog converter converts the digital data fed by the processor to analog data.

- Actuator: An actuator compares the output given by the D-A Converter to the actual (expected) output stored in it and stores the approved output.

Embedded Systems – Processors

Processor is the heart of an embedded system. It is the basic unit that takes inputs and produces an output after processing the data. For an embedded system designer, it is necessary to have the knowledge of both microprocessors and microcontrollers.

Processors in a System

A processor has two essential units:

- Program Flow Control Unit (CU).

- Execution Unit (EU).

The CU includes a fetch unit for fetching instructions from the memory. The EU has circuits that implement the instructions pertaining to data transfer operation and data conversion from one form to another. The EU includes the Arithmetic and Logical Unit (ALU) and also the circuits that execute instructions for a program control task such as interrupt, or jump to another set of instructions. A processor runs the cycles of fetch and executes the instructions in the same sequence as they are fetched from memory.

Types of Processors

Processors can be of the following categories:

1. General Purpose Processor (GPP):

- Microprocessor

- Microcontroller

- Embedded Processor

- Digital Signal Processor

- Media Processor

2. Application Specific System Processor (ASSP).

3. Application Specific Instruction Processors (ASIPs).

4. GPP core(s) or ASIP core(s) on either an Application Specific Integrated Circuit (ASIC) or a Very Large Scale Integration (VLSI) circuit.

Microprocessor

A microprocessor is a single VLSI chip having a CPU. In addition, it may also have other units such as coaches, floating point processing arithmetic unit, and pipelining units that help in faster processing of instructions. Earlier generation microprocessors' fetch-and-execute cycle was guided by a clock frequency of order of ~1 MHz. Processors now operate at a clock frequency of 2GHz.

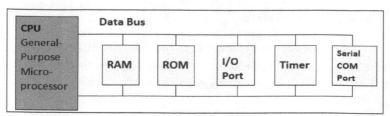

Figure: A Simple Block Diagram of a Microprocessor.

Microcontroller

A microcontroller is a single-chip VLSI unit (also called microcomputer) which, although having limited computational capabilities, possesses enhanced input/output capability and a number of on-chip functional units.

CPU	RAM	ROM
I/O Port	Timer	Serial COM Port

Microcontrollers are particularly used in embedded systems for real-time control applications with on-chip program memory and devices.

Microprocessor Vs. Microcontroller

Let us now take a look at the most notable differences between a microprocessor and a microcontroller.

Microprocessor	Microcontroller
Microprocessors are multitasking in nature. Can perform multiple tasks at a time. For example, on computer we can play music while writing text in text editor.	Single task oriented. For example, a washing machine is designed for washing clothes only.
RAM, ROM, I/O Ports, and Timers can be added externally and can vary in numbers.	RAM, ROM, I/O Ports, and Timers cannot be added externally. These components are to be embedded together on a chip and are fixed in numbers.
Designers can decide the number of memory or I/O ports needed.	Fixed number for memory or I/O makes a microcontroller ideal for a limited but specific task.
External support of external memory and I/O ports makes a microprocessor-based system heavier and costlier.	Microcontrollers are lightweight and cheaper than a microprocessor.
External devices require more space and their power consumption is higher.	A microcontroller-based system consumes less power and takes less space.

Embedded Systems – Architecture

The 8051 microcontrollers work with 8-bit data bus. So they can support external data memory up to 64K and external program memory of 64k at best. Collectively, 8051 microcontrollers can address 128k of external memory. When data and code lie in different memory blocks, then the architecture is referred as Harvard architecture. In case data and code lie in the same memory block, then the architecture is referred as Von Neumann architecture.

Von Neumann Architecture

The Von Neumann architecture was first proposed by a computer scientist John von Neumann. In this architecture, one data path or bus exists for both instruction and data. As a result, the CPU does one operation at a time. It either fetches an instruction from memory, or performs read/ write operation on data. So an instruction fetch and a data operation cannot occur simultaneously, sharing a common bus.

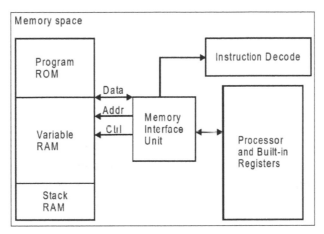

Von-Neumann architecture supports simple hardware. It allows the use of a single, sequential memory. Today's processing speeds vastly outpace memory access times, and we employ a very fast but small amount of memory (cache) local to the processor.

Harvard Architecture

The Harvard architecture offers separate storage and signal buses for instructions and data. This architecture has data storage entirely contained within the CPU, and there is no access to the instruction storage as data. Computers have separate memory areas for program instructions and data using internal data buses, allowing simultaneous access to both instructions and data. Programs needed to be loaded by an operator; the processor could not boot itself. In Harvard architecture, there is no need to make the two memories share properties.

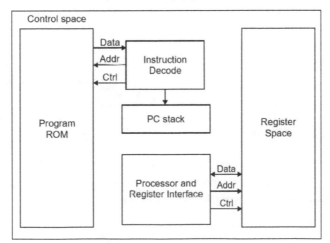

Figure: Harvard Architecture.

Von Neumann Architecture Vs. Harvard Architecture

The following points distinguish the Von Neumann Architecture from the Harvard Architecture.

Von Neumann Architecture	Harvard Architecture
Single memory to be shared by both code and data.	Separate memories for code and data.
Processor needs to fetch code in a separate clock cycle and data in another clock cycle. So it requires two clock cycles.	Single clock cycle is sufficient, as separate buses are used to access code and data.
Higher speed, thus less time consuming.	Slower in speed, thus more time-consuming.
Simple in design.	Complex in design.

CISC and RISC

CISC is a Complex Instruction Set Computer. It is a computer that can address a large number of instructions. In the early 1980s, computer designers recommended that computers should use fewer instructions with simple constructs so that they can be executed much faster within the CPU without having to use memory. Such computers are classified as Reduced Instruction Set Computer or RISC.

CISC Vs. RISC

The following points differentiate a CISC from a RISC:

CISC	RISC
Larger set of instructions. Easy to program.	Smaller set of Instructions. Difficult to program.
Simpler design of compiler, considering larger set of instructions.	Complex design of compiler.
Many addressing modes causing complex instruction formats.	Few addressing modes, fix instruction format.
Instruction length is variable.	Instruction length varies.
Higher clock cycles per second.	Low clock cycle per second.
Emphasis is on hardware.	Emphasis is on software.
Control unit implements large instruction set using micro-program unit.	Each instruction is to be executed by hardware.
Slower execution, as instructions are to be read from memory and decoded by the decoder unit.	Faster execution, as each instruction is to be executed by hardware.
Pipelining is not possible.	Pipelining of instructions is possible, considering single clock cycle.

Types of Embedded Systems

Embedded systems can be classified into different types based on performance, functional requirements and performance of the microcontroller. Embedded systems are classified into four categories based on their performance and functional requirements:

- Stand alone embedded systems,

- Real time embedded systems,

- Networked embedded systems,

- Mobile embedded systems.

Embedded Systems are classified into three types based on the performance of the microcontroller such as:

- Small scale embedded systems,

- Medium scale embedded systems,

- Sophisticated embedded systems.

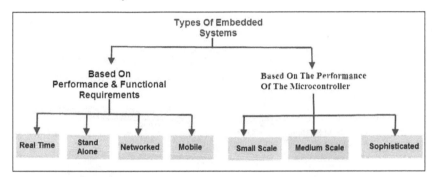

- Stand Alone Embedded Systems: Stand alone embedded systems do not require a host system like a computer, it works by itself. It takes the input from the input ports either analog or digital and processes, calculates and converts the data and gives the resulting data through the connected device-which either controls, drives and displays the connected devices. Examples for the stand alone embedded systems are mp3 players, digital cameras, video game consoles, microwave ovens and temperature measurement systems.

- Real Time Embedded Systems: A real time embedded system is defined as, a system which gives a required o/p in a particular time. These types of embedded systems follow the time deadlines for completion of a task. Real time embedded systems are classified into two types such as soft and hard real time systems.

- Networked Embedded Systems: These types of embedded systems are related to a network to access the resources. The connected network can be LAN, WAN or the internet. The connection can be any wired or wireless. This type of embedded system is the fastest growing area in embedded system applications. The embedded web server is a type of system wherein all embedded devices are connected to a web server and accessed and controlled by a web browser. Example for the LAN networked embedded system is a home security system wherein all sensors are connected and run on the protocol TCP/IP.

- Mobile Embedded Systems: Mobile embedded systems are used in portable embedded devices like cell phones, mobiles, digital cameras, mp3 players and personal digital assistants, etc. The basic limitation of these devices is the other resources and limitation of memory.

- Small Scale Embedded Systems: These types of embedded systems are designed with a single 8 or 16-bit microcontroller that may even be activated by a battery. For developing embedded software for small scale embedded systems, the main programming tools are an editor, assembler, cross assembler and integrated development environment (IDE).

- Medium Scale Embedded Systems: These types of embedded systems design with a single or 16 or 32 bit microcontroller, RISCs or DSPs. These types of embedded systems have both hardware and software complexities. For developing embedded software for medium scale embedded systems, the main programming tools are C, C++, JAVA, Visual C++, RTOS, debugger, source code engineering tool, simulator and IDE.

- Sophisticated Embedded Systems: These types of embedded systems have enormous hardware and software complexities that may need ASIPs, IPs, PLAs, scalable or configurable processors. They are used for cutting-edge applications that need hardware and software Co-design and components which have to assemble in the final system.

Applications of Embedded Systems

Embedded systems are used in different applications like automobiles, telecommunications, smart cards, missiles, satellites, computer networking and digital consumer electronics.

Embedded System Initialization

It takes just minutes for a developer to compile and run a Hello World! application on a nonembedded system. On the other hand, for an embedded developer, the task is not so trivial. It might take days before seeing a successful result. This process can be a frustrating experience for a developer new to embedded system development. Booting the target system, whether a third-party evaluation board or a custom design, can be a mystery to many newcomers. Indeed, it is daunting to pick up a programmer s reference manual for the target board and pore over tables of memory addresses and registers or to review the hardware component interconnection diagrams, wondering what it all means, what to do with the information (some of which makes little sense), and how to relate the information to running an image on the target system.

Serial Communication

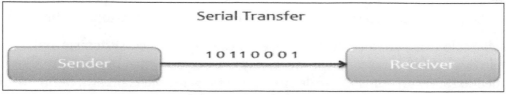

Figure: Serial Transfer.

In Telecommunication and Computer Science, serial communication is the process of sending/ receiving data in one bit at a time. It is like you are firing bullets from a machine gun to a target that's one bullet at a time.

Parallel Communication

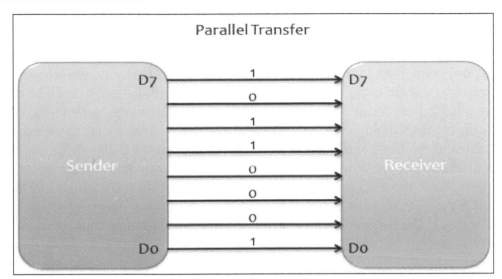

Figure: Parallel Transfer.

Parallel communication is the process of sending/receiving multiple data bits at a time through parallel channels. It is like you are firing using a shotgun to a target – where multiple bullets are fired from the same gun at a time).

Serial Vs. Parallel Communication

Now let's have a quick look at the differences between the two types of communications:

Serial Communication	Parallel Communication
1. One data bit is transceived at a time.	1. Multiple data bits are transceived at a time.
2. Slower.	2. Faster.
3. Less number of cables required to transmit data.	3. Higher number of cables required.

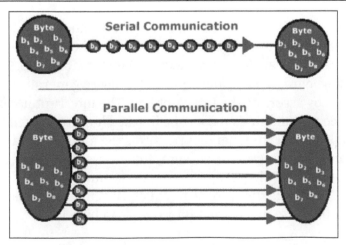

Input/Output Devices

The Address Bus

Recall from our discussion earlier about microprocessors, that every CPU has a number of pins, which work together, called an address bus. The address bus is normally used to read or write to memory, most often RAM chips. Most modern microprocessors use the address bus for more than just reading and writing to memory however. By toggling a special pin, the CPU can switch from using the address bus for accessing RAM, to using the address bus to talk to other semi-intelligent chips that are also connected to the address bus. When used in this way, we are said to be using I/O port addressing, instead of normal memory addresses. Sometimes a port will be referred to as a register, but I find this a bit confusing, since a register normally means an internal CPU register. The semi-intelligent device chips are only activate when they detect that the special I/O pin is asserted and the address bus holds the memory value that points to that specific chip. This is how most input and output occurs from devices like serial ports, parallel ports, floppy, hard drive and other controllers. Once the CPU has placed the proper address on the address bus and it asserts the special I/O pin, all RAM chips are temporarily disabled and the external I/O chips are read or written from instead. The bytes of data are actually transferred on a second set of pins called the data bus.

The Data Bus

The data bus is nothing more than a series of pins on the processor that are used to get data into, or out of, the processor chip itself. All memory and I/O devices are connected to the data bus, but depending on the current state of the address bus and other control pins on the processor, only one chip can actually be connected to the data bus at any given moment. Depending on the exact processor used, the data bus may be 4, 8, 16, 32 or perhaps 64-bits wide. A wider data bus allows the processor to read and write more bits of data in a single operation. This technique is used with PCI-based cards on PC-compatibles to achieve faster I/O operations for certain devices. In other cases however, using more bits is a waste of time, because the device connected at the other end of the data bus only supports 4 or 8 bit transfers at a time. In this case it is very important to ignore the unused bits, generally by using a bit masking operation to force the unused bits to a zero value.

Interrupt Requests

In addition to the processor using the data bus, address bus and special I/O pin to communicate with external devices; the external devices use another pin when they need the attention of the processor. This is referred to as an Interrupt Request Line or IRQ Line. For example, whenever you press a key on the keyboard, the keyboard controller device generally signals the main processor that a key is available by asserting the interrupt line. The interrupt handler must be small and efficiently designed, since in some cases it could be invoked hundreds or maybe even thousands of times a second. Generally an interrupt handler performs the minimum amount of work necessary to service the device, and then exits. At that point, the processor returns to running the process that was interrupted as if nothing happened. There are normally two different types of interrupt lines on all processors. The first is the kind we have been discussing at this point, called maskable interrupts. Maskable in this case means that interrupts can be selectively enabled or disabled by the software. The other kind of interrupt is called a non-maskable interrupt. The software can never disable this kind of interrupt. It most often used to perform the DRAM refresh on memory chips, which MUST occur at regular intervals in order to keep memory contents alive.

Memory Mapped I/O

I/O Port addressing is not the only way the processor can communicate with external devices however. Another commonly used technique is called memory mapped I/O. In this case, instead of asserting the I/O pin and addressing a data port, the processor just accesses a memory address directly. The external device can have a small amount of RAM or ROM that the processor just reads or writes as needed.

Direct Memory Access

One technique that has been used for years to speed transfer of data from main memory to an external device's memory is the direct memory access feature (DMA). The processor on the external device executes DMA transfers, without any assistance from the main processor. The processors must cooperate for this to work obviously. While the DMA transfer is in progress, the main processor is free to tend to other tasks, but should not attempt to modify the information in the buffer being transfer, until the transfer is complete. Once the transfer is stared, the main processor is free to tend to other tasks. The external processor will take over the address and data lines periodically and execute the DMA transfer. Once the transfer is complete, the external device usually notifies the main processor of this by raising an interrupt request. DMA's main advantage is that the main processor does not have to transfer data into one of its register, then save that to a memory address for each and every byte of data. Another advantage is the fact that whiles the DMA transfer is in progress, the CPU is free to work on other tasks. This leads to an apparently overall increase in speed.

Synchronous, Asynchronous and Iso-Synchronous Communication

1. In Synchronous data transfer, each basic unit of data (such as a bit) is transferred in accordance to a clock communication signal or in other words the data is transferred at a pre-decided rate. So for this data transfer method a clock signal is needed. Moreover synchronous data transfer systems usually have an error checking mechanism to guarantee data integrity over transmission.

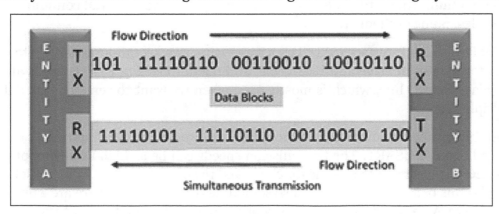

2. In Asynchronous data transfer systems, the data can be sent at irregular intervals and there is no pre-decided data rate of transmission. Special bits such as Start and stop bits are reserved to detect the start and end of data transmission in these systems and they are also equipped with an error checking mechanism.

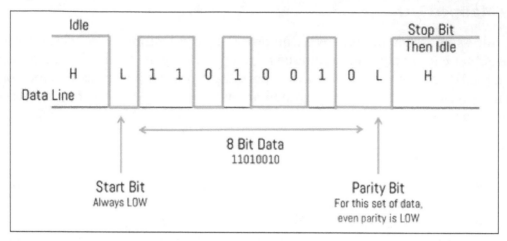

3. Isosynchronous data transfer lies somewhat in between the two other data transmission types. It sends Asynchronous data over a Synchronous transmission system. In such systems each data source is given only a fixed time to transmit its data. In that fixed interval of time, that data source can transfer data at whatever intervals it wants. If it has data which requires less time than the time allotted then it simply wastes the extra time by staying idle. Otherwise if it has data which requires more time to transmit than given then it sends the remaining data in its next turn. These systems do not have error check mechanism because it is not possible to re-transmit the data after an error due to strict timing conditions.

4. Synchronous, asynchronous, and isosynchronous transmission are not three of a kind but two unrelated pairs, where the asynchronous transmission that differs from synchronous transmission may not be the same as the asynchronous transmission that differs from isosynchronous transmission. Of course, both pairs are about timing.

Serial Communication Protocols

A variety of communication protocols have been developed based on serial communication in the past few decades. Some of them are:

- Serial Peripheral Interface (SPI): It is a three-wire based communication system. One wire each for Master to slave and Vice-versa, and one for clock pulses. There is an additional SS (Slave Select) line, which is mostly used when we want to send/receive data between multiple ICs.

- Inter-Integrated Circuit (I2C): Pronounced eye-two-see or eye-square-see, this is an advanced form of USART. The transmission speeds can be as high as a whopping 400KHz. The I2C bus has two wires – one for clock, and the other is the data line, which is bi-directional – this being the reason it is also sometimes (not always – there are a few conditions) called Two Wire Interface (TWI). It is a pretty new and revolutionary technology invented by Philips.

- FireWire: Developed by Apple, they are high-speed buses capable of audio/video transmission. The bus contains a number of wires depending upon the port, which can be either a 4-pin one, or a 6-pin one, or an 8-pin one.

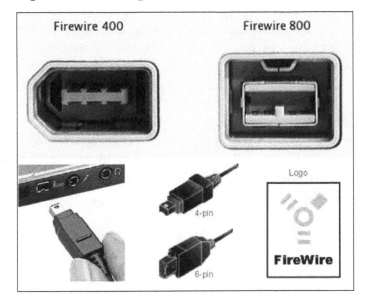

- Ethernet: Used mostly in LAN connections, the bus consists of 8 lines, or 4 Tx/Rx pairs.

- Universal Serial Bus (USB): This is the most popular of all. Is used for virtually all type of connections. The bus has 4 lines: V_{cc}, Ground, Data⁺, and Data-.

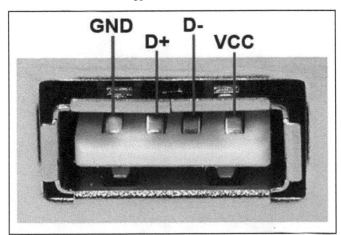

Figure: USB Pins.

- Recommended Standard 232 (RS-232): The RS-232 is typically connected using a DB9 connector, which has 9 pins, out of which 5 are input, 3 are output, and one is Ground.

Building an Embedded System

We embed 3 basic kinds of computing engines into our systems: microprocessor, microcomputer and microcontrollers. The microcomputer and other hardware are connected via A system bus is a single computer bus that connects the major components of a computer system. The technique was developed to reduce costs and improve modularity. It combines the functions of a data bus to carry information, an address bus to determine where it should be sent, and a control bus to determine its operation. The system bus is further classified int address, data and control bus. The microprocessor controls the whole system by executing a set of instructions call firmware that is stored in ROM. An instruction set, or instruction set architecture (ISA), is the part of the computer architecture related to programming, including the native data types, instructions, registers, addressing modes, memory architecture, interrupt and exception handling, and external I/O. An ISA includes a specification of the set of opcodes (machine language), and the native commands implemented by a particular processor. To run the application, when power is first turned ON, the microprocessor addresses a predefined location and fetches, decodes, and executes the instruction one after the other. The implementation of a microprocessor based embedded system combines the individual pieces into an integrated whole as shown in figure, which represents the architecture for a typical embedded system and identifies the minimal set of necessary components.

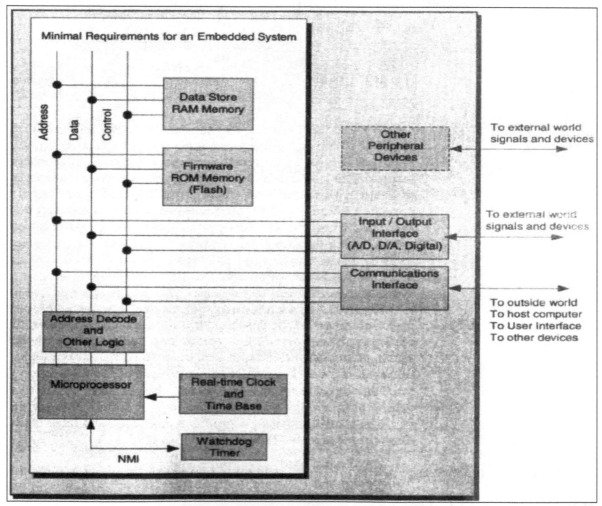

Figure: A Microprocessor Based Embedded System.

Embedded Design and Development Process

Figure shows a high level flow through the development process and identifies the major elements of the development life cycle.

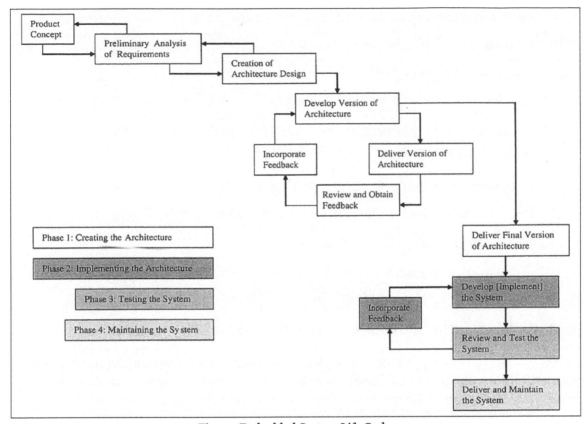

Figure: Embedded System Life Cycle.

The traditional design approach has been traverse the two sides of the accompanying diagram separately are:

- Design the hardware components.

- Design the software components.

- Bring the two together.

- Spend time testing and debugging the system.

The major areas of the design process are:

- Ensuring a sound software and hardware specification.

- Formulating the architecture for the system to be designed.

- Partitioning the h/w and s/w.

- Providing an iterative approach to the design of h/w and s/w.

The important steps in developing an embedded system are:

- Requirement definition,

- System specification,

- Functional design,

- Architectural design,
- Prototyping.

The major aspects in the development of embedded applications are:

- Digital hardware and software architecture.
- Formal design, development, and optimization process.
- Safety and reliability.
- Digital hardware and software/firmware design.
- The interface to physical world analog and digital signals.
- Debug, troubleshooting and test of our design.

Embedded applications are intended to work with the physical world, sensing various analog and digital signals while controlling, manipulating or responding to others.

Exemplary Applications of each Type of Embedded System

Embedded systems have very diversified applications. A few select application areas of embedded systems are Telecom, Smart Cards, Missiles and Satellites, Computer Networking, Digital Consumer Electronics, and Automotive. Figure shows the applications of embedded systems in these areas.

Figure: Applications of Embedded Systems.

Challenges in Embedded System Design

Figure shows one possible organization for an embedded system. In addition to the CPU and memory hierarchy, there are a variety of interfaces that enable the system to measure, manipulate, and otherwise interact with the external environment. Some differences with desktop computing may be:

- The human interface may be as simple as a flashing light or as complicated as real-time robotic vision.

- The diagnostic port may be used for diagnosing the system that is being controlled — not just for diagnosing the computer.

- Special-purpose field programmable (FPGA), application specific (ASIC), or even non-digital hardware may be used to increase performance or safety.

- Software often has a fixed function, and is specific to the application.

In addition to the emphasis on interaction with the external world, embedded systems also provide functionality specific to their applications. Instead of executing spreadsheets, word processing and engineering analysis, embedded systems typically execute control laws, finite state machines, and signal processing algorithms. They must often detect and react to faults in both the computing and surrounding electromechanical systems, and must manipulate application-specific user interface devices. In order to make the discussion more concrete, we shall discuss four example systems. Each example portrays a real system in current production, but has been slightly genericized to represent a broader cross-section of applications as well as protect proprietary interests. The four examples are a Signal Processing system, a Mission Critical control system, a Distributed control system, and a Small consumer electronic system. The Signal Processing and Mission Critical systems are representative of traditional military/ aerospace embedded systems, but in fact are becoming more applicable to general commercial applications over time.

An example of:	Signal Processing	Mission Critical	Distributed	Small
Computing speed	1 GFLOPS	10-100 MIPS	1-10 MIPS	100,000 IPS
I/O Transfer Rates	1 Gb/sec	10 Mb/sec	100 Kb/sec	1 Kb/sec
Memory Size	32-128 MB	16-32 MB	1-16 MB	1 KB
Units Sold	10-500	100-1000	100-10,000	1,000,000+
Development Cost	$20M-$100M	$10M-$50M	$1M-$10M	$100K-$1M
Lifetime	15-30 years	20-30 years	25-50 years	10-15 years
Environment	Vibration, Heat	Heat, Vibration, Lightning	Dirt, Fire	Over-voltage, Heat, Vibration
Cost Sensitivity	$1000	$100	$10	$0.05
Other Constraints	Size, weight, power	Size, weight	Size	Size, weight, power
Safety	–	Redundancy	Mechanical Safety	–
Maintenance	Frequent repairs	Aggressive fault detection/maintenance	Scheduled maintenance	"Never" breaks
Digital content	Digital except for signal I/O	- ½ Digital	- ½ Digital	Single digital chip; rest is analog/power
Certification authorities	Customer	Federal Government	Development team	Customer; Federal Government
Repair time goal	1-12 hours	30 minutes	4 min.-12 hours	1-4 hours
Initial cycle time	3-5 years	4-10 years	2-4 years	0.1-4 years
Product variants	1-5	5-20	10-10,000	3-10

Engineering allocation method	Per-product budget	Per-product budget	Allocation from large pool	Demand-driven daily from small pool
Other possible examples in this category	Radar/Sonar Video Medical imaging	Jet engines Manned spacecraft Nuclear power	High-rise elevators Trains/trams/subways Air conditioning	Automotive auxilliaries Consumer electronics Smart I/O

Using these four examples to illustrate points, the following sections describe the different areas of concern for embedded system design: computer design, system-level design, life-cycle support, business model support, and design culture adaptation. Desktop computing design methodology and tool support is to a large degree concerned with initial design of the digital system itself. To be sure, experienced designers are cognizant of other aspects, but with the recent emphasis on quantitative design (e.g.,) life-cycle issues that aren't readily quantified could be left out of the optimization process. However, such an approach is insufficient to create embedded systems that can effectively compete in the marketplace. This is because in many cases the issue is not whether design of an immensely complex system is feasible, but rather whether a relatively modest system can be highly optimized for life-cycle cost and effectiveness. While traditional digital design CAD tools can make a computer designer more efficient, they may not deal with the central issue — embedded design is about the system, not about the computer.

In desktop computing, design often focuses on building the fastest CPU, then supporting it as required for maximum computing speed. In embedded systems the combination of the external interfaces (sensors, actuators) and the control or sequencing algorithms is or primary importance. The CPU simply exists as a way to implement those functions. The following experiment should serve to illustrate this point: ask a roomful of people what kind of CPU is in the personal computer or workstation they use. Then ask the same people which CPU is used for the engine controller in their car (and whether the CPU type influenced the purchasing decision). In high-end embedded systems, the tools used for desktop computer design are invaluable. However, many embedded systems both large and small must meet additional requirements that are beyond the scope of what is typically handled by design automation. These additional needs fall into the categories of special computer design requirements, system level requirements, life-cycle support issues, business model compatibility, and design culture issues.

Computer Design Requirements

Embedded computers typically have tight constraints on both functionality and implementation. In particular, they must guarantee real time operation reactive to external events, conform to size and weight limits, budget power and cooling consumption, satisfy safety and reliability requirements, and meet tight cost targets.

1. Real time/reactive operation: Real time system operation means that the correctness of a computation depends, in part, on the time at which it is delivered. In many cases the system design must take into account worst case performance. Predicting the worst case may be difficult on complicated architectures, leading to overly pessimistic estimates erring on the side of caution. The Signal Processing and Mission Critical example systems have a significant requirement for real time operation in order to meet external I/O and control stability requirements. Reactive computation means that the software executes in response to external events. These events may be

periodic, in which case scheduling of events to guarantee performance may be possible. On the other hand, many events may be aperiodic, in which case the maximum event arrival rate must be estimated in order to accommodate worst case situations. Most embedded systems have a significant reactive component.

- Design challenge: Worst case design analyses without undue pessimism in the face of hardware with statistical performance characteristics (e.g., cache memory).

2. Small size, low weight: Many embedded computers are physically located within some larger artifact. Therefore, their form factor may be dictated by aesthetics, form factors existing in pre-electronic versions, or having to fit into interstices among mechanical components. In transportation and portable systems, weight may be critical for fuel economy or human endurance. Among the examples, the Mission Critical system has much more stringent size and weight requirements than the others because of its use in a flight vehicle, although all examples have restrictions of this type.

- Design challenges:

  ◦ Non-rectangular, non-planar geometries.

  ◦ Packaging and integration of digital, analog, and power circuits to reduce size.

3. Safe and reliable: Some systems have obvious risks associated with failure. In mission-critical applications such as aircraft flight control, severe personal injury or equipment damage could result from a failure of the embedded computer. Traditionally, such systems have employed multiply-redundant computers or distributed consensus protocols in order to ensure continued operation after an equipment failure. However, many embedded systems that could cause personal or property damage cannot tolerate the added cost of redundancy in hardware or processing capacity needed for traditional fault tolerance techniques.

- Design challenge: Low-cost reliability with minimal redundancy.

4. Harsh environment: Many embedded systems do not operate in a controlled environment. Excessive heat is often a problem, especially in applications involving combustion (e.g., many transportation applications). Additional problems can be caused for embedded computing by a need for protection from vibration, shock, lightning, power supply fluctuations, water, corrosion, fire, and general physical abuse. For example, in the Mission Critical example application the computer must function for a guaranteed, but brief, period of time even under non-survivable fire conditions.

- Design challenges:

  ◦ Accurate thermal modelling.

  ◦ De-rating components differently for each design, depending on operating environment.

5. Cost sensitivity: Even though embedded computers have stringent requirements, cost is almost always an issue (even increasingly for military systems). Although designers of systems large and small may talk about the importance of cost with equal urgency, their sensitivity to cost changes can vary dramatically. A reason for this may be that the effect of computer costs on profitability is more a function of the proportion of cost changes compared to the total system

cost, rather than compared to the digital electronics cost alone. For example, in the Signal Processing system cost sensitivity can be estimated at approximately $1000 (i.e., a designer can make decisions at the $1000 level without undue management scrutiny). However, with in the Small system decisions increasing costs by even a few cents attract management attention due to the huge multiplier of production quantity combined with the higher percentage of total system cost it represents.

- Design challenge: Variable "design margin" to permit trade-off between product robustness and aggressive cost optimization.

6. System-level requirements: In order to be competitive in the marketplace, embedded systems require that the designers take into account the entire system when making design decisions.

End-Product Utility

The utility of the end product is the goal when designing an embedded system, not the capability of the embedded computer itself. Embedded products are typically sold on the basis of capabilities, features, and system cost rather than which CPU is used in them or cost/performance of that CPU.

One way of looking at an embedded system is that the mechanisms and their associated I/O are largely defined by the application. Then, software is used to coordinate the mechanisms and define their functionality, often at the level of control system equations or finite state machines. Finally, computer hardware is made available as infrastructure to execute the software and interface it to the external world. While this may not be an exciting way for a hardware engineer to look at things, it does emphasize that the total functionality delivered by the system is what is paramount.

- Design challenge: Software- and I/O-driven hardware synthesis (as opposed to hardware-driven software compilation/synthesis).

System Safety and Reliability

The safety and reliability of the computing hardware itself. But, it is the safety and reliability of the total embedded system that really matters. The Distributed system example is mission critical, but does not employ computer redundancy. Instead, mechanical safety backups are activated when the computer system loses control in order to safely shut down system operation. A bigger and more difficult issue at the system level is software safety and reliability. While software doesn't normally "break" in the sense of hardware, it may be so complex that a set of unexpected circumstances can cause software failures leading to unsafe situations. This is a difficult problem that will take many years to address, and may not be properly appreciated by non-computer engineers and managers involved in system design decisions.

- Design challenges:
  ◦ Reliable software.
  ◦ Cheap, available systems using unreliable components.
  ◦ Electronic vs. non-electronic design tradeoffs.

Controlling Physical Systems

The usual reason for embedding a computer is to interact with the environment, often by monitoring and controlling external machinery. In order to do this, analog inputs and outputs must be transformed to and from digital signal levels. Additionally, significant current loads may need to be switched in order to operate motors, light fixtures, and other actuators. All these requirements can lead to a large computer circuit board dominated by non-digital components. In some systems "smart" sensors and actuators (that contain their own analog interfaces, power switches, and small CPUS) may be used to off-load interface hardware from the central embedded computer. This brings the additional advantage of reducing the amount of system wiring and number of connector contacts by employing an embedded network rather than a bundle of analog wires. However, this change brings with it an additional computer design problem of partitioning the computations among distributed computers in the face of an inexpensive network with modest bandwidth capabilities.

- Design challenge: Distributed system tradeoffs among analog, power, mechanical, network, and digital hardware plus software.

Power Management

A less pervasive system-level issue, but one that is still common, is a need for power management to either minimize heat production or conserve battery power. While the push to laptop computing has produced "low-power" variants of popular CPUs, significantly lower power is needed in order to run from inexpensive batteries for 30 days in some applications, and up to 5 years in others.

- Design challenge: Ultra-low power design for long-term battery operation.

Life-Cycle Support

Figure shows one view of a product life-cycle (a simplified version of the view taken by). First a need or opportunity to deploy new technology is identified. Then a product concept is developed. This is followed by concur rent product and manufacturing process design, production, and deployment. But in many embedded systems, the designer must see past deployment and take into account support, maintenance, upgrades, and system retirement issues in order to actually create a profitable design.

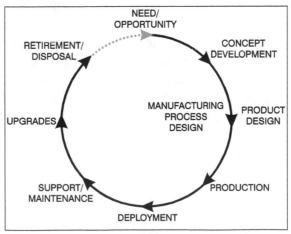

Figure: An Embedded System Lifecycle.

Component Acquisition

Because an embedded system may be more application driven than a typical technology-driven desktop computer design, there may be more leeway in component selection. Thus, component acquisition costs can be taken into account when optimizing system life-cycle cost. For example, the cost of a component generally decreases with quantity, so design decisions for multiple designs should be coordinated to share common components to the benefit of all.

- Design challenge: Life-cycle, cross-design component cost models and optimization rather than simple per-unit cost.

System Certification

Embedded computers can affect the safety as well as the performance the system. Therefore, rigorous qualification procedures are necessary in some systems after any design change in order to assess and reduce the risk of malfunction or unanticipated system failure. This additional cost can negate any savings that might have otherwise been realized by a design improvement in the embedded computer or its software. This point in particular hinders use of new technology by resynthesizing hardware components — the redesigned components cannot be used without incurring the cost of system recertification. One strategy to minimize the cost of system recertification is to delay all design changes until major system upgrades occur. As distributed embedded systems come into more widespread use, another likely strategy is to partition the system in such a way as to minimize the number of subsystems that need to be recertified when changes occur. This is a partitioning problem affected by potential design changes, technology insertion strategies, and regulatory requirements.

- Design challenge: Partitioning/synthesis to minimize recertification costs.

Logistics and Repair

Whenever an embedded computer design is created or changed, it affects the downstream maintenance of the product. A failure of the computer can cause the entire system to be unusable until the computer is repaired. In many cases embedded systems must be repairable in a few minutes to a few hours, which implies that spare components and maintenance personnel must be located close to the system. A fast repair time may also imply that extensive diagnosis and data collection capabilities must be built into the system, which may be at odds with keeping production costs low. Because of the long system lifetimes of many embedded systems, proliferation of design variations can cause significant logistics expenses. For example, if a component design is changed it can force changes in spare component inventory, maintenance test equipment, maintenance procedures, and maintenance training. Furthermore, each design change should be tested for compatibility with various system configurations, and accommodated by the configuration management database.

- Design challenge:

  ○ Designs optimized to minimize spares inventory.

  ○ High-coverage diagnosis and self-test at system level, not just digital component level.

Upgrades

Because of the long life of many embedded systems, upgrades to electronic components and software may be used to update functionality and extend the life of the embedded system with respect to competing with replacement equipment. While it may often be the case that an electronics upgrade involves completely replacing circuit boards, it is important to realize that the rest of the system will remain unchanged. Therefore, any special behaviors, interfaces, and undocumented features must be taken into account when performing the upgrade. Also, upgrades may be subject to recertification requirements. Of special concern is software in an upgraded system. Legacy software may not be executable on upgraded replacement hardware, and may not be readily cross-compiled to the new target CPU. Even worse, timing behavior is likely to be different on newer hardware, but may be both undocumented and critical to system operation.

- Design challenge: Ensuring complete interface, timing, and functionality compatibility when upgrading designs.

Long-Term Component Availability

When embedded systems are more than a few years old, some electronic components may no longer be available for production of new equipment or replacements. This problem can be especially troublesome with obsolete processors and small-sized dynamic memory chips. When a product does reach a point at which spare components are no longer economically available, the entire embedded computer must sometimes be redesigned or upgraded. This redesign might need to take place even if the system is no longer in production, depending on the availability of a replacement system. This problem is a significant concern on the distributed example system.

- Design challenge: Cost-effectively update old designs to incorporate new components.

Business Model

The business models under which embedded systems are developed can vary as widely as the applications themselves. Costs, cycle time, and the role of product families are all crucial business issues that affect design decisions.

1. Design vs. production costs: Design costs, also called Non-Recurring Engineering costs (NRE), are of major importance when few of a particular embedded system are being built. Conversely, production costs are important in high-volume production. Embedded systems vary from single units to millions of units, and so span the range of tradeoffs between design versus production costs. At the low-volume end of the spectrum, CAD tools can help designers complete their work with a minimum of effort. However, at the high-volume end of the spectrum the designs may be simple enough and engineering cost such a small fraction of total system cost that extensive hand-optimization is performed in order to reduce production costs. CAD tools may be able to outperform an average engineer at all times, and a superior engineer on very large designs (because of the limits of human capacity to deal with complexity and repetition). However, in small designs some embedded computer designers believe that a superior human engineer can outperform CAD tools. In the Small system example a programmer squeezed software into a few hundred bytes of memory by hand when the compiler produced overly large output that needed more memory than was available. It can readily be debated whether CAD tools or humans are "better" designers, but

CAD tools face skepticism in areas that require extraordinary optimization for size, performance, or cost.

- Design challenge: Intelligently trade off design time versus production cost.

2. Cycle time: The cycle time between identification of a product opportunity and product deployment (also called Time to Market) can be quite long for embedded systems. In many cases the electronics are not the driving force; instead, product schedules are driven by concerns such as tooling for mechanical components and manufacturing process design. Superficially, this would seem to imply that design time for the electronics is not an overriding concern, but this is only partially true. Because the computer system may have the most malleable design, it may absorb the brunt of changes. For example, redesign of hardware was required on the Mission Critical example system when it was found that additional sensors and actuators were needed to meet system performance goals. On the Small example system, delays in making masked ROM changes in order to revise software dominate concerns about modifications (and programmable memory is too expensive). So, although the initial design is often not in the critical path to product deployment, redesign of the computer system may need to be done quickly to resolve problems.

- Design challenge: Rapid redesign to accommodate changing form factors, control algorithms, and functionality requirements.

Product Families

In many cases embedded system designs are not unique, and there are a variety of systems of various prices and capabilities forming a product family. To the extent that system designers can reuse components, they lower the total cost of all systems in the product family. However, there is a dynamic tension between overly general solutions that satisfy a large number of niche requirements, and specifically optimized designs for each point in a product family space. Also, there may be cases in which contradictory requirements between similar systems prevent the use of a single subsystem design. In the Mission Critical and Small examples different customers require different interfaces between the embedded system and their equipment. In the Distributed example regulatory agencies impose different safety-critical behavior requirements depending on the geographic area in which the system is deployed.

- Design challenge: Customize designs while minimizing component variant proliferation.

Design Culture

Design is a social activity as well as a technical activity. The design of desktop computers, and CPUs in particular, has matured in terms of becoming more quantitative in recent years. With this new maturity has come an emphasis on simulation and CAD tools to provide engineering tradeoffs based on accurate performance and cost predictions. Computer designers venturing into the embedded arena must realize that their culture (and the underlying tool infrastructure) are unlike what is commonly practiced in some other engineering disciplines. But, because embedded system design requires a confluence of engineering skills, successful computer designers and design methodologies must find a harmonious compromise with the techniques and methodologies of other disciplines as well as company management. Also, in many cases the engineers building embedded computer systems are not actually trained in computer engineering (or, perhaps not even electrical engineering), and so are not attuned to the culture and methodologies of desktop computer design.

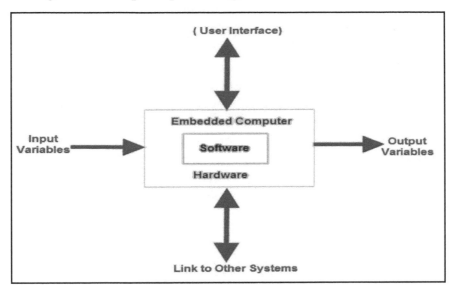

1. Computer culture vs. other cultures: A specific problem is that computer design tools have progressed to the point that many believe it is more cost-effective to do extensive simulation than build successive prototypes. However, in the mechanical arena much existing practice strongly favors prototyping with less exhaustive up-front analysis. Thus, it may be difficult to convince project managers (who may be application area specialists rather than computer specialists) to spend limited capital budgets on CAD tools and defer the gratification of early prototype development in favor of simulation.

- Design challenge: Make simulation-based computer design accessible to non-specialists.

2. Accounting for cost of engineering design: One area of common concern is the effectiveness of using engineers in any design discipline. But, some computer design CAD tools are very expensive, and in general organizations have difficulty trading off capital and tool costs against engineering time. This means that computer designers may be deprived of CAD tools that would reduce the total cost of designing a system. Also, in high-volume applications engineering costs can be relatively small when compared to production costs. Often, the number of engineers is fixed, and book-kept as a constant expense that is decoupled from the profitability of any particular system design, as is the case in all four example systems. This can be referred to as the "Engineers Are Free" syndrome. But, while the cost of engineering time may have a small impact on product costs, the unavailability of enough engineers to do work on all the products being designed can have a significant opportunity cost (which is, in general, unmeasured).

- Design challenge: Improved productivity via using tools and methodologies may be better received by managers if it is perceived to increase the number of products that can be designed, rather than merely the efficiency of engineers on any given product design effort. This is a subtle but, in practice, important distinction.

3. Inertia: In general, the cost of change in an organization is high both in terms of money and organizational disruption. The computer industry can be thought of as being forced to change

by inexorable exponential growth in hardware capabilities. However, the impact of this growth seems to have been delayed in embedded system development. In part this is because of the long time that elapses between new technology introduction and wide-scale use in inexpensive systems. Thus, it may simply be that complex designs will force updated CAD tools and design methodologies to be adopted for embedded systems in the near future. On the other hand, the latest computer design technologies may not have been adopted by many embedded system makers because they aren't necessary. Tool development that concentrates on the ability to handle millions of transistors may simply not be relevant to designers of systems using 4- and 8-bit microprocessors that constitute the bulk of the embedded CPU market. And, even if they are useful, the need for them may not be compelling enough to justify the pain and up-front expense of change so long as older techniques work. That is not to say that new tools aren't needed, but rather that the force of cultural inertia will only permit adoption of low-cost tools with significant advantages to the problem at hand.

- Design challenge: Find/create design tools and methodologies that provide unique, compelling advantages for embedded design.

The 8051 Microcontroller

8051 microcontroller is an 8-bit microcontroller. Some of the aspects of 8051 microcontroller discussed in this chapter are pin diagram, memory, port configuration, interrupts, etc. This chapter has been carefully written to provide an easy understanding of these facets of 8051 microcontroller.

Development/Classification of Microcontrollers (Invisible)

Microcontrollers have gone through a silent evolution (invisible). The evolution can be rightly termed as silent as the impact or application of a microcontroller is not well known to a common user, although microcontroller technology has undergone significant change since early 1970's. Development of some popular microcontrollers is given as follows:

Intel 4004	4 bit (2300 PMOS trans, 108 kHz)	1971
Intel 8048	8 bit	1976
Intel 8031	8 bit (ROM-less)	–
Intel 8051	8 bit (Mask ROM)	1980
Microchip PIC16C64	8 bit	1985
Motorola 68HC11	8 bit (on chip ADC)	–
Intel 80C196	16 bit	1982
Atmel AT89C51	8 bit (Flash memory)	–
Microchip PIC 16F877	8 bit (Flash memory + ADC)	–

Development of Microprocessors (Visible)

Microprocessors have undergone significant evolution over the past four decades. This development is clearly perceptible to a common user, especially, in terms of phenomenal growth in capabilities of personal computers. Development of some of the microprocessors can be given as follows:

Intel 4004	4 bit (2300 PMOS transistors)	1971
Intel 8080	8 bit (NMOS)	1974
8085	8 bit	
Intel 8088	16 bit	1978
8086	16 bit	
Intel 80186	16 bit	1982
80286	16 bit	
Intel 80386	32 bit (275000 transistors)	1985

Intel 80486 SX	32 bit	1989
DX	32 bit (built in floating point unit)	
Intel 80586 I		1993
MMX		1997
Celeron II	64 bit	1999
III		2000
IV		
Z-80 (Zilog)	8 bit	1976
Motorola Power PC 601		1993
602	32-bit	1995
603		

Some of the microcontrollers of 8051 family are given as follows:

Device	On-Chip Data Memory (bytes)	On-Chip Program Memory (bytes)	16-BIT Timer/Counter	No. of Vectored Interupts	Full Duplex I/O
8031	128	Noneo	2	5	1
8032	256	none	2	6	1
8051	128	4k ROM	2	5	1
8052	256	8k ROM	3	6	1
8751	128	4k EPROM	2	5	1
8752	256	8k EPROM	3	6	1
AT89C51	128	4k Flash Memory	2	5	1
AT89C52	256	8k Flash memory	3	6	1

Various features of 8051 microcontroller are given as follows:

- 8-bit CPU.

- 16-bit Program Counter.

- 8-bit Processor Status Word (PSW).

- 8-bit Stack Pointer.

- Internal RAM of 128bytes.

- Special Function Registers (SFRs) of 128 bytes.

- 32 I/O pins arranged as four 8-bit ports (P0 - P3).

- Two 16-bit timer/counters: T0 and T1.

- Two external and three internal vectored interrupts.

- One full duplex serial I/O.

Architecture of 8051 Microcontroller

It is 8-bit microcontroller, means MC 8051 can Read, Write and Process 8 bit data. This is mostly used microcontroller in the robotics, home appliances like mp3 player, washing machines, electronic iron and industries. Mostly used blocks in the architecture of 8051 are as follows:

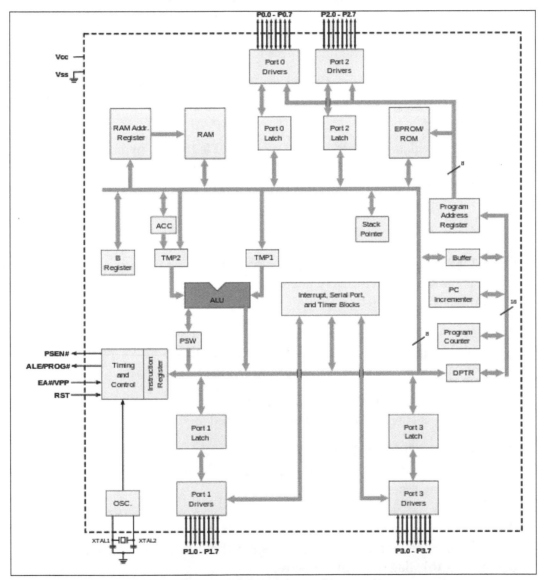

Figure: Intel 8051 Microarchitecture.

1. Oscillator and Clock Generator: All operations in a microcontroller are synchronized by the help of an oscillator clock. The oscillator clock generates the clock pulses by which all internal operations are synchronized. A resonant network connected through pins XTAL1 and XTAL2 forms up an oscillator. For this purpose a quartz crystal and capacitors are employed. The crystal run at specified maximum and minimum frequencies typically at 1 MHz to 16 MHz.

2. ALU: It is 8 bit unit. It performs arithmetic operation as addition, subtraction, multiplication, division, increment and decrement. It performs logical operations like AND, OR and EX-OR. It manipulates 8 bit and 16 bit data. It calculates address of jump locations in relative branch instruction. It performs compare, rotate and compliment operations. It consists of Boolean processor which performs bit, set, test, clear and compliment. 8051 micro controller contains 34 general purpose registers or working registers.2 of them are called math registers A & B and 32 are bank of registers.

- Accumulator (A-reg): It is 8 bit register. Its address is E0H and it is bit and byte accessible. Result of arithmetic & logic operations performed by ALU is accumulated by this register. Therefore it is called accumulator register. It is used to store 8 bit data and to hold one of operand of ALU units during arithmetical and logical operations. Most of the instructions are carried out on accumulator data. It is most versatile of 2 CPU registers.

- B-Register: It is special 8 bit math register. It is bit and byte accessible. It is used in conjunction with A register as I/P operand for ALU. It is used as general purpose register to store 8 bit data.

- PSW: It is 8 bit register. Its address is D0H and It is bit and byte accessible. It has 4 conditional flags or math flags which sets or resets according to condition of result. It has 3 control flags, by setting or resetting bit required operation or function can be achieved. The format of flag register is as shown below:

- Flag:

  ○ Carry Flag (CY): During addition and subtraction any carry or borrow is generated then carry flag is set otherwise carry flag resets. It is used in arithmetic, logical, jump, rotate and Boolean operations.

  ○ Auxiliary Carry Flag (AC): If during addition and subtraction any carry or borrow is generated from lower 4 bit to higher 4 bit then AC sets else it resets. It is used in BCD arithmetic operations.

  ○ Overflow Flag (OV): If in signed arithmetic operations result exceeds more than 7 bit than OV flag sets else resets. It is used in signed arithmetic operations only.

  ○ Parity Flag (P): If in result, even no. Of ones "1" are present than it is called even parity and parity flag sets. In result odd no. Of ones "1"are present than it is called odd parity and parity flag resets.

- Control Flags:

  ○ F0: It is user defined flag. The user defines the function of this flag. The user can set, test n clear this flag through software.

  ○ RS1 and RS0: These flags are used to select bank of register by resetting those flags which are as shown in table.

3. Program Counter (PC): The Program Counter (PC) is a 2-byte address which tells the 8051 where the next instruction to execute is found in memory. It is used to hold 16 bit address of internal RAM, external RAM or external ROM locations. When the 8051 is initialized PC always starts

at 0000h and is incremented each time an instruction is executed. It is important to note that PC isn't always incremented by one and never decremented.

4. Data Pointer Register (DTPR): It is a 16 bit register used to hold address of external or internal RAM where data is stored or result is to be stored. It is used to store 16 bit data. It is divided into2-8bit registers, DPH-data pointer higher order (83H) and DPL-data pointer lower order (82H). Each register can be used as general purpose register to store 8 bit data and can also be used as memory location. DPTR does not have single internal address. It functions as Base register in base relative addressing mode and in-direct jump.

5. Stack Pointer (SP): It is 8-bit register. It is byte addressable. Its address is 81H. It is used to hold the internal RAM memory location addresses which are used as stack memory. When the data is to be placed on stack by push instruction, the content of stack pointer is incremented by 1, and when data is retrieved from stack, content of stack of stack pointer is decremented by 1.

Special Function Registers (SFR): The 8051 microcontroller has 11 SFR divided in 4 groups:

- Timer/Counter register: 8051 microcontroller has 2-16 bit Timer/counter registers called Timer-reg-To And Timer/counter Reg-T1. Each register is 16 bit register divide into lower and higher byte register. These register are used to hold initial no. of count. All of the 4 register are byte addressable.

  ○ Timer Control Register: 8051 microcontroller has two 8-bit timer control register i.e. TMOD and TCON register. TMOD Register is 8-bit register. Its address is 89H. It is byte addressable. It used to select mode and control operation of time by writing control word.

  ○ TCON Register: It is 8-bit register. Its address is 88H. It is byte addressable. Its MSB 4-bit are used to control operation of timer/ counter and LSB 4-bit are used for external interrupt control.

- Serial Data Register: 8051 micro controller has 2 serial data register viz. SBUF and SCON.

  ○ Serial Buffer Register (SBUF): It is 8-bit register. It is byte addressable. Its address is 99H. It is used to hold data which is to be transferred serially.

  ○ Serial Control Register (SCON): It is 8-bit register. It is bit/byte addressable. Its address is 98H. The 8-bit loaded into this register controls the operation of serial communication.

- Interrupt Register: 8051 μC has 2 8-bit interrupt register.

  ○ Interrupt Enable Register (IE): It is 8-bit register. It is bit/byte addressable. Its address is A8H.it is used to enable and disable function of interrupt.

  ○ Interrupt Priority Register (IP): It is 8-bit register. It is bit/byte addressable. Its address is B8H. It is used to select low or high level priority of each individual interrupts.

- Power Control Register (PCON): it is 8-bit register. It is byte addressable .Its address is 87H. Its bits are used to control mode of power saving circuit, either idle or power down mode and also one bit is used to modify baud rate of serial communication.

Pin Diagram

The pin diagram of 8051 microcontroller looks as follows:

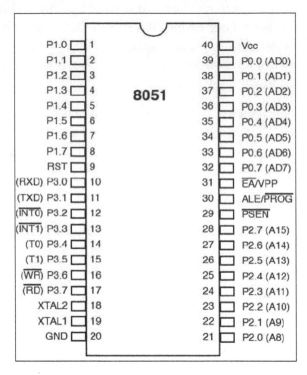

- Pins 1 to 8: These pins are known as Port 1. This port doesn't serve any other functions. It is internally pulled up, bi-directional I/O port.

- Pin 9: It is a RESET pin, which is used to reset the microcontroller to its initial values.

- Pins 10 to 17: These pins are known as Port 3. This port serves some functions like interrupts, timer input, control signals, serial communication signals RxD and TxD, etc.

- Pins 18 & 19: These pins are used for interfacing an external crystal to get the system clock.

- Pin 20: This pin provides the power supply to the circuit.

- Pins 21 to 28: These pins are known as Port 2. It serves as I/O port. Higher order address bus signals are also multiplexed using this port.

- Pin 29: This is PSEN pin which stands for Program Store Enable. It is used to read a signal from the external program memory.

- Pin 30: This is EA pin which stands for External Access input. It is used to enable/disable the external memory interfacing.

- Pin 31: This is ALE pin which stands for Address Latch Enable. It is used to demultiplex the address-data signal of port.

- Pins 32 to 39: These pins are known as Port 0. It serves as I/O port. Lower order address and data bus signals are multiplexed using this port.

- Pin 40: This pin is used to provide power supply to the circuit.

8051 microcontrollers have 4 I/O ports each of 8-bit, which can be configured as input or output. Hence, total 32 input/output pins allow the microcontroller to be connected with the peripheral devices.

1. Pin Configuration: The pin can be configured as 1 for input and 0 for output as per the logic state.

- Input/Output (I/O) pin: All the circuits within the microcontroller must be connected to one of its pins except P0 port because it does not have pull-up resistors built-in.

- Input pin: Logic 1 is applied to a bit of the P register. The output FE transistor is turned off and the other pin remains connected to the power supply voltage over a pull-up resistor of high resistance.

2. Port 0: The P0 (zero) port is characterized by two functions:

- When the external memory is used then the lower address byte (addresses A0A7) is applied on it, else all bits of this port are configured as input/output.

- When P0 port is configured as an output then other ports consisting of pins with built-in pull-up resistor connected by its end to 5V power supply, the pins of this port have this resistor left out.

3. Input Configuration: If any pin of this port is configured as an input, then it acts as if it "floats", i.e. the input has unlimited input resistance and in-determined potential.

4. Output Configuration: When the pin is configured as an output, then it acts as an "open drain". By applying logic 0 to a port bit, the appropriate pin will be connected to ground (0V), and applying logic 1, the external output will keep on "floating". In order to apply logic 1 (5V) on this output pin, it is necessary to build an external pullup resistor.

5. Port 1: P1 is a true I/O port as it doesn't have any alternative functions as in P0, but this port can be configured as general I/O only. It has a built-in pull-up resistor and is completely compatible with TTL circuits.

6. Port 2: P2 is similar to P0 when the external memory is used. Pins of this port occupy addresses intended for the external memory chip. This port can be used for higher address byte with addresses A8-A15. When no memory is added then this port can be used as a general input/output port similar to Port 1.

7. Port 3: In this port, functions are similar to other ports except that the logic 1 must be applied to appropriate bit of the P3 register.

8. Pins Current Limitations: When pins are configured as an output (i.e. logic 0), then the single port pins can receive a current of 10mA.

- When these pins are configured as inputs (i.e. logic 1), then built-in pull-up resistors provide very weak current, but can activate up to 4 TTL inputs of LS series.

- If all 8 bits of a port are active, then the total current must be limited to 15mA (port P0: 26mA).

- If all ports (32 bits) are active, then the total maximum current must be limited to 71mA.

Memory

Internal RAM

Internal RAM has memory 128-byte. Internal RAM is organized into three distinct areas: 32 bytes working registers from address 00h to 1Fh 16 bytes bit addressable occupies RAM byte address 20h to 2Fh, altogether 128 addressable bits General purpose RAM from 30h to 7Fh.

Internal ROM

Data memory and program code memory both are in different physical memory but both have the same addresses. An internal ROM occupied addresses from 0000h to 0FFFh. PC addresses program codes from 0000h to 0FFFh. Program addresses higher than 0FFFh that exceed the internal ROM capacity will cause 8051 architecture to fetch codes bytes from external program memory.

28 bytes of Internal RAM Structure (Lower Address Space)

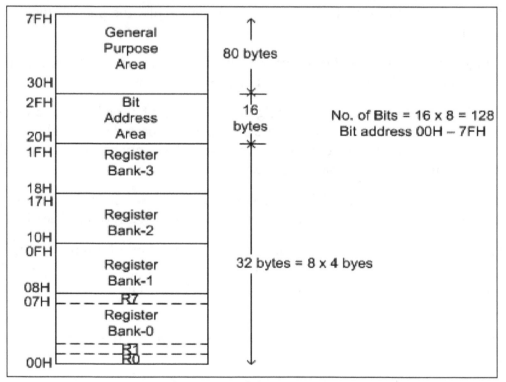

Figure: Internal RAM Structure.

The lower 32 bytes are divided into 4 separate banks. Each register bank has 8 registers of one byte each. A register bank is selected depending upon two bank select bits in the PSW register. Next 16bytes are bit addressable. In total, 128bits (16X8) are available in bit addressable area. Each bit can be accessed and modified by suitable instructions. The bit addresses are from 00H (LSB of the first byte in 20H) to 7FH (MSB of the last byte in 2FH). Remaining 80bytes of RAM are available for general purpose.

Internal Data Memory and Special Function Register (SFR) Map

Figure: Internal Data Memory Map.

The special function registers (SFRs) are mapped in the upper 128 bytes of internal data memory address. Hence there is an address overlap between the upper 128 bytes of data RAM and SFRs. Please note that the upper 128 bytes of data RAM are present only in the 8052 family. The lower128 bytes of RAM (00H - 7FH) can be accessed both by direct or indirect addressing while the upper 128 bytes of RAM (80H - FFH) are accessed by indirect addressing. The SFRs (80H - FFH) are accessed by direct addressing only. This feature distinguishes the upper 128 bytes of memory from the SFRs, as shown in figure.

SFR Map

The set of Special Function Registers (SFRs) contains important registers such as Accumulator, Register B, I/O Port latch registers, Stack pointer, Data Pointer, Processor Status Word (PSW) and various control registers. Some of these registers are bit addressable (they are marked with a * in the diagram below). The detailed map of various registers is shown in the following figure:

Address:

F8H								
F0H	B*							
E8H								
E0H	ACC*							
D8H								
D0H	PSW*							
C8H	(T2CON)*		(RCAP2L)	(RCAP2H)	(TL2)	(TH2)		
C0H								
B8H	IP*							
B0H	P3*							
A8H	IE*							
A0H	P2*							
98H	SCON*	SBUF						
90H	P1*							

88H	TCON*		TMOD	TLo		TL1		THo	TH1			
8oH	Po*		SP	DPL		DPH						PCON

It should be noted that all registers appearing in the first column are bit addressable. The bit address of a bit in the register is calculated as follows:

Bit address of 'b' bit of register 'R' is,

Address of register 'R' + b

where $0 \le b \le 7$.

Processor Status Word (PSW) Address=DoH

Figure: Processor Status Word.

PSW register stores the important status conditions of the microcontroller. It also stores the bank select bits (RS1 & RS0) for register bank selection.

Power Saving Modes of Operation

8051 has two power saving modes. They are:

- Idle Mode,

- Power Down mode.

The two power saving modes are entered by setting two bits IDL and PD in the special function register (PCON) respectively. The structure of PCON register is as follows:

PCON: Address 87H

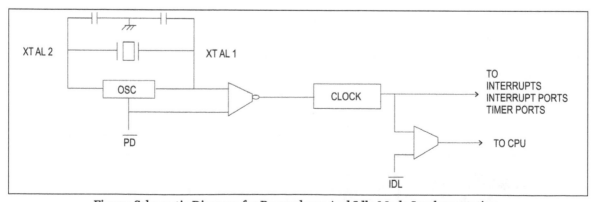

Figure: Schematic Diagram for Power down And Idle Mode Implementation.

Idle Mode

Idle mode is entered by setting IDL bit to 1 (i.e. $\overline{\text{IDL}} = 0$). The clock signal is gated off to CPU, but not to the interrupt, timer and serial port functions. The CPU status is preserved entirely. SP, PC, PSW, Accumulator and other registers maintain their data during IDLE mode. The port pins hold their logical states they had at the time Idle was initiated. ALE and $\overline{\text{PSEN}}$ are held at logic high levels.

- Ways to Exit Idle Mode:

    - Activation of any enabled interrupt will clear PCON.0 bit and hence the Idle Mode is exited. The program goes to the Interrupt Service Routine (ISR). After RETI is executed at the end of the ISR, the next instruction will start from the one following the instruction that enabled Idle Mode.

    - A hardware reset exits the idle mode. The CPU starts from the instruction following the instruction that invoked the 'Idle' mode.

Power Down Mode

The Power down Mode is entered by setting the PD bit to 1. The internal clock to the entire microcontroller is stopped (frozen). However, the program is not dead. The Power down Mode is exited (PCON.1 is cleared to 0) by Hardware Reset only. The CPU starts from the next instruction where the Power down Mode was invoked. Port values are not changed/ overwritten in power down mode. V_{cc} can be reduced to as low as 2V in Power Down mode. However, V_{cc} has to be restored to normal value before Power Down mode is exited.

Memory Organisation

The 8051 has two types of memory and these are Program Memory and Data Memory. Program Memory (ROM) is used to permanently save the program being executed, while Data Memory (RAM) is used for temporarily storing data and intermediate results created and used during the operation of the microcontroller. Depending on the model in use (we are still talking about the 8051 microcontroller family in general) at most a few Kb of ROM and 128 or 256 bytes of RAM is used. All 8051 microcontrollers have a 16-bit addressing bus and are capable of addressing 64 kb memory. It is neither a mistake nor a big ambition of engineers who were working on basic core development. It is a matter of smart memory organization which makes these microcontrollers a real "programmers' goody".

Program Memory

The first models of the 8051 microcontroller family did not have internal program memory. It was added as an external separate chip. These models are recognizable by their label beginning with 803 (for example 8031 or 8032). All later models have a few Kbyte ROM embedded. Even though such an amount of memory is sufficient for writing most of the programs, there are situations when it is necessary to use additional memory as well. A typical example are so called lookup tables. They are used in cases when equations describing some processes are too complicated or when there is no time for solving them. In such cases all necessary estimates and approximates are executed in advance and the final results are put in the tables (similar to logarithmic tables).

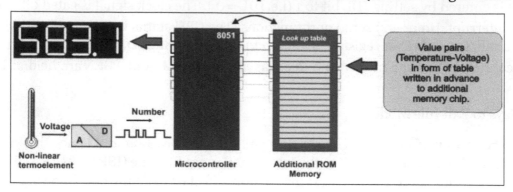

The way microcontroller handle external memory depends on the EA pin logic state:

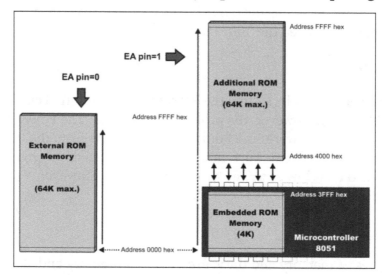

EA = 0 in this case, the microcontroller completely ignores internal program memory and executes only the program stored in external memory. EA = 1 in this case, the microcontroller executes first the program from built-in ROM, and then the program stored in external memory. In both cases, P0 and P2 are not available for use since being used for data and address transmission. Besides, the ALE and PSEN pins are also used.

Data Memory

As already mentioned, Data Memory is used for temporarily storing data and intermediate results created and used during the operation of the microcontroller. Besides, RAM memory built in the 8051 family includes many registers such as hardware counters and timers, input/output ports, serial data buffers etc. The previous models had 256 RAM locations, while for the later models this number was incremented by additional 128 registers. However, the first 256 memory locations (addresses 0-FFh) are the heart of memory common to all the models belonging to the 8051 family. Locations available to the user occupy memory space with addresses 0-7Fh, i.e. first 128 registers. This part of RAM is divided in several blocks. The first block consists of 4 banks each including 8 registers denoted by R0-R7. Prior to accessing any of these registers, it is necessary to select the bank containing it. The next memory block (address 20h2Fh) is bit- addressable, which means that each bit has its own address (0-7Fh). Since there are 16 such registers, this block contains in total of 128 bits with separate addresses (address of bit 0 of the 20h byte is 0, while address of bit 7 of the 2Fh byte is 7Fh). The third group of registers occupy addresses 2Fh-7Fh, i.e. 80 locations, and does not have any special functions or features.

Additional RAM

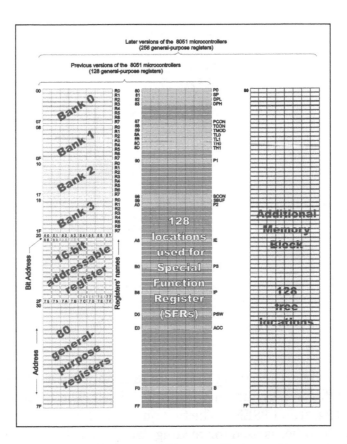

In order to satisfy the programmers' constant hunger for Data Memory, the manufacturers decided to embed an additional memory block of 128 locations into the latest versions of the 8051 microcontrollers. However, it's not as simple as it seems to be The problem is that electronics performing addressing has 1 byte (8 bits) on disposal and is capable of reaching only the first 256 locations, therefore. In order to keep already existing 8-bit architecture and compatibility with other existing models a small trick was done. What does it mean? It means that additional memory block shares the same addresses with locations intended for the SFRs (80h- FFh). In order to differentiate between these two physically separated memory spaces, different ways of addressing are used. The SFRs memory locations are accessed by direct addressing, while additional RAM memory locations are accessed by indirect addressing.

Memory Expansion

In case memory (RAM or ROM) built in the microcontroller is not sufficient, it is possible to add two external memory chips with capacity of 64Kb each. P2 and P3 I/O ports are used for their addressing and data transmission.

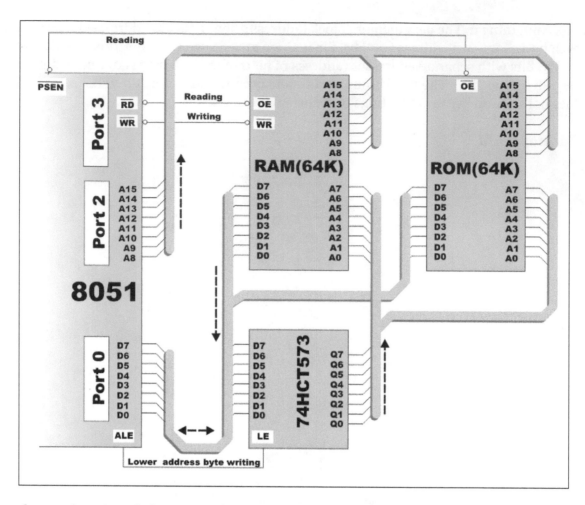

From the user's point of view, everything works quite simply when properly connected because most operations are performed by the microcontroller itself. The 8051 microcontroller has two pins for data read RD#(P3.7) and PSEN#. The first one is used for reading data from external data memory (RAM), while the other is used for reading data from external program memory (ROM). Both pins are active low. A typical example of memory expansion by adding RAM and ROM chips (Hardward architecture), is shown in figure. Even though additional memory is rarely used with the latest versions of the microcontrollers, we will describe in short what happens when memory chips are connected according to the previous schematic. The whole process described below is performed automatically. When the program during execution encounters an instruction which resides in external memory (ROM), the microcontroller will activate its control output ALE and set the first 8 bits of address (A0-A7) on P0. IC circuit 74HCT573 passes the first 8 bits to memory address pins.

A signal on the ALE pin latches the IC circuit 74HCT573 and immediately afterwards 8 higher bits of address (A8-A15) appear on the port. In this way, a desired location of additional program memory is addressed. It is left over to read its content. Port P0 pins are configured as inputs, the PSEN pin is activated and the microcontroller reads from memory chip. Similar occurs when it is necessary to read location from external RAM. Addressing is performed in the same way, while read and write are performed via signals appearing on the control outputs RD (is short for read) or WR (is short for write).

Interfacing External Memory

If external program/data memory are to be interfaced, they are interfaced in the following way:

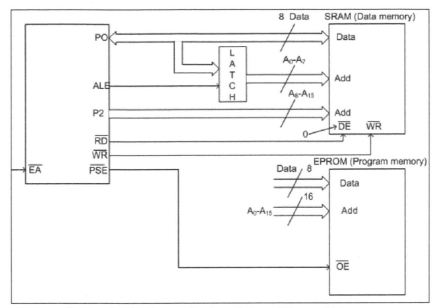

Figure: Circuit Diagram for Interfacing of External Memory.

External program memory is fetched if either of the following two conditions is satisfied.

- $\overline{EA}$ (Enable Address) is low. The microcontroller by default starts searching for program from external program memory.

- PC is higher than FFFH for 8051 or 1FFFH for 8052.

$\overline{PSEN}$ tells the outside world whether the external memory fetched is program memory or data memory. $\overline{EA}$ is user configurable. $\overline{PSEN}$ is processor controlled.

8051 Instruction Set and Programming

8051 Addressing Modes

8051 has four addressing modes:

1. Immediate Addressing: Data is immediately available in the instruction. For example:

ADD A, #77; Adds 77 (decimal) to A and stores in A.

ADD A, #4DH; Adds 4D (hexadecimal) to A and stores in A.

MOV DPTR, #1000H; Moves 1000 (hexadecimal) to data pointer.

2. Register Addressing: This way of addressing accesses the bytes in the current register bank. Data is available in the register specified in the instruction. The register bank is decided by 2 bits of Processor Status Word (PSW). For example:

ADD A, R0; Adds content of R0 to A and stores in A.

3. Direct Addressing: The address of the data is available in the instruction. For example:

MOV A, 088H; Moves content of SFR TCON (address 088H)to A.

4. Register Indirect Addressing: The address of data is available in the R0 or R1 registers as specified in the instruction. For example:

MOV A, @R0 moves content of address pointed by R0 to A.

External Data Addressing

Pointer used for external data addressing can be either R0/R1 (256 byte access) or DPTR (64kbyte access). For example:

MOVX A, @R0; Moves content of 8-bit address pointed by R0 to A.

MOVX A, @DPTR; Moves content of 16-bit address pointed by DPTR to A.

External Code Addressing

Sometimes we may want to store non-volatile data into the ROM e.g. look-up tables. Such data may require reading the code memory. This may be done as follows:

MOVC A, @A+DPTR; Moves content of address pointed by A+DPTR to A.

MOVC A, @A+PC; Moves content of address pointed by A+PC to A.

Port Configuration

Each port of 8051 has bidirectional capability. Port 0 is called 'true bidirectional port' as it floats (tristated) when configured as input. Port-1, 2, 3 are called 'quasi bidirectional port'.

Port-0 Pin Structure

Port -0 has 8 pins (P0.0-P0.7). The structure of a Port-0 pin is shown in figure.

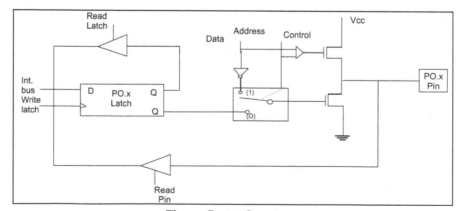

Figure: Port-0 Structure.

Port-0 can be configured as a normal bidirectional I/O port or it can be used for address/data interfacing for accessing external memory. When control is '1', the port is used for address/ data interfacing. When the control is '0', the port can be used as a normal bidirectional I/O port. Let us assume that control is '0'. When the port is used as an input port, '1' is written to the latch. In this situation both the output MOSFETs are 'off'. Hence the output pin floats. This high impedance pin can be pulled up or low by an external source. When the port is used as an output port, a '1' written to the latch again turns 'off' both the output MOSFETs and causes the output pin to float. An external pull-up is required to output a '1'. But when '0' is written to the latch, the pin is pulled down by the lower MOSFET. Hence the output becomes zero. When the control is '1', address/data bus controls the output driver MOSFETs. If the address/ data bus (internal) is '0', the upper MOSFET is 'off' and the lower MOSFET is 'on'. The output becomes '0'. If the address/data bus is '1', the upper transistor is 'on' and the lower transistor is 'off'. Hence the output is '1'. Hence for normal address/data interfacing (for external memory access) no pull-up resistors are required. Port-0 latch is written to with 1's when used for external memory access.

Port-1 Pin Structure

Port-1 has 8 pins (P1.1-P1.7). The structure of a port-1 pin is shown in figure.

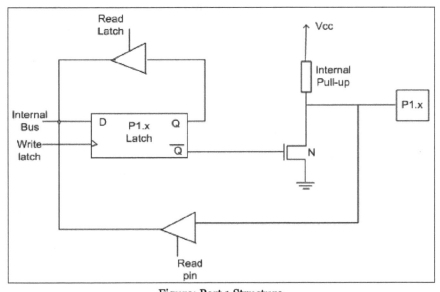

Figure: Port 1 Structure.

Port-1 does not have any alternate function i.e. it is dedicated solely for I/O interfacing. When used as output port, the pin is pulled up or down through internal pull-up. To use port-1 as input port, '1' has to be written to the latch. In this input mode when '1' is written to the pin by the external device then it read fine. But when '0' is written to the pin by the external device then the external source must sink current due to internal pull-up. If the external device is not able to sink the current the pin voltage may rise, leading to a possible wrong reading.

PORT-2 Pin Structure

Port-2 has 8-pins (P2.0-P2.7). The structure of a port-2 pin is shown in figure.

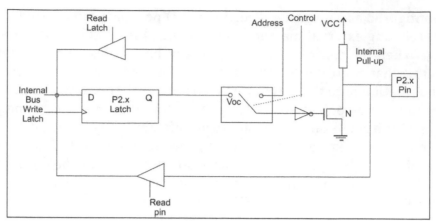

Figure: Port 2 Structure.

Port-2 is used for higher external address byte or a normal input/output port. The I/O operation is similar to Port-1. Port-2 latch remains stable when Port-2 pin are used for external memory access. Here again due to internal pull-up there is limited current driving capability.

PORT-3 Pin Structure

Port-3 has 8 pin (P3.0-P3.7). Port-3 pins have alternate functions. The structure of a port3 pin is shown in figure.

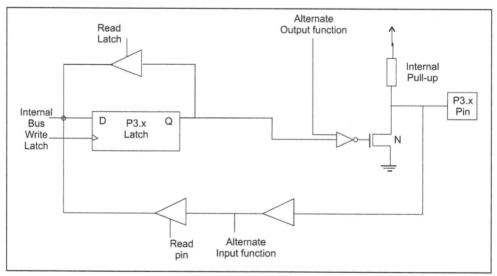

Figure: Port 3 Structure.

Each pin of Port-3 can be individually programmed for I/O operation or for alternate function. The alternate function can be activated only if the corresponding latch has been written to '1'. To use the port as input port, '1' should be written to the latch. This port also has internal pull-up and limited current driving capability. Alternate functions of Port-3 pins are:

P3.0	RxD
P3.1	TxD
P3.2	$\overline{INT0}$

P3.3	$\overline{INT1}$
P3.4	T0
P3.5	T1
P3.6	$\overline{WR}$
P3.7	$\overline{RD}$

- Port 1, 2, 3 each can drive 4 LS TTL inputs.

- Port-0 can drive 8 LS TTL inputs in address /data mode. For digital output port, it needs external pull-up resistors.

- Ports-1,2and 3 pins can also be driven by open-collector or open-drain outputs.

- Each Port 3 bit can be configured either as a normal I/O or as a special function bit.

Reading a Port (Port-Pins) Versus Reading a Latch

There is a subtle difference between reading a latch and reading the output port pin. The status of the output port pin is sometimes dependant on the connected load. For instance if a port is configured as an output port and a '1' is written to the latch, the output pin should also show '1'. If the output is used to drive the base of a transistor, the transistor turns 'on'. If the port pin is read, the value will be '0' which is corresponding to the base-emitter voltage of the transistor.

- Reading a Latch: Usually the instructions that read the latch, read a value, possibly change it, and then rewrite it to the latch. These are called "read-modify-write" instructions. Examples of a few instructions are:

ORL P2, A; P2 <-- P2 or A

MOV P2.1, C; Move carry bit to PX.Y bit.

In this the latch value of P2 is read, is modified such that P2.1 is the same as Carry and is then written back to P2 latch.

- Reading a Pin: Examples of a few instructions that read port pin, are:

MOV A, P0; Move port-0 pin values to A

MOV A, P1; Move port-1 pin values to A

Accessing External Memory

Access to external program memory uses the signal $\overline{PSEN}$ (Program store enable) as the read strobe. Access to external data memory uses $\overline{RD}$ or $\overline{WR}$ (alternate function of P3.7 and P3.6). For external program memory, always 16 bit address is used. For example:

MOVC A, @ A+DPTR

MOVC A, @ A+PC

Access to external data memory can be either 8-bit address or 16-bit address:

8-bit address- MOVX A, @Rp where Rp is either R0 or R1

MOVX @Rp, A

16 bit address- MOVX A,@DPTR

MOV X @DPTR, A

The external memory access in 8051 can be shown by a schematic diagram as given in figure.

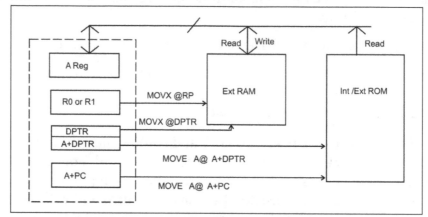

Figure: Schematic Diagram of External Memory Access.

If an 8-bit external address is used for data memory (i.e. MOVX @Rp) then the content of Port-2 SFR remains at Port-2 pins throughout the external memory cycle. This facilitates memory paging as the upper 8 bit address remains fixed. During any access to external memory, the CPU writes FFH to Port-0 latch (SFR). If the user writes to Port-0 during an external memory fetch, the incoming byte is corrupted. External program memory is accessed under the following condition:

• Whenever $\overline{EA}$ is low.

• Whenever PC contains a number higher than 0FFFH (for 8051) or 1FFF (for 8052).

Some typical use of code/program memory access:

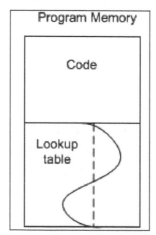

Figure: Program Memory Showing the Storage of Lookup Table.

External program memory can be not only used to store the code, but also for lookup table of various functions required for a particular application. Mathematical functions such as Sine, Square root, Exponential, etc. can be stored in the program memory (Internal or external) and these functions can be accessed using MOVC instruction.

Timers/Counters

8051 has two 16-bit programmable UP timers/counters. They can be configured to operate either as timers or as event counters. The names of the two counters are T0 and T1 respectively. The timer content is available in four 8-bit special function registers, viz, TL0, TH0, TL1 and TH1 respectively. In the "timer" function mode, the counter is incremented in every machine cycle. Thus, one can think of it as counting machine cycles. Hence the clock rate is 1/12th of the oscillator frequency. In the "counter" function mode, the register is incremented in response to a 1 to 0 transition at its corresponding external input pin (T0 or T1). It requires 2 machine cycles to detect a high to low transition. Hence maximum count rate is 1/24th of oscillator frequency. The operation of the timers/counters is controlled by two special function registers, TMOD and TCON respectively.

- Timer Mode control (TMOD) Special Function Register: TMOD register is not bit addressable.

TMOD Address: 89 H

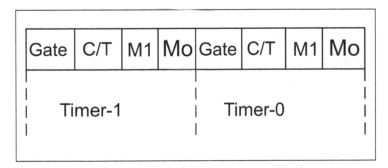

Various bits of TMOD are described as follows:

- Gate: This is an OR Gate enabled bit which controls the effect of $\overline{INT1/0}$ on START/STOP of Timer. It is set to one ('1') by the program to enable the interrupt to start/stop the timer. If TR1/0 in TCON is set and signal on $\overline{INT1/0}$ pin is high then the timer starts counting using either internal clock (timer mode) or external pulses (counter mode).

- $C/\overline{T}$: It is used for the selection of Counter/Timer mode.

- Mode Select Bits: M1 and M0 are mode select bits.

M1	M0	Mode
0	0	Mode 0
0	1	Mode 1
1	0	Mode 2
1	1	Mode 3

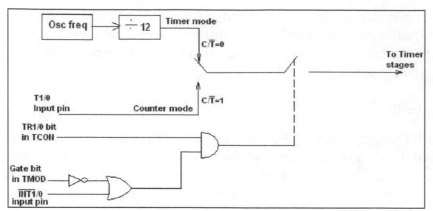

Figure: Timer/Counter Control Logic.

- Timer Control (TCON) Special Function Register: TCON is bit addressable. The address of TCON is 88H. It is partly related to Timer and partly to interrupt.

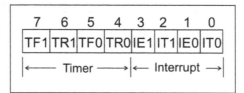

Figure: TCON Register.

The various bits of TCON are as follows:

- TF1: Timer1 overflow flag. It is set when timer rolls from all 1s to 0s. It is cleared when processor vectors to execute ISR located at address 001BH.

- TR1: Timer1 run control bit. Set to 1 to start the timer/counter.

- TF0: Timer0 overflow flag. (Similar to TF1).

- TR0: Timer0 run control bit.

- IE1: Interrupt1 edge flag. Set by hardware when an external interrupt edge is detected. It is cleared when interrupt is processed.

- IE0: Interrupt0 edge flag. (Similar to IE1).

- IT1: Interrupt1 type control bit. Set/ cleared by software to specify falling edge/low level triggered external interrupt.

- IT0: Interrupt0 type control bit. (Similar to IT1).

Timers can operate in four different modes. They are as follows:

- Timer Mode-0: In this mode, the timer is used as a 13-bit UP counter as follows:

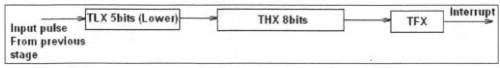

Figure: Operation of Timer on Mode-0.

The lower 5 bits of TLX and 8 bits of THX are used for the 13 bit count. Upper 3 bits of TLX are ignored. When the counter rolls over from all 0's to all 1's, TFX flag is set and an interrupt is generated. The input pulse is obtained from the previous stage. If TR1/0 bit is 1 and Gate bit is 0, the counter continues counting up. If TR1/0 bit is 1 and Gate bit is 1, then the operation of the counter is controlled by $\overline{INTX}$ input. This mode is useful to measure the width of a given pulse fed to $\overline{INTX}$ input.

- Timer Mode-1: This mode is similar to mode-0 except for the fact that the Timer operates in 16-bit mode.

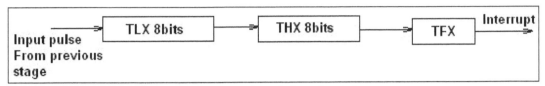

Figure: Operation of Timer in Mode 1.

- Timer Mode-2: (Auto-Reload Mode): This is a 8 bit counter/timer operation. Counting is performed in TLX while THX stores a constant value. In this mode when the timer overflows i.e. TLX becomes FFH, it is fed with the value stored in THX. For example if we load THX with 50H then the timer in mode 2 will count from 50H to FFH. After that 50H is again reloaded. This mode is useful in applications like fixed time sampling.

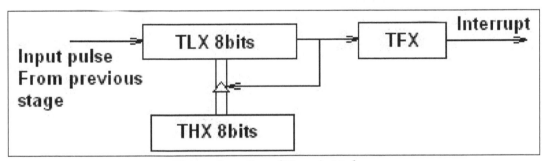

Figure: Operation of Timer in Mode 2.

- Timer Mode-3: Timer 1 in mode-3 simply holds its count. The effect is same as setting TR1=0. Timer0 in mode-3 establishes TL0 and TH0 as two separate counters.

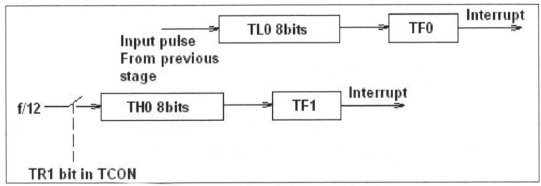

Figure: Operation of Timer in Mode 3.

Control bits TR1 and TF1 are used by Timer-0 (higher 8 bits) (TH0) in Mode-3 while TR0 and TF0 are available to Timer-0 lower 8 bits (TL0).

Interrupts

8051 provides five vectored interrupts. They are:

- $\overline{\text{INT0}}$

- TF0

- $\overline{\text{INT1}}$

- TF1

- RI/TI

Out of these, $\overline{\text{INT0}}$ and $\overline{\text{INT1}}$ are external interrupts whereas Timer and Serial port interrupts are generated internally. The external interrupts could be negative edge triggered or low level triggered. All these interrupt, when activated, set the corresponding interrupt flags. Except for serial interrupt, the interrupt flags are cleared when the processor branches to the Interrupt Service Routine (ISR). The external interrupt flags are cleared on branching to Interrupt Service Routine (ISR), provided the interrupt is negative edge triggered. For low level triggered external interrupt as well as for serial interrupt, the corresponding flags have to be cleared by software by the programmer. The schematic representation of the interrupts is as follows:

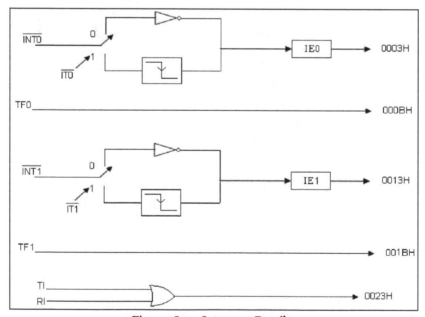

Figure: 8051 Interrupt Details.

Each of these interrupts can be individually enabled or disabled by 'setting' or 'clearing' the corresponding bit in the IE (Interrupt Enable Register) SFR. IE contains a global enable bit EA which enables/disables all interrupts at once.

7	6	5	4	3	2	1	0
EA	——	ET2	ES	ET1	EX1	ET0	EX0

Figure: Interrupt Enable register (IE): Address: A8H.

EX0 → $\overline{\text{INT0}}$ interrupt (External) enable bit.

ET0 → Timer-0 interrupt enable bit.

EX1 → $\overline{\text{INT1}}$ interrupt (External) enable bit.

ET1 → Timer-1 interrupt enable bit.

ES → Serial port interrupt enable bit.

ET2 → Timer-2 interrupt enable bit.

EA → Enable/Disable all.

Setting '1' → Enable the corresponding interrupt.

Setting '0' → Disable the corresponding interrupt.

Priority Level Structure

Each interrupt source can be programmed to have one of the two priority levels by setting (high priority) or clearing (low priority) a bit in the IP (Interrupt Priority) Register. A low priority interrupt can itself be interrupted by a high priority interrupt, but not by another low priority interrupt. If two interrupts of different priority levels are received simultaneously, the request of higher priority level is served. If the requests of the same priority level are received simultaneously, an internal polling sequence determines which request is to be serviced. Thus, within each priority level, there is a second priority level determined by the polling sequence, as follows:

Source	Priority level
IE0	Highest
TF0	
IE1	
TF1	
RI + TI	Lowest

Interrupt Priority register (IP)

7	6	5	4	3	2	1	0
——	——	PT2	PS	PT1	PX1	PT0	PX0

'0' → low priority

'1' → high priority

Interrupt Handling

The interrupt flags are sampled at P2 of S5 of every instruction cycle (Note that every instruction cycle has six states each consisting of P1 and P2 pulses). The samples are polled during the next machine cycle (or instruction cycle). If one of the flags was set at S5P2 of the preceding instruction cycle, the polling detects it and the interrupt process generates a long call (LCALL) to the appropriate vector location of the interrupt. The LCALL is generated provided this hardware generated LCALL is not blocked by any one of the following conditions.

- An interrupt of equal or higher priority level is already in progress.

- The current polling cycle is not the final cycle in the execution of the instruction in progress.

- The instruction in progress is RETI or any write to IE or IP registers.

When an interrupt comes and the program is directed to the interrupt vector address, the Program Counter (PC) value of the interrupted program is stored (pushed) on the stack. The required Interrupt Service Routine (ISR) is executed. At the end of the ISR, the instruction RETI returns the value of the PC from the stack and the originally interrupted program is resumed. Reset is a non-maskable interrupt. A reset is accomplished by holding the RST pin high for at least two machine cycles. On resetting the program starts from 0000H and some flags are modified as follows:

Register	Value(Hex) on Reset
PC	0000H
DPTR	0000H
A	00H
B	00H
SP	07H
PSW	00H
Ports P0-3 Latches	FFH
IP	XXX 00000 b
IE	0 XX 00000 b
TCON	00H
TMOD	00H
TH0	00H
TH0	00H
TH1	00H
TL1	00H
SCON	00H
SBUF	XX H
PCON	0 XXXX XXX b

The schematic diagram of the detection and processing of interrupts is given as follows:

Instruction Cycles →

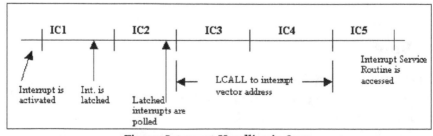

Figure: Interrupt Handling in 8051.

It should be noted that the interrupt which is blocked due to the three conditions mentioned before is not remembered unless the flag that generated interrupt is not still active when the above blocking conditions are removed, i.e., every polling cycle is new.

Jump and Call Instructions

There are 3 types of jump instructions. They are:

- Relative Jump,

- Short Absolute Jump,

- Long Absolute Jump.

Relative Jump

Jump that replaces the PC (program counter) content with a new address that is greater than (the address following the jump instruction by 127 or less) or less than (the address following the jump by 128 or less) is called a relative jump. Schematically, the relative jump can be shown as follows:

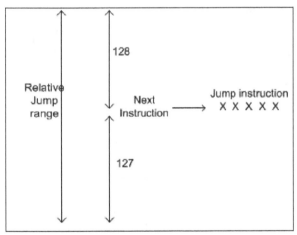

Figure: Relative Jump.

- Advantages of the Relative Jump:

  ◦ Only 1 byte of jump address needs to be specified in the 2's complement form, i.e. for jumping ahead, the range is 0 to 127 and for jumping back, the range is - 1 to -128.

  ◦ Specifying only one byte reduces the size of the instruction and speeds up program execution.

  ◦ The program with relative jumps can be relocated without reassembling to generate absolute jump addresses.

- Disadvantages of the Absolute Jump: Short jump range (-128 to 127 from the instruction following the jump instruction).

- Instructions that use Relative Jump:

  SJMP <relative address>

(The remaining relative jumps are conditional jumps)

JC <relative address>

JNC <relative address>

JB bit, <relative address>

JNB bit, <relative address>

JBC bit, <relative address>

CJNE <destination byte>, <source byte>, <relative address>

DJNZ <byte>, <relative address>

JZ <relative address>

JNZ <relative address>

Short Absolute Jump

In this case only 11bits of the absolute jump address are needed. The absolute jump address is calculated in the following manner. In 8051, 64 kbyte of program memory space is divided into 32 pages of 2 kbyte each. The hexadecimal addresses of the pages are given as follows:

Page (Hex)	Address (Hex)
00	0000 - 07FF
01	0800 - 0FFF
02	1000 - 17FF
03	1800 - 1FFF
.	.
1E	F000 - F7FF
1F	F800 - FFFF

It can be seen that the upper 5bits of the program counter (PC) hold the page number and the lower 11bits of the PC hold the address within that page. Thus, an absolute address is formed by taking page numbers of the instruction (from the program counter) following the jump and attaching the specified 11bits to it to form the 16-bit address.

- Advantage: The instruction length becomes 2 bytes.

However, difficulty is encountered when the next instruction following the jump instruction begins from a fresh page (at X000H or at X800H). This does not give any problem for the forward jump, but results in an error for the backward jump. In such a case the assembler prompts the user to relocate the program suitably.

Example of short absolute jump: -

ACALL <address 11>

AJMP <address 11>

Long Absolute Jump/Call

Applications that need to access the entire program memory from 0000H to FFFFH use long absolute jump. Since the absolute address has to be specified in the op-code, the instruction length is 3 bytes (except for JMP @ A+DPTR). This jump is not relocatable. Example:

> LCALL <address 16>
>
> LJMP <address 16>
>
> JMP @A+DPTR

Serial Interface

The serial port of 8051 is full duplex, i.e., it can transmit and receive simultaneously. The register SBUF is used to hold the data. The special function register SBUF is physically two registers. One is, write-only and is used to hold data to be transmitted out of the 8051 via TXD. The other is, read-only and holds the received data from external sources via RXD. Both mutually exclusive registers have the same address 099H.

Serial Port Control Register (SCON)

Register SCON controls serial data communication.

Address: 098H (Bit addressable)

SM0	SM1	SM2	REN	TB8	RB8	TI	RI

Mode select bits:

SM0	SM1	Mode
0	0	Mode 0
0	1	Mode 1
1	0	Mode 2
1	1	Mode 3

- SM2: Multi processor communication bit.
- REN: Receive enable bit.
- TB8: Transmitted bit 8 (Normally we have 0-7 bits transmitted/received).
- RB8: Received bit 8.
- TI: Transmit interrupt flag.
- RI: Receive interrupt flag.

Power Mode Control Register

Register PCON controls processor power down, sleep modes and serial data band rate. Only one bit of PCON is used with respect to serial communication. The seventh bit (b7) (SMOD) is used to generate the baud rate of serial communication.

Address: 87H

b7							bo
SMOD	–	–	–	GFI	GFo	PD	IDL

- SMOD: Serial baud rate modify bit.

- GF1: General purpose user flag bit 1.

- GFo: General purpose user flag bit 0.

- PD: Power down bit.

- IDL: Idle mode bit.

Data Transmission

Transmission of serial data begins at any time when data is written to SBUF. Pin P3.1 (Alternate function bit TXD) is used to transmit data to the serial data network. TI is set to 1 when data has been transmitted. This signifies that SBUF is empty so that another byte can be sent.

Data Reception

Reception of serial data begins if the receive enable bit is set to 1 for all modes. Pin P3.0 (Alternate function bit RXD) is used to receive data from the serial data network. Receive interrupt flag, RI, is set after the data has been received in all modes. The data gets stored in SBUF register from where it can be read.

Serial Data Transmission Modes

Mode-0: In this mode, the serial port works like a shift register and the data transmission works synchronously with a clock frequency of $f_{osc}/12$. Serial data is received and transmitted through RXD. 8 bits are transmitted/ received at a time. Pin TXD outputs the shift clock pulses of frequency $f_{osc}/12$, which is connected to the external circuitry for synchronization. The shift frequency or baud rate is always 1/12 of the oscillator frequency.

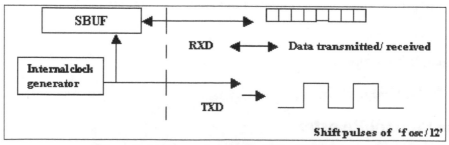

Figure: Data Transmission/Reception in Mode-0.

- Mode-1 (standard UART mode): In mode-1, the serial port functions as a standard Universal Asynchronous Receiver Transmitter (UART) mode. 10 bits are transmitted through TXD or received through RXD. The 10 bits consist of one start bit (which is usually '0'), 8 data bits (LSB is sent first/received first), and a stop bit (which is usually '1'). Once received, the stop bit goes into RB8 in the special function register SCON. The baud rate is variable. The following figure shows the way the bits are transmitted/ received.

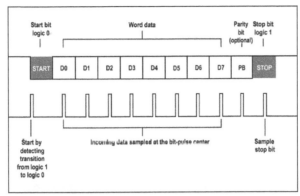

Figure: Data Transmission Format in UART Mode.

Bit time= $1/f_{baud}$

In receiving mode, data bits are shifted into the receiver at the programmed baud rate. The data word (8- bits) will be loaded to SBUF if the following conditions are true:

- RI must be zero. (i.e., the previously received byte has been cleared from SBUF).

- Mode bit SM2 = 0 or stop bit = 1.

After the data is received and the data byte has been loaded into SBUF, RI becomes one.

Mode-1 baud rate generation: Timer-1 is used to generate baud rate for mode-1 serial communication by using overflow flag of the timer to determine the baud frequency. Timer-1 is used in timer mode-2 as an auto-reload 8-bit timer. The data rate is generated by timer-1 using the following formula.

$$f_{baud} = \frac{2^{SMOD}}{32} \times \frac{fosc}{12 \times \left[256 - (TH1)\right]}$$

where, SMOD is the 7th bit of PCON register and f_{osc} is the crystal oscillator frequency of the microcontroller.

It can be noted that f_{osc}/ (12 X [256- (TH1)]) is the timer overflow frequency in timer mode-2, which is the auto-reload mode. If timer-1 is not run in mode-2, then the baud rate is,

$$f_{baud} = \frac{2^{SMOD}}{32} \times \left(timer - 1 \text{ overflow frequency}\right)$$

Timer-1 can be run using the internal clock, f_{osc}/12 (timer mode) or from any external source via pin T1 (P3.5) (Counter mode).

Example: If standard baud rate is desired, then 11.0592 MHz crystal could be selected. To get a standard 9600 baud rate, the setting of TH1 is calculated as follows.

Assuming SMOD to be '0':

$$9600 = \frac{2^0}{32} \times \frac{11.0592 \times 10^6}{12 \times (256 - TH1)}$$

or

$$256 - TH1 = \frac{1}{32} \times \frac{11.0592 \times 10^6}{12 \times 9600} = 3$$

or

$$TH1 = 256 - 3 = 253 = FDH$$

In mode-1, if SM2 is set to 1, no receive interrupt (RI) is generated unless a valid stop bit is received.

Serial Data Mode-2-Multiprocessor Mode

In this mode 11 bits are transmitted through TXD or received through RXD. The various bits are as follows, a start bit (usually '0'), 8 data bits (LSB first), a programmable 9th (TB8 or RB8) bit and a stop bit (usually '1'). While transmitting, the 9th data bit (TB8 in SCON) can be assigned the value '0' or '1'. For example, if the information of parity is to be transmitted, the parity bit (P) in PSW could be moved into TB8. On reception of the data, the 9th bit goes into RB8 in 'SCON', while the stop bit is ignored. The baud rate is programmable to either 1/32 or 1/64 of the oscillator frequency.

$$f_{baud} = \left(2^{SMOD} / 64\right) f_{osc}.$$

Mode-3-Multi Processor Mode with Variable Baud Rate

In this mode 11 bits are transmitted through TXD or received through RXD. The various bits are, a start bit (usually '0'), 8 data bits (LSB first), a programmable 9 th bit and a stop bit (usually '1'). Mode-3 is same as mode-2, except the fact that the baud rate in mode-3 is variable (i.e., just as in mode-1).

$$f_{baud} = \left(2^{SMOD} / 32\right) * \left(fosc / 12 \ (256 - TH1)\right).$$

This baud rate holds when Timer-1 is programmed in Mode-2.

Counters and Timers

As you already know, the microcontroller oscillator uses quartz crystal for its operation. As the frequency of this oscillator is precisely defined and very stable, pulses it generates are always of the same width, which makes them ideal for time measurement. Such crystals are also used in quartz watches. In order to measure time between two events it is sufficient to count up pulses coming from this oscillator. That is exactly what the timer does. If the timer is properly programmed, the value stored in its register will be incremented (or decremented) with each coming pulse, i.e. once per each machine cycle. A single machine-cycle instruction lasts for 12 quartz oscillator periods, which means that by embedding quartz with oscillator frequency of 12MHz, a number stored in the timer register will be changed million times per second, i.e. each microsecond. The 8051 microcontroller has 2 timers/counters called T0 and T1. As their names suggest, their main purpose is to measure time and count external events. Besides, they can be used for generating clock pulses to be used in serial communication, so called Baud Rate.

Timer T0

The timer T0 consists of two registers – TH0 and TL0 representing a low and a high byte of one 16-digit binary number.

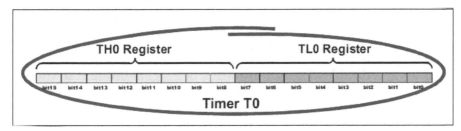

Accordingly, if the content of the timer T0 is equal to 0 (T0=0) then both registers it consists of will contain 0. If the timer contains for example number 1000 (decimal), then the TH0 register (high byte) will contain the number 3, while the TL0 register (low byte) will contain decimal number 232.

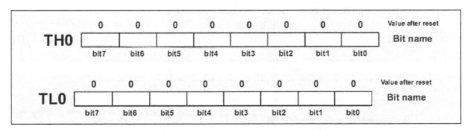

Formula used to calculate values in these two registers is very simple:

TH0 × 256 + TL0 = T.

Matching the previous example it would be as follows:

3 × 256 + 232 = 1000.

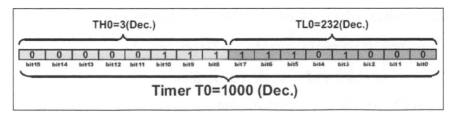

Since the timer T0 is virtually 16-bit register, the largest value it can store is 65 535. In case of exceeding this value, the timer will be automatically cleared and counting starts from 0. This condition is called an overflow. Two registers TMOD and TCON are closely connected to this timer and control its operation.

TMOD Register (Timer Mode)

The TMOD register selects the operational mode of the timers T0 and T1. As seen in figure below, the low 4 bits (bit0 – bit3) refer to the timer 0, while the high 4 bits (bit4 – bit7) refer to the timer 1. There are 4 operational modes and each of them is described herein.

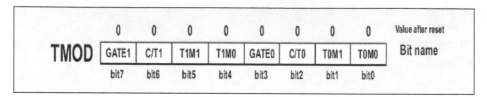

Bits of this register have the following function:

- GATE1 enables and disables Timer 1 by means of a signal brought to the INT1 pin (P3.3):

    ◦ 1 – Timer 1 operates only if the INT1 bit is set.

    ◦ 0 – Timer 1 operates regardless of the logic state of the INT1 bit.

- C/T1 selects pulses to be counted up by the timer/counter 1:

    ◦ 1 – Timer counts pulses brought to the T1 pin (P3.5).

    ◦ 0 – Timer counts pulses from internal oscillator.

- T1M1 and T1M0 are the two bits that select the operational mode of the Timer 1.

T1M1	T1M0	Mode	Description
0	0	0	13-bit timer
0	1	1	16-bit timer
1	0	2	8-bit auto-reload
1	1	3	Split mode

- GATE0 enables and disables Timer 1 using a signal brought to the INT0 pin (P3.2):

    ◦ 1 – Timer 0 operates only if the INT0 bit is set.

    ◦ 0 – Timer 0 operates regardless of the logic state of the INT0 bit.

- C/T0 selects pulses to be counted up by the timer/counter 0:

    ◦ 1 – Timer counts pulses brought to the T0 pin (P3.4).

    ◦ 0 – Timer counts pulses from internal oscillator.

- T0M1 and T0M0 are the two bits that select the operational mode of the Timer 0.

ToM1	ToMo	Mode	Description
0	0	0	13-bit timer
0	1	1	16-bit timer
1	0	2	8-bit auto-reload
1	1	3	Split mode

Timer 0 in Mode 0 (13-Bit Timer)

This is one of the rarities being kept only for the purpose of compatibility with the previous versions of microcontrollers. This mode configures timer 0 as a 13-bit timer which consists of all 8 bits of TH0 and the lower 5 bits of TL0. As a result, the Timer 0 uses only 13 of 16 bits. How does it operate? Each coming pulse causes the lower register bits to change their states. After receiving 32 pulses, this register is loaded and automatically cleared, while the higher byte (TH0) is incremented by 1. This process is repeated until registers count up 8192 pulses. After that, both registers are cleared and counting starts from 0.

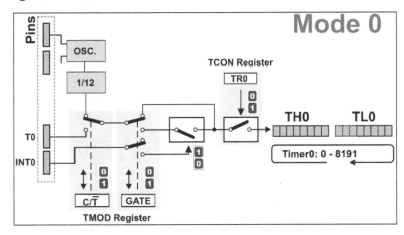

Timer 0 in Mode 1 (16-Bit Timer)

Mode 1 configures timer 0 as a 16-bit timer comprising all the bits of both registers TH0 and TL0. That's why this is one of the most commonly used modes. Timer operates in the same way as in mode 0, with difference that the registers count up to 65 536 as allowable by the 16 bits.

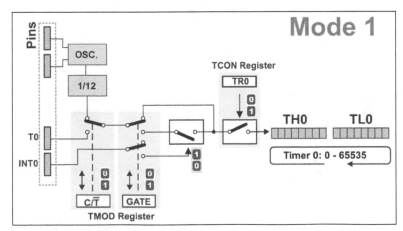

Timer 0 in Mode 2 (Auto-Reload Timer)

Mode 2 configures timer 0 as an 8-bit timer. Actually, timer 0 uses only one 8-bit register for counting and never counts from 0, but from an arbitrary value (0-255) stored in another (TH0) register. The following example shows the advantages of this mode. Suppose it is necessary to constantly count up 55 pulses generated by the clock. If mode 1 or mode 0 is used, It is necessary to write the number 200 to the timer registers and constantly check whether an overflow has occurred, i.e. whether they reached the value 255. When it happens, it is necessary to rewrite the number 200 and repeat the whole procedure. The same procedure is automatically performed by the microcontroller if set in mode 2. In fact, only the TL0 register operates as a timer, while another (TH0) register stores the value from which the counting starts. When the TL0 register is loaded, instead of being cleared, the contents of TH0 will be reloaded to it. Referring to the previous example, in order to register each 55th pulse, the best solution is to write the number 200 to the TH0 register and configure the timer to operate in mode 2.

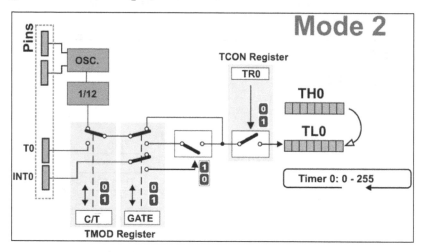

Timer 0 in Mode 3 (Split Timer)

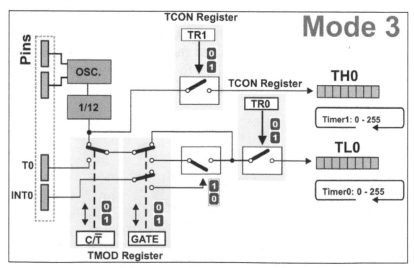

Mode 3 configures timer 0 so that registers TL0 and TH0 operate as separate 8-bit timers. In other words, the 16-bit timer consisting of two registers TH0 and TL0 is split into two independent 8-bit timers. This mode is provided for applications requiring an additional 8-bit timer or counter. The TL0 timer turns into timer 0, while the TH0 timer turns into timer 1. In addition, all the control bits of 16-bit Timer 1 (consisting of the TH1 and TL1 register), now control the 8-bit Timer 1. Even though the 16-bit Timer 1 can still be configured to operate in any of modes (mode 1, 2 or 3), it is no longer possible to disable it as there is no control bit to do it. Thus, its operation is restricted when timer 0 is in mode 3. The only application of this mode is when two timers are used and the 16-bit Timer 1 the operation of which is out of control is used as a baud rate generator.

Timer Control (TCON) Register

TCON register is also one of the registers whose bits are directly in control of timer operation. Only 4 bits of this register are used for this purpose, while rest of them is used for interrupt control.

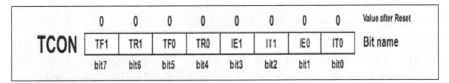

- TF1 bit is automatically set on the Timer 1 overflow.

- TR1 bit enables the Timer 1.

  - 1 – Timer 1 is enabled.

  - 0 – Timer 1 is disabled.

- TF0 bit is automatically set on the Timer 0 overflow.

- TR0 bit enables the timer 0.

  - 1 – Timer 0 is enabled.

  - 0 – Timer 0 is disabled.

Use of Timer 0

In order to use timer 0, it is first necessary to select it and configure the mode of its operation. Bits of the TMOD register are in control of it:

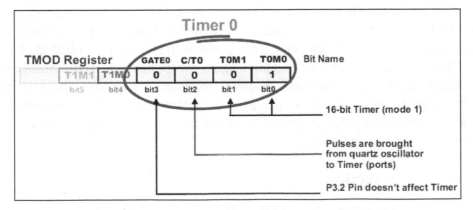

Referring to figure above, the timer 0 operates in mode 1 and counts pulses generated by internal clock the frequency of which is equal to 1/12 the quartz frequency.

Turn on the timer:

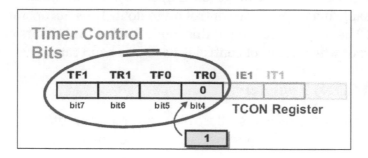

The TR0 bit is set and the timer starts operation. If the quartz crystal with frequency of 12MHz is embedded then its contents will be incremented every microsecond. After 65.536 microseconds, the both registers the timer consists of will be loaded. The microcontroller automatically clears them and the timer keeps on repeating procedure from the beginning until the TR0 bit value is logic zero (0).

How to 'Read' a Timer?

Depending on application, it is necessary either to read a number stored in the timer registers or to register the moment they have been cleared.

- It is extremely simple to read a timer by using only one register configured in mode 2 or 3. It is sufficient to read its state at any moment.

- It is somehow complicated to read a timer configured to operate in mode 2. Suppose the lower byte is read first (TL0), then the higher byte (TH0). The result is:

    TH0 = 15 TL0 = 255

Everything seems to be ok, but the current state of the register at the moment of reading was:

    TH0 = 14 TL0 = 255

In case of negligence, such an error in counting (255 pulses) may occur for not so obvious but quite logical reason. The lower byte is correctly read (255), but at the moment the program counter was about to read the higher byte TH0, an overflow occurred and the contents of both registers have been changed (TH0: 14→15, TL0: 255→0). This problem has a simple solution. The higher byte should be read first, then the lower byte and once again the higher byte. If the number stored in the higher byte is different then this sequence should be repeated. It's about a short loop consisting of only 3 instructions in the program. There is another solution as well. It is sufficient to simply turn the timer off while reading is going on (the TR0 bit of the TCON register should be cleared), and turn it on again after reading is finished.

Timer 0 Overflow Detection

Usually, there is no need to constantly read timer registers. It is sufficient to register the moment they are cleared, i.e. when counting starts from 0. This condition is called an overflow. When it occurs, the TF0 bit of the TCON register will be automatically set. The state of this bit can be constantly checked from within the program or by enabling an interrupt which will stop the main program execution when this bit is set. Suppose it is necessary to provide a program delay of 0.05 seconds (50 000 machine cycles), i.e. time when the program seems to be stopped:

First a number to be written to the timer registers should be calculated:

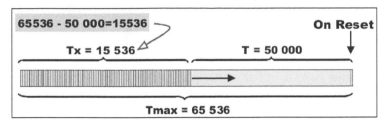

Then it should be written to the timer registers TH0 and TL0:

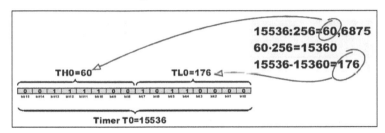

When enabled, the timer will resume counting from this number. The state of the TF0 bit, i.e. whether it is set, is checked from within the program. It happens at the moment of overflow, i.e. after exactly 50.000 machine cycles or 0.05 seconds.

How to Measure Pulse Duration?

Suppose it is necessary to measure the duration of an operation, for example how long a device has been turned on? Look again at the figure illustrating the timer and pay attention to the function of the GATE0 bit of the TMOD register. If it is cleared then the state of the P3.2 pin doesn't affect timer operation. If GATE0 = 1 the timer will operate until the pin P3.2 is cleared. Accordingly, if this pin is supplied with 5V through some external switch at the moment the device is being turned on, the timer will measure duration of its operation, which actually was the objective.

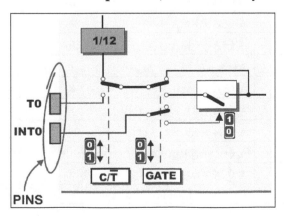

How to Count up Pulses?

Similarly to the previous example, the answer to this question again lies in the TCON register. This time it's about the C/To bit. If the bit is cleared the timer counts pulses generated by the internal oscillator, i.e. measures the time passed. If the bit is set, the timer input is provided with pulses from the P3.4 pin (To). Since these pulses are not always of the same width, the timer cannot be used for time measurement and is turned into a counter, therefore. The highest frequency that could be measured by such a counter is 1/24 frequency of used quartz-crystal.

Timer 1

Timer 1 is identical to timer 0, except for mode 3 which is a hold-count mode. It means that they have the same function, their operation is controlled by the same registers TMOD and TCON and both of them can operate in one out of 4 different modes.

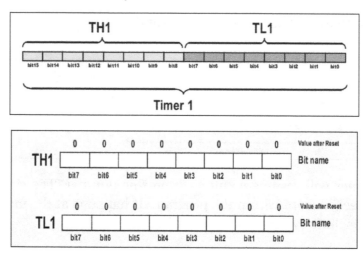

Different Instructions of 8051

Arithmetic Instructions

Mnemonics	Description	Bytes	Instruction Cycles
ADD A, Rn	A ← A + Rn	1	1
ADD A, direct	A ← A + (direct)	2	1
ADD A, @Ri	A ← A + @Ri	1	1
ADD A, #data	A ← A + data	2	1
ADDC A, Rn	A ← A + Rn + C	1	1
ADDC A, direct	A ← A + (direct) + C	2	1
ADDC A, @Ri	A ← A + @Ri + C	1	1
ADDC A, #data	A ← A + data + C	2	1
DA A	Decimal adjust accumulator	1	1

DIV AB	Divide A by B A ← quotient B ← remainder	1	4
DEC A	A ← A -1	1	1
DEC Rn	Rn ← Rn - 1	1	1
DEC direct	(direct) ← (direct) - 1	2	1
DEC @Ri	@Ri ← @Ri - 1	1	1
INC A	A ← A+1	1	1
INC Rn	Rn ← Rn + 1	1	1
INC direct	(direct) ← (direct) + 1	2	1
INC @Ri	@Ri ← @Ri +1	1	1
INC DPTR	DPTR ← DPTR +1	1	2
MUL AB	Multiply A by B A ← low byte (A*B) B ← high byte (A* B)	1	4
SUBB A, Rn	A ← A - Rn - C	1	1
SUBB A, direct	A ← A - (direct) - C	2	1
SUBB A, @Ri	A ← A - @Ri - C	1	1
SUBB A, #data	A ← A - data - C	2	1

Logical Instructions

Mnemonics	Description	Bytes	Instruction Cycles
ANL A, Rn	A ← A AND Rn	1	1
ANL A, direct	A ← A AND (direct)	2	1
ANL A, @Ri	A ← A AND @Ri	1	1
ANL A, #data	A ← A AND data	2	1
ANL direct, A	(direct) ← (direct) AND A	2	1
ANL direct, #data	(direct) ← (direct) AND data	3	2
CLR A	A ← 00H	1	1
CPL A	A ← A	1	1
ORL A, Rn	A ← A OR Rn	1	1
ORL A, direct	A ← A OR (direct)	1	1
ORL A, @Ri	A ← A OR @Ri	2	1
ORL A, #data	A ← A OR data	1	1
ORL direct, A	(direct) ← (direct) OR A	2	1
ORL direct, #data	(direct) ← (direct) OR data	3	2
RL A	Rotate accumulator left	1	1

RLC A	Rotate accumulator left through carry	1	1
RR A	Rotate accumulator right	1	1
RRC A	Rotate accumulator right through carry	1	1
SWAP A	Swap nibbles within Acumulator	1	1
XRL A, Rn	A ← A EXOR Rn	1	1
XRL A, direct	A ← A EXOR (direct)	1	1
XRL A, @Ri	A ← A EXOR @Ri	2	1
XRL A, #data	A ← A EXOR data	1	1
XRL direct, A	(direct) ← (direct) EXOR A	2	1
XRL direct, #data	(direct) ← (direct) EXOR data	3	2

Data Transfer Instructions

Mnemonics	Description	Bytes	Instruction Cycles
MOV A, Rn	A ← Rn	1	1
MOV A, direct	A ← (direct)	2	1
MOV A, @Ri	A ← @Ri	1	1
MOV A, #data	A ← data	2	1
MOV Rn, A	Rn ← A	1	1
MOV Rn, direct	Rn ← (direct)	2	2
MOV Rn, #data	Rn ← data	2	1
MOV direct, A	(direct) ← A	2	1
MOV direct, Rn	(direct) ← Rn	2	2
MOV direct1, direct2	(direct1) ← (direct2)	3	2
MOV direct, @Ri	(direct) ← @Ri	2	2
MOV direct, #data	(direct) ← #data	3	2
MOV @Ri, A	@Ri ← A	1	1
MOV @Ri, direct	@Ri ← (direct)	2	2
MOV @Ri, #data	@Ri data	2	1
MOV DPTR, #data16	DPTR ← data16	3	2
MOVC A, @A+DPTR	A ← Code byte pointed by A + DPTR	1	2

MOVC A, @A+PC	A ← Code byte pointed by A + PC	1	2
MOVC A, @Ri	A ← Code byte pointed by Ri 8-bit address)	1	2
MOVX A, @DPTR	A ← External data pointed by DPTR	1	2
MOVX @Ri, A	@Ri ← A (External data - 8bit address)	1	2
MOVX @DPTR, A	@DPTR ← A(External data - 16 bit address)	1	2
PUSH direct	(SP) ← (direct)	2	2
POP direct	(direct) ← (SP)	2	2
XCH Rn	Exchange A with Rn	1	1
XCH direct	Exchange A with direct byte	2	1
XCH @Ri	Exchange A with indirect RAM	1	1
XCHD A, @Ri	Exchange least significant nibble of A with that of indirect RAM	1	1

Boolean Variable Instructions

Mnemonics	Description	Bytes	Instruction Cycles
CLR C	C-bit ← 0	1	1
CLR bit	bit ← 0	2	1
SET C	C ← 1	1	1
SET bit	bit ← 1	2	1
CPL C	C ← $\overline{C-bit}$	1	1
CPL bit	bit ← $\overline{bit}$	2	1
ANL C, /bit	C ← C . $\overline{bit}$	2	1
ANL C, bit	C ← C. bit	2	1
ORL C, /bit	C ← C + $\overline{bit}$	2	1
ORL C, bit	C ← C + bit	2	1
MOV C, bit	C ← bit	2	1
MOV bit, C	bit ← C	2	2

Program Branching Instructions

Mnemonics	Description	Bytes	Instruction Cycles
ACALL addr11	PC + 2 → (SP) ; addr 11 → PC	2	2
AJMP addr11	Addr11 → PC	2	2
CJNE A, direct, rel	Compare with A, jump (PC + rel) if not equal	3	2

CJNE A, #data, rel	Compare with A, jump (PC + rel) if not equal	3	2
CJNE Rn, #data, rel	Compare with Rn, jump (PC + rel) if not equal	3	2
CJNE @Ri, #data, rel	Compare with @Ri A, jump (PC + rel) if not equal	3	2
DJNZ Rn, rel	Decrement Rn, jump if not zero	2	2
DJNZ direct, rel	Decrement (direct), jump if not zero	3	2
JC rel	Jump (PC + rel) if C bit = 1	2	2
JNC rel	Jump (PC + rel) if C bit = 0	2	2
JB bit, rel	Jump (PC + rel) if bit = 1	3	2
JNB bit, rel	Jump (PC + rel) if bit = 0	3	2
JBC bit, rel	Jump (PC + rel) if bit = 1	3	2
JMP @A+DPTR	A+DPTR $\rightarrow$ PC	1	2
JZ rel	If A=0, jump to PC + rel	2	2
JNZ rel	If A $\neq$ 0 , jump to PC + rel	2	2
LCALL addr16	PC + 3 $\rightarrow$ (SP), addr16 $\rightarrow$ PC	3	2
LJMP addr 16	Addr16 $\rightarrow$ PC	3	2
NOP	No operation	1	1
RET	(SP) $\rightarrow$ PC	1	2
RETI	(SP) $\rightarrow$ PC, Enable Interrupt	1	2
SJMP rel	PC + 2 + rel $\rightarrow$ PC	2	2
JMP @A+DPTR	A+DPTR $\rightarrow$ PC	1	2
JZ rel	If A = 0. jump PC+ rel	2	2
JNZ rel	If A $\neq$ 0, jump PC + rel	2	2
NOP	No operation	1	1

Microprocessors

The electronic devices used by a computer to perform its work are known as microprocessors. Microprocessors are used to perform the various arithmetic and logic operations of a computer. The topics elaborated in this chapter will help in gaining a better perspective about the different types of microprocessors such as Intel 8085 and Intel 8086.

A microprocessor is a programmable electronics chip that has computing and decision making capabilities similar to central processing unit of a computer. Any microprocessor based systems having limited number of resources are called microcomputers. Nowadays, microprocessor can be seen in almost all types of electronics devices like mobile phones, printers, washing machines etc. Microprocessors are also used in advanced applications like radars, satellites and flights. Due to the rapid advancements in electronic industry and large scale integration of devices results in a significant cost reduction and increase application of microprocessors and their derivatives.

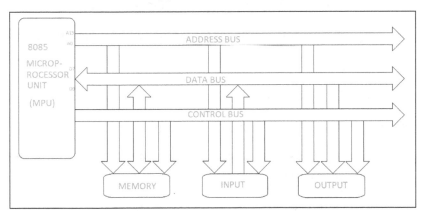

Figure: Microprocessor-Based System.

- Bit: A bit is a single binary digit.

- Word: A word refers to the basic data size or bit size that can be processed by the arithmetic and logic unit of the processor. A 16-bit binary number is called a word in a 16-bit processor.

- Bus: A bus is a group of wires/lines that carry similar information.

- System Bus: The system bus is a group of wires/lines used for communication between the microprocessor and peripherals.

- Memory Word: The number of bits that can be stored in a register or memory element is called a memory word.

- Address Bus: It carries the address, which is a unique binary pattern used to identify a memory location or an I/O port. For example, an eight bit address bus has eight lines and thus it can address $2^8 = 256$ different locations. The locations in hexadecimal format can be written as 00H – FFH.

- Data Bus: The data bus is used to transfer data between memory and processor or between I/O device and processor. For example, an 8-bit processor will generally have an 8-bit data bus and a 16-bit processor will have 16-bit data bus.

- Control Bus: The control bus carry control signals, which consists of signals for selection of memory or I/O device from the given address, direction of data transfer and synchronization of data transfer in case of slow devices.

A typical microprocessor consists of arithmetic and logic unit (ALU) in association with control unit to process the instruction execution. Almost all the microprocessors are based on the principle of store-program concept. In store-program concept, programs or instructions are sequentially stored in the memory locations that are to be executed. To do any task using a microprocessor, it is to be programmed by the user. So the programmer must have idea about its internal resources, features and supported instructions. Each microprocessor has a set of instructions, a list which is provided by the microprocessor manufacturer. The instruction set of a microprocessor is provided in two forms: binary machine code and mnemonics. Microprocessor communicates and operates in binary numbers 0 and 1. The set of instructions in the form of binary patterns is called a machine language and it is difficult for us to understand. Therefore, the binary patterns are given abbreviated names, called mnemonics, which forms the assembly language. The conversion of assembly-level language into binary machine-level language is done by using an application called assembler.

- Technology Used: The semiconductor manufacturing technologies used for chips are:

  ◦ Transistor-Transistor Logic (TTL),

  ◦ Emitter Coupled Logic (ECL),

  ◦ Complementary Metal-Oxide Semiconductor (CMOS).

- Classification of Microprocessors: Based on their specification, application and architecture microprocessors are classified.

  ◦ Based on Size of Data Bus:

    ▫ 4-bit microprocessor,

    ▫ 8-bit microprocessor,

    ▫ 16-bit microprocessor,

    ▫ 32-bit microprocessor.

  ◦ Based on Application:

    ▫ General-Purpose Microprocessor: Used in general computer system and can be used by programmer for any application. Examples, 8085 to Intel Pentium.

    ▫ Microcontroller: Microprocessor with built-in memory and ports and can be programmed for any generic control application. Example, 8051.

    ▫ Special-Purpose Processors: Designed to handle special functions required for an application. Examples, digital signal processors and application-specific integrated circuit (ASIC) chips.

- ○ Based on Architecture:

  - □ Reduced Instruction Set Computer (RISC) processors,

  - □ Complex Instruction Set Computer (CISC) processors.

Intel 8085

The 8085 microprocessor is an 8-bit processor available as a 40-pin IC package and uses +5 V for power. It can run at a maximum frequency of 3 MHz. Its data bus width is 8-bit and address bus width is 16-bit, thus it can address $2^{16} = 64$ KB of memory. The internal architecture of 8085 is shown is figure.

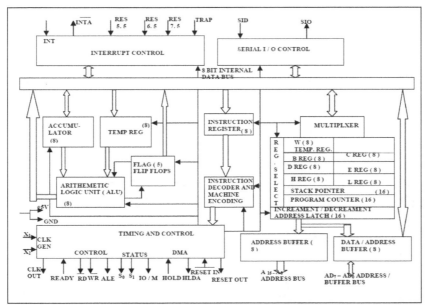

Figure: Internal Architecture of 8085.

Arithmetic and Logic Unit

The ALU performs the actual numerical and logical operations such as Addition (ADD), Subtraction (SUB), AND, OR etc. It uses data from memory and from Accumulator to perform operations. The results of the arithmetic and logical operations are stored in the accumulator.

Registers

The 8085 includes six registers, one accumulator and one flag register, as shown in Figure. In addition, it has two 16-bit registers: stack pointer and program counter. They are briefly described as follows. The 8085 has six general-purpose registers to store 8-bit data; these are identified as B, C, D, E, H and L. they can be combined as register pairs-BC, DE and HL to perform some 16-bit operations. The programmer can use these registers to store or copy data into the register by using data copy instructions.

ACCUMULATOR A (8)		FLAG REGISTER
B (8)		C (8)
D (8)		E (8)
H (8)		L (8)
Stack Pointer (SP)		(16)
Program Counter (PC)		(16)

Data Bus   Address Bus

8 Lines Bidirectional   16 Lines unidirectional

Figure: Register organisation.

Accumulator

The accumulator is an 8-bit register that is a part of ALU. This register is used to store 8-bit data and to perform arithmetic and logical operations. The result of an operation is stored in the accumulator. The accumulator is also identified as register A.

Flag Register

The ALU includes five flip-flops, which are set or reset after an operation according to data condition of the result in the accumulator and other registers. They are called Zero (Z), Carry (CY), Sign (S), Parity (P) and Auxiliary Carry (AC) flags. Their bit positions in the flag register are shown in Figure. The microprocessor uses these flags to test data conditions.

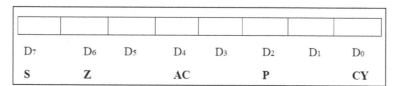

D_7	D_6	D_5	D_4	D_3	D_2	D_1	D_0
S	Z		AC		P		CY

For example, after an addition of two numbers, if the result in the accumulator is larger than 8-bit, the flip-flop uses to indicate a carry by setting CY flag to 1. When an arithmetic operation results in zero, Z flag is set to 1. The S flag is just a copy of the bit D7 of the accumulator. A negative number has a 1 in bit D7 and a positive number has a 0 in 2's complement representation. The AC flag is set to 1, when a carry result from bit D3 and passes to bit D4. The P flag is set to 1, when the result in accumulator contains even number of 1s.

Program Counter (PC)

This 16-bit register deals with sequencing the execution of instructions. This register is a memory pointer. The microprocessor uses this register to sequence the execution of the instructions. The function of the program counter is to point to the memory address from which the next byte is to be fetched. When a byte is being fetched, the program counter is automatically incremented by one to point to the next memory location.

Stack Pointer (SP)

The stack pointer is also a 16-bit register, used as a memory pointer. It points to a memory location in R/W memory, called stack. The beginning of the stack is defined by loading 16- bit address in the stack pointer.

Instruction Register/Decoder

It is an 8-bit register that temporarily stores the current instruction of a program. Latest instruction sent here from memory prior to execution. Decoder then takes instruction and decodes or interprets the instruction. Decoded instruction then passed to next stage.

Control Unit

Generates signals on data bus, address bus and control bus within microprocessor to carry out the instruction, which has been decoded. Typical buses and their timing are described as follows:

- Data Bus: Data bus carries data in binary form between microprocessor and other external units such as memory. It is used to transmit data i.e. information, results of arithmetic etc between memory and the microprocessor. Data bus is bidirectional in nature. The data bus width of 8085 microprocessor is 8-bit i.e. 28 combination of binary digits and are typically identified as D0 – D7. Thus size of the data bus determines what arithmetic can be done. If only 8-bit wide then largest number is 11111111 (255 in decimal). Therefore, larger numbers have to be broken down into chunks of 255. This slows microprocessor.

- Address Bus: The address bus carries addresses and is one way bus from microprocessor to the memory or other devices. 8085 microprocessor contain 16-bit address bus and are generally identified as A0-A15. The higher order address lines (A8 – A15) are unidirectional and the lower order lines (A0 – A7) are multiplexed (time-shared) with the eight data bits (D0 – D7) and hence, they are bidirectional.

- Control Bus: Control bus are various lines which have specific functions for coordinating and controlling microprocessor operations. The control bus carries control signals partly unidirectional and partly bidirectional. The following control and status signals are used by 8085 processor:

  ○ ALE (output): Address Latch Enable is a pulse that is provided when an address appears on the AD0 – AD7 lines, after which it becomes 0.

  ○ $\overline{RD}$ (Active low output): The Read signal indicates that data are being read from the selected I/O or memory device and that they are available on the data bus.

  ○ $\overline{WR}$ (Active low output): The Write signal indicates that data on the data bus are to be written into a selected memory or I/O location.

  ○ IO/$\overline{M}$ (Output): It is a signal that distinguished between a memory operation and an

I/O operation. When $IO/\overline{M} = 0$ it is a memory operation and $IO/\overline{M} = 1$ it is an I/O operation.

○ S1 and So (output): These are status signals used to specify the type of operation being performed; they are listed in table.

Table: Status Signals and Associated Operations.

S1	So	States
0	0	Halt
0	1	Write
1	0	Read
1	1	Fetch

The schematic representation of the 8085 bus structure is as shown in figure. The microprocessor performs primarily four operations:

• Memory Read: Reads data (or instruction) from memory.

• Memory Write: Writes data (or instruction) into memory.

• I/O Read: Accepts data from input device.

• I/O Write: Sends data to output device.

The 8085 processor performs these functions using address bus, data bus and control bus as shown in figure.

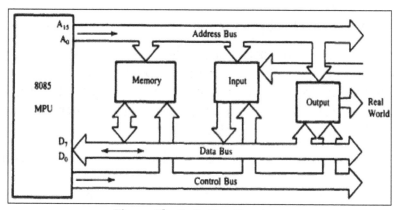

Figure: The 8085 Bus Structure.

8085 Pin Description

Properties

• It is a 8-bit microprocessor.

• Manufactured with N-MOS technology.

• 40 pin IC package.

• It has 16-bit address bus and thus has 2^{16} = 64 KB addressing capability.

- Operate with 3 MHz single-phase clock.

- +5 V single power supply.

The logic pin layout and signal groups of the 8085nmicroprocessor are shown in figure. All the signals are classified into six groups:

- Address bus,

- Data bus,

- Control & status signals,

- Power supply and frequency signals,

- Externally initiated signals,

- Serial I/O signals.

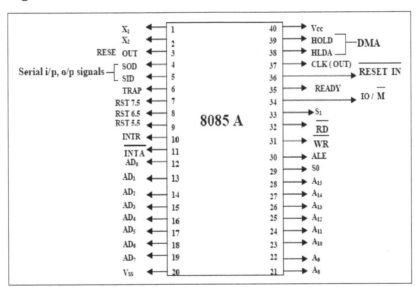

Figure: 8085 Microprocessor Pin Layout and Signal Groups.

Address and Data Buses

- A8 – A15 (output, 3-state): Most significant eight bits of memory addresses and the eight bits of the I/O addresses. These lines enter into tri-state high impedance state during HOLD and HALT modes.

- AD0 – AD7 (input/output, 3-state): Lower significant bits of memory addresses and the eight bits of the I/O addresses during first clock cycle. Behaves as data bus during third and fourth clock cycle. These lines enter into tri-state high impedance state during HOLD and HALT modes.

Control and Status Signals

- ALE: Address latch enable.

- $\overline{\text{RD}}$: Read control signal.

- $\overline{\text{WR}}$: Write control signal.

- $\text{IO}/\overline{\text{M}}$, S1 and S0: Status signals.

Power Supply and Clock Frequency

- V_{cc}: +5 V power supply.

- V_{ss}: Ground reference.

- X1, X2: A crystal having frequency of 6 MHz is connected at these two pins.

- CLK: Clock output.

Externally Initiated and Interrupt Signals

- $\overline{\text{RESET IN}}$: When the signal on this pin is low, the PC is set to 0, the buses are tristated and the processor is reset.

- RESET OUT: This signal indicates that the processor is being reset. The signal can be used to reset other devices.

- READY: When this signal is low, the processor waits for an integral number of clock cycles until it goes high.

- HOLD: This signal indicates that a peripheral like DMA (direct memory access) controller is requesting the use of address and data bus.

- HLDA: This signal acknowledges the HOLD request.

- INTR: Interrupt request is a general-purpose interrupt.

- $\overline{\text{INTA}}$: This is used to acknowledge an interrupt.

- RST 7.5, RST 6.5, RST 5, 5 – restart interrupt: These are vectored interrupts and have highest priority than INTR interrupt.

- TRAP: This is a non-maskable interrupt and has the highest priority.

Serial I/O Signals

- Serial Input Signal (SID): Bit on this line is loaded to D7 bit of register A using RIM instruction.

- Serial Output Signal (SOD): Output SOD is set or reset by using SIM instruction.

Instruction Set and Execution in 8085

Based on the design of the ALU and decoding unit, the microprocessor manufacturer provides instruction set for every microprocessor. The instruction set consists of both machine code and mnemonics. An instruction is a binary pattern designed inside a microprocessor to perform a specific function. The entire group of instructions that a microprocessor supports is called instruction set. Microprocessor instructions can be classified based on the parameters such functionality, length and operand addressing.

- Classification based on Functionality:

  ○ Data Transfer Operations: This group of instructions copies data from source to destination. The content of the source is not altered.

  ○ Arithmetic Operations: Instructions of this group perform operations like addition, subtraction, increment & decrement. One of the data used in arithmetic operation is stored in accumulator and the result is also stored in accumulator.

  ○ Logical Operations: Logical operations include AND, OR, EXOR, NOT. The operations like AND, OR and EXOR uses two operands, one is stored in accumulator and other can be any register or memory location. The result is stored in accumulator. NOT operation requires single operand, which is stored in accumulator.

  ○ Branching Operations: Instructions in this group can be used to transfer program sequence from one memory location to another either conditionally or unconditionally.

  ○ Machine Control Operations: Instruction in this group control execution of other instructions and control operations like interrupt, halt etc.

- Classification based on Length:

  ○ One-Byte Instructions: Instruction having one byte in machine code. Examples are depicted in table.

  ○ Two-Byte Instructions: Instruction having two byte in machine code. Examples are depicted in table.

  ○ Three-Byte Instructions: Instruction having three byte in machine code. Examples are depicted in table.

Table: Examples of One Byte Instructions.

Opcode	Operand	Machine code/Hex code
MOV	A, B	78
ADD	M	86

Table: Examples of Two Byte Instructions.

Opcode	Operand	Machine code/Hex code	Byte description
MVI	A, 7FH	3E	First byte
		7F	Second byte
ADI	0FH	C6	First byte
		0F	Second byte

Table: Examples of Three Byte Instructions.

Opcode	Operand	Machine code/Hex code	Byte description
JMP	9050H	C3	First byte
		50	Second byte

		90	Third byte
LDA	8850H	3A	First byte
		50	Second byte
		88	Third byte

Addressing Modes in Instructions

The process of specifying the data to be operated on by the instruction is called addressing. The various formats for specifying operands are called addressing modes. The 8085 has the following five types of addressing:

Immediate Addressing

In this mode, the operand given in the instruction-a byte or word – transfers to the destination register or memory location. Example: MVI A, 9AH.

- The operand is a part of the instruction.

- The operand is stored in the register mentioned in the instruction.

Memory Direct Addressing

Memory direct addressing moves a byte or word between a memory location and register. The memory location address is given in the instruction. Example: LDA 850FH. This instruction is used to load the content of memory address 850FH in the accumulator.

Register Direct Addressing

Register direct addressing transfer a copy of a byte or word from source register to destination register. Example: MOV B, C. It copies the content of register C to register B.

Indirect Addressing

Indirect addressing transfers a byte or word between a register and a memory location. Example: MOV A, M. Here the data is in the memory location pointed to by the contents of HL pair. The data is moved to the accumulator.

Implicit Addressing

In this addressing mode the data itself specifies the data to be operated upon. Example: CMA. The instruction complements the content of the accumulator. No specific data or operand is mentioned in the instruction.

Instruction Execution and Timing Diagram

Each instruction in 8085 microprocessor consists of two part- operation code (opcode) and oper-and. The opcode is a command such as ADD and the operand is an object to be operated on, such as a byte or the content of a register.

- Instruction Cycle: The time taken by the processor to complete the execution of an instruction. An instruction cycle consists of one to six machine cycles.

- Machine Cycle: The time required to complete one operation; accessing either the memory or I/O device. A machine cycle consists of three to six T-states.

- T-State: Time corresponding to one clock period. It is the basic unit to calculate execution of instructions or programs in a processor.

To execute a program, 8085 performs various operations as:

- Opcode fetch,

- Operand fetch,

- Memory read/write,

- I/O read/write.

External communication functions are:

- Memory read/write,

- I/O read/write,

- Interrupt request acknowledge.

Opcode Fetch Machine Cycle

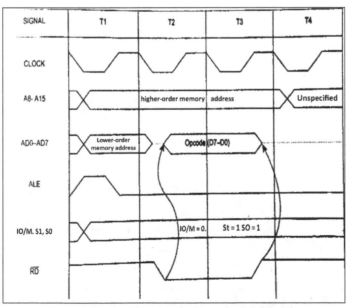

Figure: Timing Diagram for Opcode Fetch Cycle.

It is the first step in the execution of any instruction. The timing diagram of this cycle is given in Figure. The following points explain the various operations that take place and the signals that are changed during the execution of opcode fetch machine cycle.

- T1 Clock Cycle:

  ○ The content of PC is placed in the address bus; AD0-AD7 lines contains lower bit address and A8 – A15 contains higher bit address.

  ○ IO / $\overline{\text{M}}$ signal is low indicating that a memory location is being accessed. S1 and S0 also changed to the levels as indicated in table.

  ○ ALE is high, indicates that multiplexed AD0 – AD7 act as lower order bus.

- T2 Clock Cycle:

  ○ Multiplexed address bus is now changed to data bus.

  ○ The $\overline{\text{RD}}$ signal is made low by the processor. This signal makes the memory device load the data bus with the contents of the location addressed by the processor.

- T3 Clock Cycle:

  ○ The opcode available on the data bus is read by the processor and moved to the instruction register.

  ○ The $\overline{\text{RD}}$ signal is deactivated by making it logic 1.

- T4 Clock Cycle:

  ○ The processor decode the instruction in the instruction register and generate the necessary control signals to execute the instruction. Based on the instruction further operations such as fetching, writing into memory etc. takes place.

Memory Read Machine Cycle

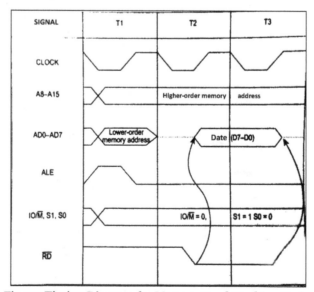

Figure: Timing Diagram for Memory Read Machine Cycle.

The memory read cycle is executed by the processor to read a data byte from memory. The machine cycle is exactly same to opcode fetch except: a) It has three T-states b) The S0 signal is set to 0. The timing diagram of this cycle is given in figure.

Memory Write Machine Cycle

The memory write cycle is executed by the processor to write a data byte in a memory location. The processor takes three T-states and $\overline{WR}$ signal is made low. The timing diagram of this cycle is given in figure.

I/O Read Cycle

The I/O read cycle is executed by the processor to read a data byte from I/O port or from peripheral, which is I/O mapped in the system. The 8-bit port address is placed both in the lower and higher order address bus. The processor takes three T-states to execute this machine cycle. The timing diagram of this cycle is given in figure.

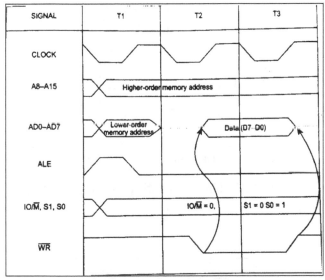

Figure: Timing Diagram for Memory Write Machine Cycle.

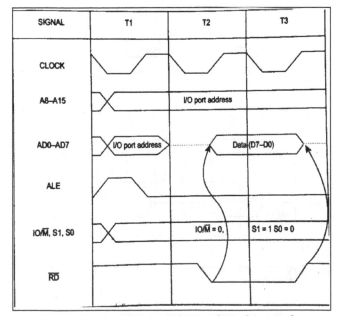

Figure: Timing Diagram I/O Read Machine Cycle.

I/O Write Cycle

The I/O write cycle is executed by the processor to write a data byte to I/O port or to a peripheral, which is I/O mapped in the system. The processor takes three T-states to execute this machine cycle. The timing diagram of this cycle is given in figure.

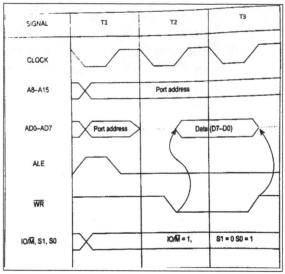

Figure: Timing Diagram I/O Write Machine Cycle.

Example: Timing diagram for IN 80H. The instruction and the corresponding codes and memory locations are given in Table.

Table: IN instruction.

Address	Mnemonics	Opcode
800F	IN 80H	DB
8010		80

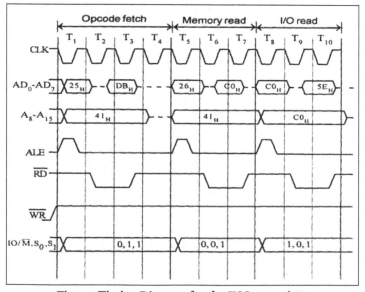

Figure: Timing Diagram for the IN Instruction.

- During the first machine cycle, the opcode DB is fetched from the memory, placed in the instruction register and decoded.

- During second machine cycle, the port address 80H is read from the next memory location.

- During the third machine cycle, the address 80H is placed in the address bus and the data read from that port address is placed in the accumulator.

8085 Interrupts

Interrupt Structure

Interrupt is the mechanism by which the processor is made to transfer control from its current program execution to another program having higher priority. The interrupt signal may be given to the processor by any external peripheral device. The program or the routine that is executed upon interrupt is called interrupt service routine (ISR). After execution of ISR, the processor must return to the interrupted program. Key features in the interrupt structure of any microprocessor are as follows:

- Number and types of interrupt signals available.

- The address of the memory where the ISR is located for a particular interrupt signal. This address is called interrupt vector address (IVA).

- Masking and unmasking feature of the interrupt signals.

- Priority among the interrupts.

- Timing of the interrupt signals.

- Handling and storing of information about the interrupt program (status information).

Types of Interrupts

Interrupts are classified based on their maskability, IVA and source. They are classified as:

- Vectored and Non-Vectored Interrupts:

  - Vectored interrupts require the IVA to be supplied by the external device that gives the interrupt signal. This technique is vectoring, is implemented in number of ways.

  - Non-vectored interrupts have fixed IVA for ISRs of different interrupt signals.

- Maskable and Non-Maskable Interrupts:

  - Maskable interrupts are interrupts that can be blocked. Masking can be done by software or hardware means.

  - Non-maskable interrupts are interrupts that are always recognized; the corresponding ISRs are executed.

- Software and Hardware Interrupts:

  - Software interrupts are special instructions, after execution transfer the control to predefined ISR.

○ Hardware interrupts are signals given to the processor, for recognition as an interrupt and execution of the corresponding ISR.

Interrupt Handling Procedure

The following sequence of operations takes place when an interrupt signal is recognized:

- Save the PC content and information about current state (flags, registers etc.) in the stack.

- Load PC with the beginning address of an ISR and start to execute it.

- Finish ISR when the return instruction is executed.

- Return to the point in the interrupted program where execution was interrupted.

Interrupt Sources and Vector Addresses in 8085

- Software Interrupts: 8085 instruction set includes eight software interrupt instructions called Restart (RST) instructions. These are one byte instructions that make the processor execute a subroutine at predefined locations. Instructions and their vector addresses are given in table.

Table: Software interrupts and their vector addresses.

Instruction	Machine hex code	Interrupt Vector Address
RST 0	C7	0000H
RST 1	CF	0008H
RST 2	D7	0010H
RST 3	DF	0018H
RST 4	E7	0020H
RST 5	EF	0028H
RST 6	F7	0030H
RST 7	FF	0032H

The software interrupts can be treated as CALL instructions with default call locations. The concept of priority does not apply to software interrupts as they are inserted into the program as instructions by the programmer and executed by the processor when the respective program lines are read.

- Hardware Interrupts and Priorities: 8085 have five hardware interrupts – INTR, RST 5.5, RST 6.5, RST 7.5 and TRAP. Their IVA and priorities are given in table.

Table: Hardware interrupts of 8085.

Interrupt	Interrupt vector address	Maskable or nonmaskable	Edge or level triggered	Priority
TRAP	0024H	Non-makable	Level	1
RST 7.5	003CH	Maskable	Rising edge	2
RST 6.5	0034H	Maskable	Level	3

| RST 5.5 | 002CH | Maskable | Level | 4 |
| INTR | Decided by hardware | Maskable | Level | 5 |

Masking of Interrupts

Masking can be done for four hardware interrupts INTR, RST 5.5, RST 6.5, and RST 7.5. The masking of 8085 interrupts is done at different levels. Figure shows the organization of hardware interrupts in the 8085.

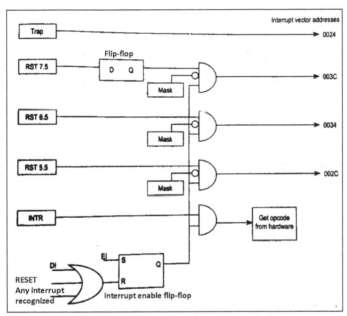

Figure: Interrupt Structure of 8085.

The figure is explained by the following five points:

- The maskable interrupts are by default masked by the Reset signal. So no interrupt is recognized by the hardware reset.

- The interrupts can be enabled by the EI instruction.

- The three RST interrupts can be selectively masked by loading the appropriate word in the accumulator and executing SIM instruction. This is called software masking.

- All maskable interrupts are disabled whenever an interrupt is recognized.

- All maskable interrupts can be disabled by executing the DI instruction.

RST 7.5 alone has a flip-flop to recognize edge transition. The DI instruction reset interrupt enable flip-flop in the processor and the interrupts are disabled. To enable interrupts, EI instruction has to be executed.

SIM Instruction

The SIM instruction is used to mask or unmask RST hardware interrupts. When executed, the SIM instruction reads the content of accumulator and accordingly mask or unmask the interrupts.

The format of control word to be stored in the accumulator before executing SIM instruction is as shown in figure.

Bit position	D7	D6	D5	D4	D3	D2	D1	D0
Name	SOD	SDE	X	R7.5	MSE	M7.5	M6.5	M5.5
Explanation	Serial data to be sent	Serial data enable-set to 1 for sending	Not used	Reset RST 7.5 flip-flop	Mask set enable- Set to 1 to mask interrupts	Set to 1 to mask RST 7.5	Set to 1 to mask RST 6.5	Set to 1 to mask RST 5.5

In addition to masking interrupts, SIM instruction can be used to send serial data on the SOD line of the processor. The data to be send is placed in the MSB bit of the accumulator and the serial data output is enabled by making D6 bit to 1.

RIM Instruction

RIM instruction is used to read the status of the interrupt mask bits. When RIM instruction is executed, the accumulator is loaded with the current status of the interrupt masks and the pending interrupts. The format and the meaning of the data stored in the accumulator after execution of RIM instruction is shown in figure. In addition RIM instruction is also used to read the serial data on the SID pin of the processor. The data on the SID pin is stored in the MSB of the accumulator after the execution of the RIM instruction.

Bit Position	D7	D6	D5	D4	D3	D2	D1	D0
Name	SID	I7.5	I6.5	I5.5	IE	M7.5	M6.5	M5.5
Explanation	Serial input data in the SID pin	Set to 1 if RST 7.5 is pending	Set to 1 if RST 6.5 is pending	Set to 1 if RST 5.5 is pending	Set to 1 if interrupts are enabled	Set to 1 if RST 7.5 is masked	Set to 1 if RST 6.5 is masked	Set to 1 if RST 5.5 is masked

Example: Write an assembly language program to enables all the interrupts in 8085 after reset.

> EI: Enable interrupts

> MVI A, 08H: Unmask the interrupts

> SIM: Set the mask and unmask using SIM instruction

Timing of Interrupts

The interrupts are sensed by the processor one cycle before the end of execution of each instruction. An interrupts signal must be applied long enough for it to be recognized. The longest instruction of the 8085 takes 18 clock periods. So, the interrupt signal must be applied for at least 17.5 clock periods. This decides the minimum pulse width for the interrupt signal. The maximum pulse width for the interrupt signal is decided by the condition that the interrupt signal must not be recognized once again. This is under the control of the programmer.

Interfacing with 8085

The programs and data that are executed by the microprocessor have to be stored in ROM/ EPROM and RAM, which are basically semiconductor memory chips. The programs and data that are stored in ROM/EPROM are not erased even when power supply to the chip is removed. Hence, they are called non-volatile memory. They can be used to store permanent programs. In a RAM, stored programs and data are erased when the power supply to the chip is removed. Hence, RAM is called volatile memory. RAM can be used to store programs and data that include, programs written during software development for a microprocessor based system, program written when one is learning assembly language programming and data enter while testing these programs. Input and output devices, which are interfaced with 8085, are essential in any microprocessor based system. They can be interfaced using two schemes: I/O mapped I/O and memory-mapped I/O. In the I/O mapped I/O scheme, the I/O devices are treated differently from memory. In the memory-mapped I/O scheme, each I/O device is assumed to be a memory location.

Interfacing Memory Chips with 8085

8085 has 16 address lines (A0-A15), hence a maximum of 64 KB (= 2^{16} bytes) of memory locations can be interfaced with it. The memory address space of the 8085 takes values from 0000H to FFFFH. The 8085 initiates set of signals such as $IO/\overline{M}$, $\overline{RD}$ and $\overline{WR}$ when it wants to read from and write into memory. Similarly, each memory chip has signals such as $\overline{CE}$ or $\overline{CS}$ (chip enable or chip select), $\overline{OE}$ or $\overline{RD}$ (output enable or read) and WE or WR (write enable or write) associated with it.

- Generation of Control Signals for Memory: When the 8085 wants to read from and write into memory, it activates $IO/\overline{M}$, $\overline{RD}$ and $\overline{WR}$ signals as shown in table.

Table: Status Of $IO/\overline{M}$, $\overline{RD}$ And $\overline{WR}$ Signals during Memory Read and Write Operations.

$IO/\overline{M}$	$\overline{RD}$	$\overline{WR}$	Operation
0	0	1	8085 reads data from memory
0	1	0	8085 writes data into memory

Using $IO/\overline{M}$, $\overline{RD}$ and $\overline{WR}$ signals, two control signals $\overline{MEMR}$ (memory read) and $\overline{MEMW}$ (memory write) are generated. Figure shows the circuit used to generate these signals.

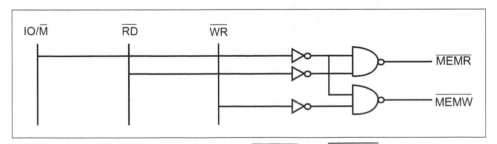

Figure: Circuit used to Generate $\overline{MEMR}$ and $\overline{MEMW}$ Signals.

When is IO/$\overline{\text{M}}$ high, both memory control signals are deactivated irrespective of the status of $\overline{\text{RD}}$ and $\overline{\text{WR}}$ signals. Example: Interface an IC 2764 with 8085 using NAND gate address decoder such that the address range allocated to the chip is 0000H – 1FFFH.

- Specification of IC 2764:
    - ○ 8 KB (8 x 2^{10} byte) EPROM chip
    - ○ 13 address lines (2^{13} bytes = 8 KB)
- Interfacing:
    - ○ 13 address lines of IC are connected to the corresponding address lines of 8085.
    - ○ Remaining address lines of 8085 are connected to address decoder formed using logic gates, the output of which is connected to the $\overline{\text{CE}}$ pin of IC.
    - ○ Address range allocated to the chip is shown in table.
    - ○ Chip is enabled whenever the 8085 places an address allocated to EPROM chip in the address bus. This is shown in figure.

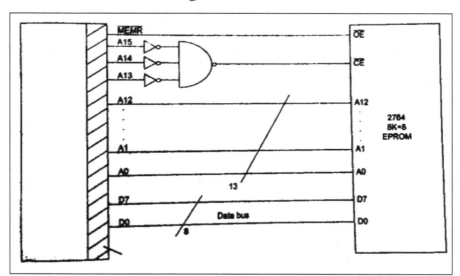

Figure: Interfacing IC 2764 with the 8085.

Table: Address Allocated to IC 2764.

A15	A14	A13	A12	A11	A10	A9	A8	A7	A6	A5	A4	A3	A1	A0	Address
0	0	0	0	0	0	0	0	0	0	0	0	0	0	0	0000H
0	0	0	0	0	0	0	0	0	0	0	0	0	0	1	0001H
-	-	-	-	-	-	-	-	-	-	-	-	-	-	-	-
-	-	-	-	-	-	-	-	-	-	-	-	-	-	-	-
-	-	-	-	-	-	-	-	-	-	-	-	-	-	-	-

0	0	0	1	1	1	1	1	1	1	1	1	1	1	0	1FFEH
0	0	0	1	1	1	1	1	1	1	1	1	1	1	1	1FFFH

Example: Interface a 6264 IC (8K x 8 RAM) with the 8085 using NAND gate decoder such that the starting address assigned to the chip is 4000H.

- Specification of IC 6264:

  - 8K x 8 RAM

  - 8 KB = 2^{13} bytes

  - 13 address lines

The ending address of the chip is 5FFFH (since 4000H + 1FFFH = 5FFFH). When the address 4000H to 5FFFH are written in binary form, the values in the lines A15, A14, A13 are 0, 1 and 0 respectively. The NAND gate is designed such that when the lines A15 and A13 carry 0 and A14 carries 1, the output of the NAND gate is 0. The NAND gate output is in turn connected to the $\overline{CE1}$ pin of the RAM chip. A NAND output of 0 selects the RAM chip for read or write operation, since CE2 is already 1 because of its connection to +5V. Figure shows the interfacing of IC 6264 with the 8085.

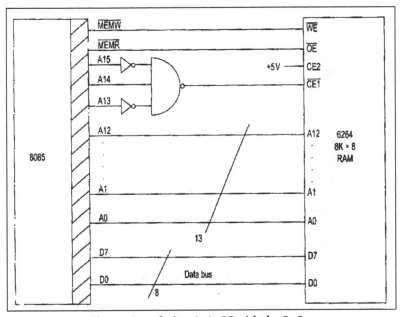

Figure: Interfacing 6264 IC with the 8085.

Example: Interface two 6116 ICs with the 8085 using 74LS138 decoder such that the starting addresses assigned to them are 8000H and 9000H, respectively.

- Specification of IC 6116:

  - 2 K x 8 RAM

  - 2 KB = 2^{11} bytes

  - 11 address lines

6116 has 11 address lines and since 2 KB, therefore ending addresses of 6116 chip 1 is and chip 2 are 87FFH and 97FFH, respectively. Table shows the address range of the two chips.

Table: Address Range for IC 6116.

A15	A14	A13	A11	A10	A9	A8	A7	A6	A5	A4	A3	A2	A1	A0	Address
1	0	0	0	0	0	0	0	0	0	0	0	0	0	0	8000H
–	–	–	–	–	–	–	–	–	–	–	–	–	–	–	–
–	–	–	–	–	–	–	–	–	–	–	–	–	–	–	–
1	0	0	0	1	1	1	1	1	1	1	1	1	1	1	87FFH (RAM chip 1)
1	0	0	1	0	0	0	0	0	0	0	0	0	0	0	9000H
–	–	–	–	–	–	–	–	–	–	–	–	–	–	–	–
–	–	–	–	–	–	–	–	–	–	–	–	–	-	–	–
1	0	0	1	1	1	1	1	1	1	1	1	1	1	1	97FFH (RAM chip 2)

- Interfacing:

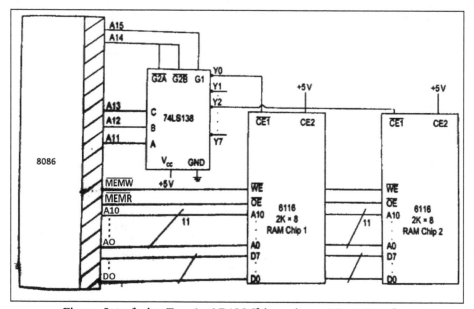

Figure: Interfacing Two 6116 RAM Chips using 74LS138 Decoder.

- ○ Figure shows the interfacing.

- ○ A0 – A10 lines of 8085 are connected to 11 address lines of the RAM chips.

- ○ Three address lines of 8085 having specific value for a particular RAM are connected to the three select inputs (C, B and A) of 74LS138 decoder.

- ○ Table shows that A13=A12=A11=0 for the address assigned to RAM 1 and A13=0, A12=1 and A11=0 for the address assigned to RAM 2.

- ○ Remaining lines of 8085 which are constant for the address range assigned to the two RAM are connected to the enable inputs of decoder.

- ○ When 8085 places any address between 8000H and 87FFH in the address bus, the select inputs C, B and A of the decoder are all 0. The Y0 output of the decoder is also 0, selecting RAM 1.

- ○ When 8085 places any address between 9000H and 97FFH in the address bus, the select inputs C, B and A of the decoder are 0, 1 and 0. The Y2 output of the decoder is also 0, selecting RAM 2.

Peripheral Mapped I/O Interfacing

In this method, the I/O devices are treated differently from memory chips. The control signals I/O read $\left(\overline{IOR}\right)$ and I/O write $\left(\overline{IOW}\right)$, which are derived from the $IO/\overline{M}$, $\overline{RD}$ and $\overline{WR}$ signals of the 8085, are used to activate input and output devices, respectively. Generation of these control signals is shown in Figure. Table shows the status of $IO/\overline{M}$, $\overline{RD}$ and $\overline{WR}$ signals during I/O read and I/O write operation.

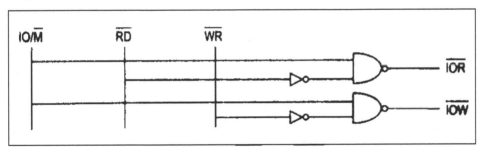

Figure: Generation Of $\overline{IOR}$ and $\overline{IOW}$ Signals.

IN instruction is used to access input device and OUT instruction is used to access output device. Each I/O device is identified by a unique 8-bit address assigned to it. Since the control signals used to access input and output devices are different, and all I/O device use 8-bit address, a maximum of 256 (2^8) input devices and 256 output devices can be interfaced with 8085.

Table: Status Of $\overline{IOR}$ and $\overline{IOW}$ Signals in 8085.

$IO/\overline{M}$	$\overline{RD}$	$\overline{WR}$	$\overline{IOR}$	$\overline{IOW}$	Operation
1	0	1	0	1	I/O read operation
1	1	0	1	0	I/O write operation
0	X	X	1	1	Memory read or write operation

Example: Interface an 8-bit DIP switch with the 8085 such that the address assigned to the DIP switch if F0H. IN instruction is used to get data from DIP switch and store it in accumulator. Steps involved in the execution of this instruction are:

- Address F0H is placed in the lines A0 – A7 and a copy of it in lines A8 – A15.

- The $\overline{IOR}$ signal is activated ($\overline{IOR}$ = 0), which makes the selected input device to place its data in the data bus.

- The data in the data bus is read and store in the accumulator.

Table: The Interfacing of DIP Switch.

A7	A6	A5	A4	A3	A2	A1	A0	
1	1	1	1	0	0	0	0	= F0H

A0 – A7 lines are connected to a NAND gate decoder such that the output of NAND gate is 0. The output of NAND gate is ORed with the $\overline{\text{IOR}}$ signal and the output of OR gate is connected to $\overline{1G}$ and $\overline{2G}$ of the 74LS244. When 74LS244 is enabled, data from the DIP switch is placed on the data bus of the 8085. The 8085 read data and store in the accumulator. Thus data from DIP switch is transferred to the accumulator.

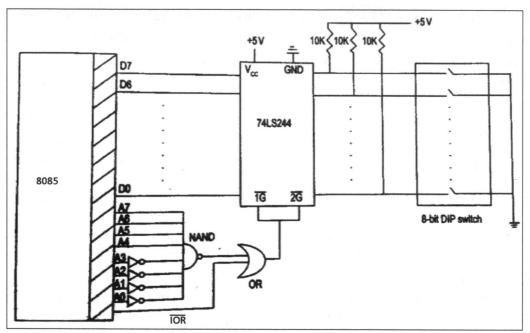

Figure: Interfacing of 8-bit DIP Switch with 8085.

Memory Mapped I/O Interfacing

In memory-mapped I/O, each input or output device is treated as if it is a memory location. The $\overline{\text{MEMR}}$ and $\overline{\text{MEMW}}$ control signals are used to activate the devices. Each input or output device is identified by unique 16-bit address, similar to 16-bit address assigned to memory location. All memory related instruction like LDA 2000H, LDAX B, MOV A, M can be used. Since the I/O devices use some of the memory address space of 8085, the maximum memory capacity is lesser than 64 KB in this method. Example: Interface an 8-bit DIP switch with the 8085 using logic gates such that the address assigned to it is F0F0H. Since a 16-bit address has to be assigned to a DIP switch, the memory-mapped I/O technique must be used. Using LDA F0F0H instruction, the data from the 8-bit DIP switch can be transferred to the accumulator. The steps involved are:

- The address F0F0H is placed in the address bus A0 – A15.

- The $\overline{\text{MEMR}}$ signal is made low for some time.

- The data in the data bus is read and stored in the accumulator.

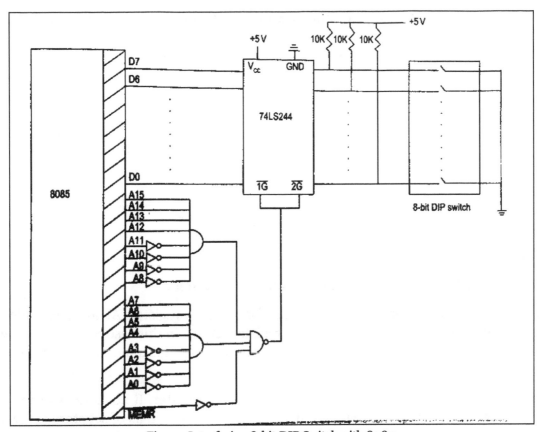

Figure: Interfacing 8-bit DIP Switch with 8085.

When 8085 executes the instruction LDA F0F0H, it places the address F0F0H in the address lines A0 – A15 as:

A15	A14	A13	A12	A11	A10	A9	A8	A7	A6	A5	A4	A3	A2	A1	A0	
1	1	1	1	0	0	0	0	1	1	1	1	0	0	0	0	= F0F0H

The address lines are connected to AND gates. The output of these gates along with $\overline{\text{MEMR}}$ signal are connected to a NAND gate, so that when the address F0F0H is placed in the address bus and $\overline{\text{MEMR}}$ = 0 its output becomes 0, thereby enabling the buffer 74LS244. The data from the DIP switch is placed in the 8085 data bus. The 8085 reads the data from the data bus and stores it in the accumulator.

Intel 8086

8086 has a powerful set of registers containing general purpose and special purpose registers. All the registers of 8086 are 16-bit registers. The general purpose registers, can be used either 8-bit registers or 16-bit registers. The general purpose registers are either used for holding the data, variables and intermediate results temporarily or for other purpose like counter or for storing offset address for some particular addressing modes etc. The special purpose registers are used as segment registers, pointers, index registers or as offset storage registers for particular addressing modes. Figure shows register organization of 8086. We will categorize the register set into four groups as follows:

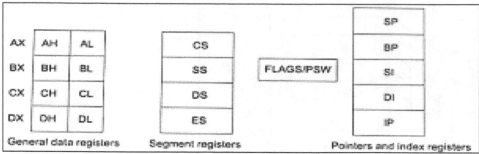

Figure: Register Organization of 8086 Microprocessor.

General Data Registers

The registers AX, BX, CX, and DX are the general 16-bit registers.

- AX Register: Accumulator register consists of two 8-bit registers AL and AH, which can be combined together and used as a 16- bit register AX. AL in this case contains the low-order byte of the word, and AH contains the high order byte. Accumulator can be used for I/O operations, rotate and string manipulation.

- BX Register: This register is mainly used as a base register. It holds the starting base location of a memory region within a data segment. It is used as offset storage for forming physical address in case of certain addressing mode.

- CX Register: It is used as default counter or count register in case of string and loop instructions.

- DX Register: Data register can be used as a port number in I/O operations and implicit operand or destination in case of few instructions. In integer 32-bit multiply and divide instruction the DX register contains high-order word of the initial or resulting number.

Segment Registers

To complete 1Mbyte memory is divided into 16 logical segments. The complete 1Mbyte memory segmentation is as shown in figure. Each segment contains 64Kbyte of memory. There are four segment registers.

- Code Segment (CS) is a 16-bit register containing address of 64 KB segment with processor instructions. The processor uses CS segment for all accesses to instructions referenced by instruction pointer (IP) register. CS register cannot be changed directly. The CS register is automatically updated during far jump, far call and far return instructions. It is used for addressing a memory location in the code segment of the memory, where the executable program is stored.

- Stack Segment (SS) is a 16-bit register containing address of 64KB segment with program stack. By default, the processor assumes that all data referenced by the stack pointer (SP) and base pointer (BP) registers is located in the stack segment. SS register can be changed directly using POP instruction. It is used for addressing stack segment of memory. The stack segment is that segment of memory, which is used to store stack data.

- Data Segment (DS) is a 16-bit register containing address of 64KB segment with program data. By default, the processor assumes that all data referenced by general registers (AX, BX, CX, and DX) and index register (SI, DI) is located in the data segment. DS register can be changed directly using POP and LDS instructions. It points to the data segment memory where the data is resided.

- Extra Segment (ES) is a 16-bit register containing address of 64KB segment, usually with program data. By default, the processor assumes that the DI register references the ES segment in string manipulation instructions. ES register can be changed directly using POP and LES instructions. It also refers to segment which essentially is another data segment of the memory. It also contains data.

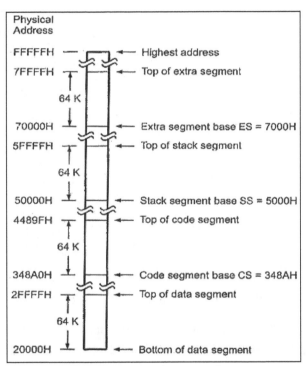

Figure: Memory Segmentation.

Pointers and Index Registers

The pointers contain within the particular segments. The pointers IP, BP, SP usually contain offsets within the code, data and stack segments respectively.

- Stack Pointer (SP) is a 16-bit register pointing to program stack in stack segment.

- Base Pointer (BP) is a 16-bit register pointing to data in stack segment. BP register is usually used for based, based indexed or register indirect addressing.

- Source Index (SI) is a 16-bit register. SI is used for indexed, based indexed and register indirect addressing, as well as a source data addresses in string manipulation instructions.

- Destination Index (DI) is a 16-bit register. DI is used for indexed, based indexed and register indirect addressing, as well as a destination data address in string manipulation instructions.

Flag Register

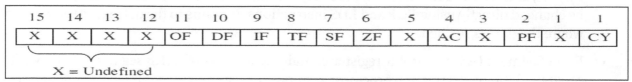

Figure: Flag Register of 8086.

Flags Register determines the current state of the processor. They are modified automatically by CPU after mathematical operations, this allows to determine the type of the result, and to determine conditions to transfer control to other parts of the program. The 8086 flag register as shown in the figure. 8086 has 9 active flags and they are divided into two categories:

- Conditional flags: Conditional flags are as follows:

  ○ Carry Flag (CY): This flag indicates an overflow condition for unsigned integer arithmetic. It is also used in multiple-precision arithmetic.

  ○ Auxiliary Flag (AC): If an operation performed in ALU generates a carry/barrow from lower nibble (i.e. D0 – D3) to upper nibble (i.e. D4 – D7), the AC flag is set i.e. carry given by D3 bit to D4 is AC flag. This is not a general-purpose flag, it is used internally by the Processor to perform Binary to BCD conversion.

  ○ Parity Flag (PF): This flag is used to indicate the parity of result. If lower order 8-bits of the result contains even number of 1's, the Parity Flag is set and for odd number of 1's, the Parity flag is reset.

  ○ Zero Flag (ZF): It is set; if the result of arithmetic or logical operation is zero else it is reset.

  ○ Sign Flag (SF): In sign magnitude format the sign of number is indicated by MSB bit. If the result of operation is negative, sign flag is set.

- Control Flags: Control flags are set or reset deliberately to control the operations of the execution unit. Control flags are as follows:

  ○ Trap Flag (TF): It is used for single step control. It allows user to execute one instruction of a program at a time for debugging. When trap flag is set, program can be run in single step mode.

  ○ Interrupt Flag (IF): It is an interrupt enable/disable flag. If it is set, the maskable interrupt of 8086 is enabled and if it is reset, the interrupt is disabled. It can be set by executing instruction sit and can be cleared by executing CLI instruction.

  ○ Direction Flag (DF): It is used in string operation. If it is set, string bytes are accessed from higher memory address to lower memory address. When it is reset, the string bytes are accessed from lower memory address to higher memory address.

8086 Architecture

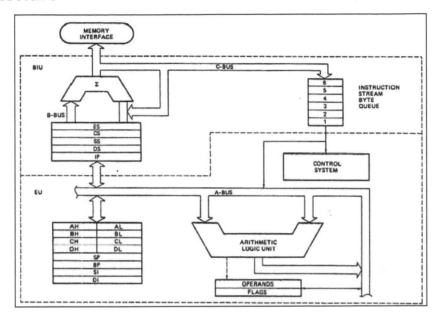

The 8086 is mainly divided into mainly two blocks:

- Execution Unit (EU),
- Bus interface Unit (BIU),

Dividing the work between these two will speed up the processing.

Execution Unit (EU)

The execution unit tells the BIU where to fetch instructions or data from:

- Decodes instructions,
- Executes instructions,

The Execution unit contains:

- Control circuitry,
- ALU,
- FLAGS,
- General purpose Registers,
- Pointer and Index Registers,

1. Control Circuitry:

- It directs internal operations.
- A decoder in the EU translates instructions fetched from memory into series of actions which the EU carries out.

2. Arithmetic Logic Unit: 16 bit ALU is used to carry the operations.

- ADD

- SUBTRACT

- XOR

- INCREMENT

- DECREMENT

- COMPLEMENT

- SHIFT BINARY NUMBERS

3. Flag Registers:

- A flag is a flip flop that indicates some condition produced by execution of an instruction or controls certain operation of the EU.

- It is 16 bit.

- It has nine active flags.

- It can be divided into two types: conditional flags and control flags.

- Conditional Flags:

  - Carry Flag (CY): This flag indicates an overflow condition for unsigned integer arithmetic. It is also used in multiple-precision arithmetic.

  - Auxiliary Flag (AC): If an operation performed in ALU generates a carry/barrow from lower nibble (i.e. $D_0 - D_3$) to upper nibble (i.e. $D_4 - D_7$), the AC flag is set i.e. carry given by D_3 bit to D_4 is AC flag. This is not a general-purpose flag, it is used internally by the Processor to perform Binary to BCD conversion.

  - Parity Flag (PF): This flag is used to indicate the parity of result. If lower order 8-bits of the result contains even number of 1's, the Parity Flag is set and for odd number of 1's, the Parity flag is reset.

  - Zero Flag (ZF): It is set; if the result of arithmetic or logical operation is zero else it is reset.

  - Sign Flag (SF): In sign magnitude format the sign of number is indicated by MSB bit. If the result of operation is negative, sign flag is set.

- Control Flags: Control flags are set or reset deliberately to control the operations of the execution unit. Control flags are as follows:

  - Trap Flag (TF): It is used for single step control. It allows user to execute one instruction of a program at a time for debugging. When trap flag is set, program can be run in single step mode.

○ Interrupt Flag (IF): It is an interrupt enable/disable flag. If it is set, the maskable interrupt of 8086 is enabled and if it is reset, the interrupt is disabled. It can be set by executing instruction sit and can be cleared by executing CLI instruction.

○ Direction Flag (DF): It is used in string operation. If it is set, string bytes are accessed from higher memory address to lower memory address. When it is reset, the string bytes are accessed from lower memory address to higher memory address.

4. General Purpose Registers: The 8086 general purpose registers are similar to those of earlier generations 8080 and 8085 .It was designed in such a way that many programs written for 8080 and 8085 could easily be translated to run on 8086.The advantage of using internal registers for the temporary storage of data is that since data already in the EU., it can be accessed much more quickly than it could be accessed from external memory. The registers AX, BX, CX, and DX are the general 16-bit registers.

- AX Register: Accumulator register consists of two 8-bit registers AL and AH, which can be combined together and used as a 16- bit register AX. AL in this case contains the low-order byte of the word, and AH contains the high order byte. Accumulator can be used for I/O operations, rotate and string manipulation.

- BX Register: This register is mainly used as a base register. It holds the starting base location of a memory region within a data segment. It is used as offset storage for forming physical address in case of certain addressing mode.

- CX Register: It is used as default counter or count register in case of string and loop instructions.

- DX Register: Data register can be used as a port number in I/O operations and implicit operand or destination in case of few instructions. In integer 32-bit multiply and divide instruction the DX register contains high-order word of the initial or resulting number.

Bus Interface Unit (BIU)

The BIU sends out:

- Addresses,

- Fetches instructions from memory,

- Read data from ports and memory.

The BIU handles all transfer of data and addresses on the buses for the Execution Unit. The Bus interface unit contains:

- Instruction Queue,

- Instruction Pointer,

- Segment Registers,

- Address Generator.

Instruction Queue

BIU gets upto 6 bytes of next instructions and stores them in the instruction queue. When EU executes instructions and is ready for its next instruction, then it simply reads the instruction from this instruction queue resulting in increased execution speed. Fetching the next instruction while the current instruction executes is called pipelining. (Based on FIFO). This is much faster than sending out an addresses to the system memory and waiting for memory to send back the next instruction byte or bytes .here the queue will be dumped and then reloaded from the new address.

Segment Register

The 8086 20 bit addresses So it can address upto 2^{20} in memory (1 Mbyte) but at any instant it can address upto 4 64 KB segments. This four segments holds the upper 16 bits of the starting address of four memory segments that the 8086 is working with it at particular time .The BIU always inserts zeros for the lowest 4 bits of the 20 bit starting address. Example : If the code segment register contains 348AH then the code segment starts at 348A0H .In other words a 64Kbyte segment can be located anywhere within 1MByte address Space but the segment will always starts at an address with zeros in the lowest 4 bits.

Stack

Stack is a section of memory set aside to store addresses and data while subprogram executes is often called segment base. The stack segment register always holds the upper 16 bit starting address of program stack. The extra segment register and data segment register is used to hold the upper 16 bit starting addresses of two memory segments that are used for data.

Instruction Pointer

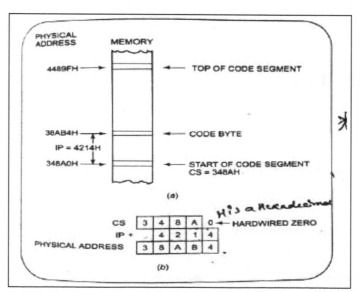

Figure: Addition of IP to CS to Produce the Physical Address of the Code Byte, (A) Diagram, (B) Computation.

Instruction Pointer holds the 16 bit address or offset of the next code byte within the code segment. The value contained in the Instruction Pointer called as Offset because the value must be added to the segment base address in CS to produce the required 20 bit address.

CS register contains the Upper 16 bit of the starting address of the code segment in the 1 Mbyte address range the instruction pointer contains a 16 bit offset which tells wherein that 64 Kbyte code segment the next instruction byte has to be fetched from.

Stack Register and Stack Pointer

Stack is a section of memory set aside to store addresses and data while subprogram executes is often called segment base. The stack segment register always holds the upper 16 bit starting address of program stack. The Stack pointer (SP) holds the 16 bit offset from the starting of the segment to the memory location where a word was most recently stored .The memory location where the word is stored is called as top of the stack.

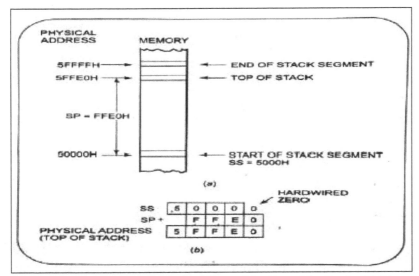

Figure: Addition of SS and SP to Produce the Physical Address of the Top of the Stock, (A) Diagram (B) Computation.

Pointer and Index Registers

In addition to stack pointer register EU has:

- Base pointer Register (BP),

- Source Pointer Register (SP),

- Destination Pointer Register (DP).

These three registers are used to store temporary storage of data like general purpose registers. They hold the 16 bit offset data of the data word in one of the segment.

Programming Model

How can a 20-bit address be obtained, if there are only 16-bit registers? However, the largest register is only 16 bits (64k); so physical addresses have to be calculated. These calculations are done in hardware within the microprocessor. The 16-bit contents of segment register gives the starting/base address of particular segment. To address a specific memory location within a segment we need an offset address. The offset address is also 16-bit wide and it is provided by one of the associated pointer or index register. To be able to program a microprocessor, one does not need to know all of its hardware architectural features. What is important to the programmer is being aware of the various registers within the device and to understand their purpose, functions, operating capabilities, and limitations. The above figure illustrates the software architecture of the 8086 microprocessor. From this diagram, we see that it includes fourteen16-bit internal registers: the instruction pointer (IP), four data registers (AX, BX, CX, and DX), two pointer registers (BP and SP), two index registers (SI and DI), four segment registers (CS, DS, SS, and ES) and status register (SR), with nine of its bits implemented as status and control flags.

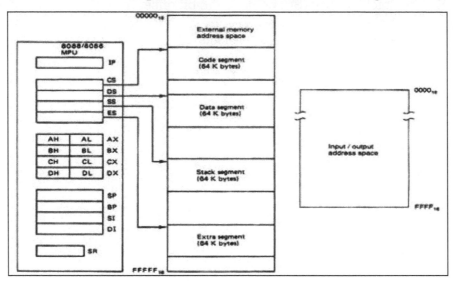

The point to note is that the beginning segment address must begin at an address divisible by 16.Also note that the four segments need not be defined separately. It is allowable for all four segments to completely overlap (CS = DS = ES = SS).

Logical and Physical Address

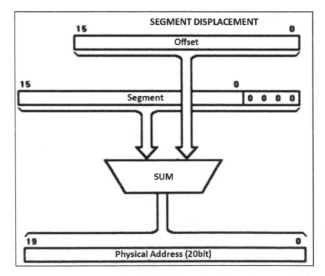

Addresses within a segment can range from address 00000h to address 0FFFFh. This corresponds to the 64K-bytelength of the segment. An address within a segment is called an offset or logical address. A logical address gives the displacement from the base address of the segment to the desired location within it, as opposed to its "real" address, which maps directly anywhere into the 1 MByte memory space. This "real" address is called the physical address. What is the difference between the physical and the logical address? The physical address is 20 bits long and corresponds to the actual binary code output by the BIU on the address bus lines. The logical address is an offset from location 0 of a given segment.

You should also be careful when writing addresses on paper to do so clearly. To specify the logical address XXXX in the stack segment, use the convention SS:XXXX, which is equal to [SS] * 16 + XXXX.

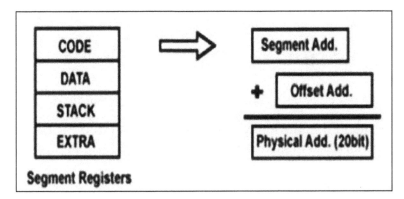

Logical address is in the form of- Base Address: Offset. Offset is the displacement of the memory location from the starting location of the segment. To calculate the physical address of the memory, BIU uses the following formula:

Physical Address = Base Address of Segment * 16 + Offset

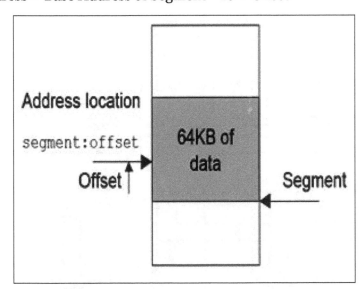

Example: The value of Data Segment Register (DS) is 2222H. To convert this 16-bit address into 20-bit, the BIU appends 0H to the LSB (by multiplying with 16) of the address. After appending, the starting address of the Data Segment becomes 22220H. Data at any location has a logical address specified as 2222H: 0016H, where 0016H is the offset, 2222 H is the value of DS.

Therefore the physical address is 22220H + 0016H: 22236 H. The following table describes the default offset values to the corresponding memory segments.

Segment	Offset Registers	Function
CS	IP	Address of the next instruction.
DS	BX, DI, SI	Address of data.
SS	SP, BP	Address in the stack.
ES	BX, DI, SI	Address of destination data (for string operations).

Some of the advantages of memory segmentation in the 8086 are as follows:

- With the help of memory segmentation a user is able to work with registers having only 16-bits.

- The data and the user's code can be stored separately allowing for more flexibility.

- Also due to segmentation the logical address range is from 0000H to FFFFH the code can be loaded at any location in the memory.

Physical Memory Organization

The 8086's 1Mbyte memory address space is divided in to two independent 512Kbyte banks: the low (even) bank and the high (odd) bank. Data bytes associated with an even address (0000016, 0000216, etc.) reside in the low bank, and those with odd addresses (0000116, 0000316, etc.) reside in the high bank. Address bits A1 through A19 select the storage location that is to be accessed. They are applied to both banks in parallel. A0and bank high enable (BHE) are used as bank-select signals. The four different cases that happen during accessing data:

Case: When a byte of data at an even address (such as X) is to be accessed:

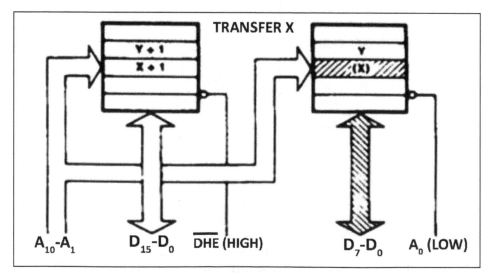

- A0 is set to logic 0 to enable the low bank of memory.

- BHE is set to logic 1 to disable the high bank.

Case: When a byte of data at an odd addresses (such as X+1) is to be accessed:

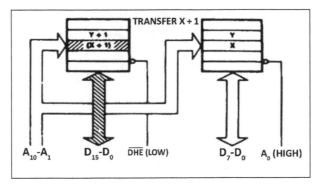

- Ao is set to logic 1 to disable the low bank of memory.

- BHE is set to logic 0 to enable the high bank.

Case: When a word of data at an even address (aligned word) is to be accessed:

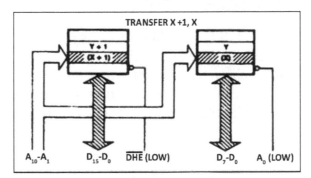

- Ao is set to logic 0 to enable the low bank of memory.

- BHE is set to logic 0 to enable the high bank.

Case: When a word of data at an odd address (misaligned word) is to be accessed, then the 8086 need two bus cycles to access it:

- During the first bus cycle, the odd byte of the word (in the high bank) is addressed:

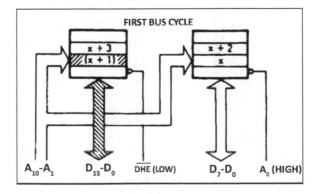

- Ao is set to logic 1 to disable the low bank of memory.

- ○ BHE is set to logic 0 to enable the high bank.

- During the second bus cycle, the odd byte of the word (in the low bank) is addressed:

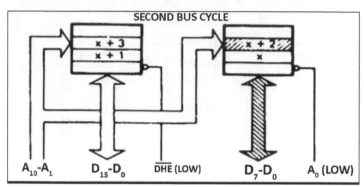

- ○ A0 is set to logic 0 to enable the low bank of memory.

- ○ BHE is set to logic 1 to disable the high bank.

Signal Description of 8086 Microprocessor

The 8086 Microprocessor is a 16-bit CPU available in 3 clock rates, i.e. 5, 8 and 10MHz, packaged in a 40 pin CERDIP or plastic package. The 8086 Microprocessor operates in single processor or multiprocessor configurations to achieve high performance. The pin configuration is as shown in figure. Some of the pins serve a particular function in minimum mode (single processor mode) and others function in maximum mode (multiprocessor mode) configuration.

			MAX MODE	MIN MODE
Vss (GND)	1	40	Vcc (5P)	
AD14	2	39	AD15	
AD13	3	38	A16/S3	
AD12	4	37	A17/S4	
AD11	5	36	A18/S5	
AD10	6	35	A19/S6	
AD9	7	34	$\overline{BHE}$/S7	
AD8	8	33	MN/$\overline{MX}$	
AD7	9	32	$\overline{RD}$	
AD6	10	31	$\overline{RQ}/\overline{GT0}$	HOLD
AD5	11	30	$\overline{RQ}/\overline{GT1}$	HLDA
AD4	12	29	$\overline{LOCK}$	$\overline{WR}$
AD3	13	28	$\overline{S2}$	M/$\overline{IO}$
AD2	14	27	$\overline{S1}$	DT/$\overline{R}$
AD1	15	26	$\overline{S0}$	$\overline{DEN}$
AD0	16	25	QS0	ALE
NMI	17	24	QS1	$\overline{INTA}$
INTR	18	23	$\overline{TEST}$	
CLK	19	22	READY	
Vss (GND)	20	21	RESET	

(8086)

The 8086 signals can be categorized in three groups. The first are the signals having common functions in minimum as well as maximum mode, the second are the signals which have special functions in minimum mode and third are the signals having special functions for maximum mode. The following signal description is common for both the minimum and maximum modes.

1. AD15-AD0: These are the time multiplexed memory I/O address and data lines. Address remains on the lines during T1 state, while the data is available on the data bus during T2, T3, TW and T4. Here T1, T2, T3, T4 and TW are the clock states of a machine cycle. TW is await state. These lines are active high and float to a tristate during interrupt acknowledge and local bus hold acknowledge cycles.

2. A19/S6, A18/S5, A17/S4, A16/S3: These are the time multiplexed address and status lines. During T1, these are the most significant address lines or memory operations. During I/O operations, these lines are low. During memory or I/O operations, status information is available on those lines for T2, T3, TW and T4 .The status of the interrupt enable flag bit(displayed on S5) is updated at the beginning of each clock cycle. The S4 and S3 combinedly indicate which segment register is presently being used for memory accesses as shown in table. These lines float to tri-state off (tristated) during the local bus hold acknowledge. The status line S6 is always low(logical). The address bits are separated from the status bits using latches controlled by the ALE signal.

Table: Bus High Enable/Status.

S4	S3	Indication
0	0	Alternate Data
0	1	Stack
1	0	Code or none
1	1	Data

3. BHE/S7 (Active Low): The bus high enable signal is used to indicate the transfer of data over the higher order (D15-D8) data bus as shown in Table. It goes low for the data transfers over D15-D8 and is used to derive chip selects of odd address memory bank or peripherals. $\overline{BHE}$ is low during T1 for read, write and interrupt acknowledge cycles, when- ever a byte is to be transferred on the higher byte of the data bus. The status information is available during T2, T3 and T4. The signal is active low and is tristated during 'hold'. It is low during T1 for the first pulse of the interrupt acknowledge cycle.

$\overline{BHE}$	A_0	Indication
0	0	Whole Word
0	1	Upper byte from or to odd address
1	0	Upper byte from or to even address
1	1	None

4. $\overline{RD}$-Read: Read signal, when low, indicates the peripherals that the processor is performing a memory or I/O read operation. $\overline{RD}$ is active low and shows the state for T2, T3, TW of any read cycle. The signal remains tristated during the 'hold acknowledge'.

5. READY: This is the acknowledgement from the slow devices or memory that they have completed the data transfer. The signal made available by the devices is synchronized by the 8284A clock generator to provide ready input to the 8086. The signal is active high.

6. INTR-Interrupt Request: This is a level triggered input. This is sampled during the last clock cycle of each instruction to determine the availability of the request. If any interrupt request is pending, the processor enters the interrupt acknowledge cycle. This can be internally masked by resetting the interrupt enable flag. This signal is active high and internally synchronized.

7. TEST: This input is examined by a 'WAIT' instruction. If the TEST input goes low, execution will continue, else, the processor remains in an idle state. The input is synchronized internally during each clock cycle on leading edge of clock.

8. NMI-Non-maskable Interrupt: This is an edge-triggered input which causes a Type2 interrrupt. The NMI is not maskable internally by software. A transition from low to high initiates the interrupt response at the end of the current instruction. This input is internally synchronized.

9. RESET: This input causes the processor to terminate the current activity and start execution from FFFF0H. The signal is active high and must be active for at least four clock cycles. It restarts execution when the RESET returns low. RESET is also internally synchronized.

10. CLK-Clock Input: The clock input provides the basic timing for processor operation and bus control activity. Its an asymmetric square wave with 33% duty cycle. The range of frequency for different 8086 versions is from 5MHz to 10MHz.

11. VCC: +5V power supply for the operation of the internal circuit. GND ground for the internal circuit.

12. MN/MX: The logic level at this pin decides whether the processor is to operate in either minimum (single processor) or maximum (multiprocessor) mode. The following pin functions are for the minimum mode operation of 8086.

13. M/IO -Memory/IO: This is a status line logically equivalent to S2 in maximum mode. When it is low, it indicates the CPU is having an I/O operation, and when it is high, it indicates that the CPU is having a memory operation. This line becomes active in the previous T4 and remains active till final T4 of the current cycle. It is tristated during local bus "hold acknowledge".

14. $\overline{\text{INTA}}$ -Interrupt Acknowledge: This signal is used as a read strobe for interrupt acknowledge cycles. In other words, when it goes low, it means that the processor has accepted the interrupt. It is active low during T2, T3 and TW of each interrupt acknowledge cycle.

15. ALE-Address latch Enable: This output signal indicates the availability of the valid address on the address/data lines, and is connected to latch enable input of latches. This signal is active high and is never tristated.

16. DT/$\overline{\text{R}}$ -Data Transmit/Receive: This output is used to decide the direction of data flow through the transreceivers (bidirectional buffers). When the processor sends out data, this signal is high and when the processor is receiving data, this signal is low. Logically, this is equivalent to S1 in maximum mode. Its timing is the same as M/I/O. This is tristated during 'hold acknowledge'.

17. $\overline{\text{DEN}}$ -Data Enable: This signal indicates the availability of valid data over the address/data lines. It is used to enable the transreceivers (bidirectional buffers) to separate the data from the

multiplexed address/data signal. It is active from the middle ofT2 until the middle of T4 DEN is tristated during 'hold acknowledge' cycle.

18. HOLD, HLDA-Hold/Hold Acknowledge: When the HOLD line goes high, it indicates to the processor that another master is requesting the bus access. The processor, after receiving the HOLD request, issues the hold acknowledge signal on HLDA pin, in the middle of the next clock cycle after completing the current bus (instruction) cycle. At the same time, the processor floats the local bus and control lines. When the processor detects the HOLD line low, it lowers the HLDA signal. HOLD is an asynchronous input, and it should be externally synchronized.

19. S2, S1, S0 -Status Lines: These are the status lines which reflect the type of operation, being carried out by the processor. These become active during T4 of the previous cycle and remain active during T1 and T2 of the current bus cycle. The status lines return to passive state during T3 of the current bus cycle so that they may again become active for the next bus cycle during T4. Any change in these lines during T3 indicates the starting of a new cycle, and return to passive state indicates end of the bus cycle. These status lines are encoded in table.

S_2	S_1	S_0	Indication
0	0	0	Interrupt Acknowledge
0	0	1	Read I/O Port
0	1	0	Write I/O Port
0	1	1	Halt
1	0	0	Code Access
1	0	1	Read memory
1	1	0	Write memory
1	1	1	Passive

20. $\overline{LOCK}$: This output pin indicates that other system bus masters will be prevented from gaining the system bus, while the $\overline{LOCK}$ signal is low. The $\overline{LOCK}$ signal is activated by the 'LOCK' prefix instruction and remains active until the completion of the next instruction. This floats to tri-state off during "hold acknowledge". When the CPU is executing a critical instruction which requires the system bus, the LOCK prefix instruction ensures that other processors connected in the system will not gain the control of the bus. The 8086, while executing the prefixed instruction, asserts the bus lock signal output, which may be connected to an external bus controller.

21. QS1, QS0-Queue Status: These lines give information about the status of the code prefetch queue. These are active during the CLK cycle after which the queue operation is performed. These are encoded as shown in table.

QS_1	QS_0	Indication
0	0	No operation
0	1	First byte of opcode from the queue
1	0	Empty queue
1	1	Subsequent byte from the queue

22. $\overline{RQ}/\overline{GT_0}$, $\overline{RQ}/\overline{GT_1}$ ReQuest/Grant: These pins are used by other local bus masters, in maxi-

mum mode, to force the processor to release the local bus at the end of the processor's current bus cycle. Each of the pins is bidirectional with $\overline{RQ}/\overline{GT}_0$ having higher priority than $\overline{RQ}/\overline{GT}_1$, $\overline{RQ}/\overline{GT}$ pins have internal pull-up resistors and may be left unconnected. The request grant sequence is as follows:

- A pulse one clock wide from another bus master requests the bus access to 8086.

- During T4 (current) or T1 (next) clock cycle, a pulse one clock wide from 8086 to the requesting master, indicates that the 8086 has allowed the local bus to float and that it will enter the "hold acknowledge" state at next clock cycle. The CPU's bus interface unit is likely to be disconnected from the local bus of the system.

- A one clock wide pulse from another master indicates to 8086 that the 'hold' request is about to end and the 8086 may regain control of the local bus at the next clock cycle.

Minimum Mode 8086 System and Timings

In a minimum mode 8086 system, the microprocessor 8086 is operated in minimum mode by strapping its MN/MX* pin to logic1. In this mode, all the control signals are given out by the microprocessor chip itself. There is a single microprocessor in the minimum mode system. The remaining components in the system are latches, transreceivers, clock generator, memory and I/O devices. Some type of chip selection logic may be required for selecting memory or I/O devices, depending upon the address map of the system.

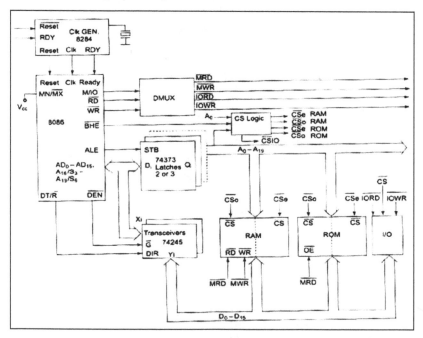

1. Latches: The latches are generally buffered output D-type flip-flops, like, 74LS373 or 8282. They are used for separating the valid address from the multiplexed address/data signals and are controlled by the ALE signal generated by 8086.

2. Transreceivers: Transreceivers are the bidirectional buffers and some times they are called as data amplifiers. They are required to separate the valid data from the time multiplexed ad-

dress/data signal. They are controlled by two signals, namely, DEN* and DT/R*. The DEN* signal indicates that the valid data is available on the data bus, while DT/R indicates the direction of data, i.e. from or to the processor.

3. Memory: The system contains memory for the monitor and users program storage. Usually, EPROMS are used for monitor storage, while RAMs for users program storage.

4. IO Devices: A system may contain I/O devices for communication with the processor as well as some special purpose I/O devices.

5. Clock Generator: The clock generator generates the clock from the crystal oscillator and then shapes it and divides to make it more precise so that it can be used as an accurate timing reference for the system. The clock generator also synchronizes some external signals with the system clock.

The general system organization is shown in figure. Since it has 20 address lines and 16 data lines, the 8086 CPU requires three octal address latches and two octal data buffers for the complete address and data separation. The working of the minimum mode configuration system can be better described in terms of the timing diagrams rather than qualitatively describing the operations. The opcode fetch and read cycles are similar. Hence the timing diagram can be categorized in two parts.

Timing Diagram for Read Cycle

The read cycle begins in T1 with the assertion of the address latch enable (ALE) signal and also M/IO* signal. During the negative going edge of this signal, the valid address is latched on the local bus. The BHE* and A0 signals address low, high or both bytes. From Tl to T4, the M/IO* signal indicates a memory or I/O operation. At T2 the address is removed from the local bus and is sent to the output. The bus is then tristated. The read (RD*) control signal is also activated in T2. The read (RD) signal causes the addressed device to enable its data bus drivers. After RD* goes low, the valid data is available on the data bus. The addressed device will drive the READY line high, when the processor returns the read signal to high level, the addressed device will again tristate its bus drivers.

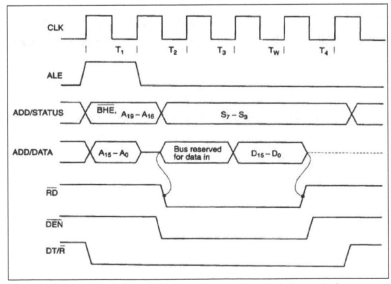

Figure: Read Cycle Timing Diagram for Minimum Mode.

Timing Diagram for Write Cycle

A write cycle also begins with the assertion of ALE and the emission of the address. The M/IO* signal is again asserted to indicate a memory or I/O operation. In T2 after sending the address in Tl the processor sends the data to be written to the addressed location. The data remains on the bus until middle of T4 state. The WR* becomes active at the beginning of T2.

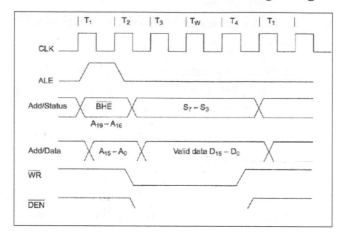

The BHE* and Ao signals are used to select the proper byte or bytes of memory or I/O word to be read or written. The M/IO*, RD* and WR* signals indicate the types of data transfer as specified in Table.

M/IO	RD	WR	Transfer Type
0	0	1	I/O read
0	1	0	I/O
1	0	1	Memory read
1	1	0	Memory write

HOLD Response Sequence

The HOLD pin is checked at the end of the each bus cycle. If it is received active by the processor before T4 of the previous cycle or during T1 state of the current cycle, the CPU activities HLDA in the next clock cycle and for the succeeding bus cycles, the bus will be given to another requesting master The control of the bus is not regained by the processor until the requesting master does not drop the HOLD pin low. When the request is dropped by the requesting master, the HLDA is dropped by the processor at the trailing edge of the next clock as shown in figure.

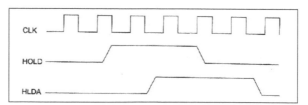

Maximum Mode 8086 System and Timings

In the maximum mode, the 8086 is operated by strapping the MN/MX* pin to ground. In this mode, the processor derives the status signals S2*, S1* and So*. Another chip called bus controller derives the control signals using this status information. In the maximum mode, there may be more than one microprocessor in the system configuration. The other components in the system are the same as in the minimum mode system. The general system organization is as shown in the figure. The basic functions of the bus controller chip IC8288, is to derive control signals like RD* and WR* (for memory and I/O devices), DEN*, DT/R*, ALE, etc. using the information made available by the processor on the status lines. The bus controller chip has input lines S2*, S1* and So* and CLK. These inputs to 8288 are driven by the CPU. It derives the outputs ALE, DEN*, DT/R*, MWTC*, AMWC*, IORC*, IOWC* and AIOWC*. The AEN*, IOB and CEN pins are specially useful for multiprocessor systems. AEN* and IOB are generally grounded. CEN pin is usually tied to +5V.

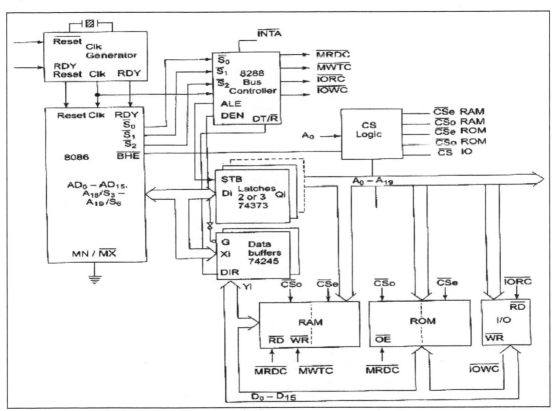

INTA* pin is used to issue two interrupt acknowledge pulses to the interrupt controller or to an interrupting device. IORC*, IOWC* are I/O read command and I/O write command signals respectively. These signals enable an IO interface to read or write the data from or to the addressed port. The MRDC*, MWTC* are memory read command and memory write command signals respectively and may be used as memory read and write signals. All these command signals instruct the memory to accept or send data from or to the bus. For both of these write command signals, the advanced signals namely AIOWC* and AMWTC* are available. They also serve the same purpose, but are activated one clock cycle earlier than the IOWC* and MWTC* signals, respectively. The maximum mode system is shown in figure. The maximum mode system timing diagrams are also divided in two portions as read (input) and write (output) timing diagrams. The address/data and address/status timings are similar to the minimum mode. ALE is asserted in T1, just like minimum mode. The only difference lies in the status signals used and the available control and advanced command signals. The figure shows the maximum mode timings for the read operation while the figure shows the same for the write operation.

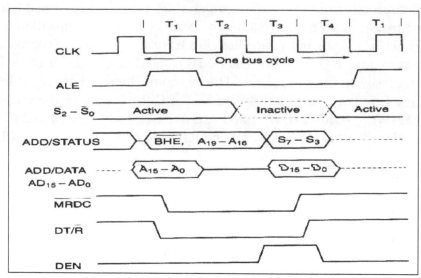
Figure: Memory Read Timing in Maximum Mode.

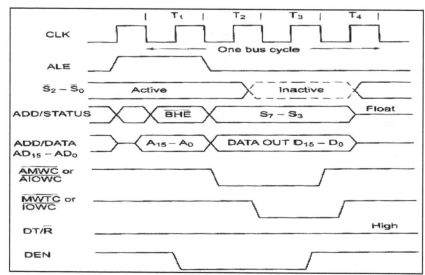
Figure: Memory Write Timing in Maximum Mode.

Intel 8255

The parallel input-output port chip 8255 is also called as programmable peripheral input-output port. The Intel's 8255 are designed for use with Intel's 8-bit, 16-bit and higher capability micro-processors. It has 24 input/output lines which may be individually programmed in two groups of twelve lines each, or three groups of eight lines. The two groups of I/O pins are named as Group A and Group B. Each of these two groups contains a subgroup of eight I/O lines called as 8-bit port and another subgroup of four lines or a 4-bit port. Thus Group A contains an 8-bit port A along with a 4-bit port C upper.

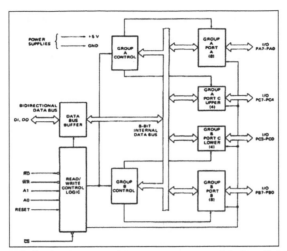

Figure: Internal Block Diagram of 8255A Programmable Parallel Port Device.

The port A lines are identified by symbols PA0-PA7 while the port C lines are identified as PC4-PC7 similarly. Group B contains an 8-bit port B, containing lines PB0- PB7 and a 4-bit port C with lower bits PC0-PC3. The port C upper and port C lower can be used in combination as an 8-bit port C. Both the port Cs is assigned the same address. Thus one may have either three 8-bit I/O ports or two 8-bit and two 4-bit I/O ports from 8255. All of these ports can function independently either as input or as output ports. This can be achieved by programming the bits of an internal register of 8255 called as control word register (CWR). The internal block diagram and the pin configuration of 8255 are shown in figure. The 8-bit data bus buffer is controlled by the read/write control logic. The read/write control logic manages all of the internal and external transfer of both data and control words. RD, WR, A1, A0 and RESET are the inputs, provided by the microprocessor to READ/WRITE control logic of 8255. The 8-bit, 3-state bidirectional buffer is used to interface the 8255 internal data bus with the external system data bus. This buffer receives or transmits data upon the execution of input or output instructions by the microprocessor. The control words or status information is also transferred through the buffer.

Pin Diagram of 8255A

The pin configuration of 8255 is shown in figure.

PA₃ — 1	40 — PA₄
PA₂ — 2	39 — PA₅
PA₁ — 3	38 — PA₆
PA₀ — 4	37 — PA₇
RD — 5	36 — WR
CS — 6	35 — Reset
GND — 7	34 — D₀
A₁ — 8	33 — D₁
A₀ — 9	32 — D₂
PC₇ — 10	31 — D₃
PC₆ — 11	30 — D₄
PC₅ — 12	29 — D₅
PC₄ — 13	28 — D₆
PC₀ — 14	27 — D₇
PC₁ — 15	26 — Vcc
PC₂ — 16	25 — PB₇
PC₃ — 17	24 — PB₆
PB₀ — 18	23 — PB₅
PB₁ — 19	22 — PB₄
PB₂ — 20	21 — PB₃

8255A Pin Configuration

The port A lines are identified by symbols PA0-PA7 while the port C lines are identified as PC4-PC7. Similarly, Group B contains an 8-bit port B, containing lines PB0-PB7 and a 4-bit port C with lower bits PC0- PC3. The port C upper and port C lower can be used in combination as an 8-bit port C.

Both the port C is assigned the same address. Thus one may have either three 8-bit I/O ports or two 8-bit and two 4-bit ports from 8255. All of these ports can function independently either as input or as output ports. This can be achieved by programming the bits of an internal register of 8255 called as control word register (CWR).

The 8-bit data bus buffer is controlled by the read/write control logic. The read/write control logic manages all of the internal and external transfers of both data and control words. RD,WR, A1, A0 and RESET are the inputs provided by the microprocessor to the READ/WRITE control logic of 8255. The 8-bit, 3-state bidirectional buffer is used to interface the 8255 internal data bus with the external system data bus. This buffer receives or transmits data upon the execution of input or output instructions by the microprocessor. The control words or status information is also transferred through the buffer. The signal description of 8255 is briefly presented as follows:

- PA7-PA0: These are eight port A lines that acts as either latched output or buffered input lines depending upon the control word loaded into the control word register.

- PC7-PC4: Upper nibble of port C lines. They may act as either output latches or input buffers lines. This port also can be used for generation of handshake lines in mode1 or mode2.

- PC3-PC0: These are the lower port C lines; other details are the same as PC7-PC4 lines.

- PB0-PB7: These are the eight port B lines which are used as latched output lines or buffered input lines in the same way as port A.

- RD: This is the input line driven by the microprocessor and should be low to indicate read operation to 8255.

- WR: This is an input line driven by the microprocessor. A low on this line indicates write operation.

- CS: This is a chip select line. If this line goes low, it enables the 8255 to respond to RD and WR signals, otherwise RD and WR signal are neglected.

- D0-D7: These are the data bus lines those carry data or control word to/from the microprocessor.

- RESET: Logic high on this line clears the control word register of 8255. All ports are set as input ports by default after reset.

- A1-A0: These are the address input lines and are driven by the microprocessor.

These lines A1-A0 with RD, WR and CS from the following operations for 8255. These address lines are used for addressing any one of the four registers, i.e. three ports and a control word register as given in table below. In case of 8086 systems, if the 8255 is to be interfaced with lower order data bus, the A0 and A1 pins of 8255 are connected with A1 and A2 respectively.

$\overline{RD}$	$\overline{WR}$	$\overline{CS}$	A_1	A_0	Input (Read) cycle
0	1	0	0	0	Port A to Data bus
0	1	0	0	1	Port B to Data bus
0	1	0	1	0	Port C to Data bus
0	1	0	1	1	CWR to Data bus

$\overline{RD}$	$\overline{WR}$	$\overline{CS}$	A_1	A_0	Input (write) cycle
1	0	0	0	0	Data bus to Port A
1	0	0	0	1	Data bus to Port B
1	0	0	1	0	Data bus to Port C
1	0	0	1	1	Data bus to CWR

$\overline{RD}$	$\overline{WR}$	$\overline{CS}$	A_1	A_0	Function
X	X	1	X	X	Data bus tristated
1	1	0	X	X	Data bus tristaed

Modes of Operation of 8255

These are two basic modes of operation of 8255. I/O mode and Bit Set-Reset mode (BSR). In I/O mode, the 8255 ports work as programmable I/O ports, while in BSR mode only port C (PC0-PC7) can be used to set or reset its individual port bits. Under the I/O mode of operation, further there are three modes of operation of 8255, so as to support different types of applications, mode 0, mode 1 and mode 2. In BSR Mode, any of the 8-bits of port C can be set or reset depending on D0 of the control word. The bit to be set or reset is selected by bit select flags D3, D2 and D1 of the CWR as given in table.

I/O Modes

Mode 0 (Basic I/O Mode)

This mode is also called as basic input/output Mode. This mode provides simple input and output capabilities using each of the threeports. Data can be simply read from and written to the input and output portsrespectively, after appropriate initialization.

D_3	D_2	D_1	Selected bits of port C
0	0	0	D_0
0	0	1	D_1
0	1	0	D_2
0	1	1	D_3
1	0	0	D_4
1	0	1	D_5
1	1	0	D_6
1	1	1	D_7

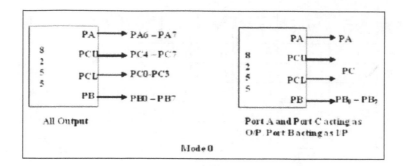

The salient features of this mode are as listed below:

- Two 8-bit ports (port A and port B) and two 4-bit ports (port C upper and lower) are available. The two 4-bit ports can be combined used as a third 8-bit port.

- Any port can be used as an input or output port.

- Output ports are latched. Input ports are not latched.

- A maximum of four ports are available so that overall 16 I/O configurations are possible.

All these modes can be selected by programming a register internal to 8255known as CWR. The control word register has two formats. The first format is valid for I/O modes of operation, i.e. modes 0, mode 1 and mode 2 while the second format is valid for bit set/reset (BSR) mode of operation. These formats are shown in following figure:

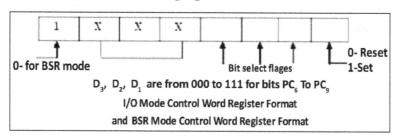

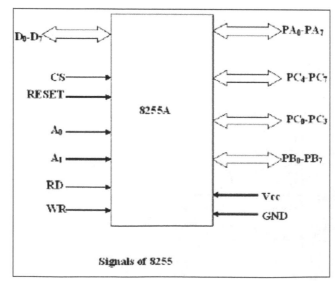

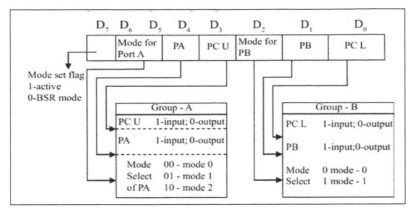

Control Word Format of 8255.

Mode 1: (Strobed Input/Output Mode)

In this mode the handshaking control the input and output action of the specified port. Port C lines PC0-PC2, provide strobe or handshake lines for port B. This group which includes port B and PC0-PC2 is called as group B for Strobed data input/output. Port C lines PC3-PC5 provides strobe lines for port A. This group including port A and PC3-PC5 from group A. Thus port C is utilized for generating handshake signals. The salient features of mode 1 are listed as follows:

- Two groups – Group A and group B are available for strobed data transfer.

- Each group contains one 8-bit data I/O port and one 4-bit control/data port.

- The 8-bit data port can be either used as input and output port. The inputs and outputs both are latched.

- Out of 8-bit port C, PC0-PC2 are used to generate control signals for port B and PC3-PC5 are used to generate control signals for port A. the lines PC6, PC7 may be used as independent data lines.

The control signals for both the groups in input and output modes are explained as follows:

Input Control Signal (Mode 1)

- STB (Strobe Input): If this lines falls to logic low level, the data available at 8- bit input port is loaded into input latches.

- IBF (Input Buffer Full): If this signal rises to logic 1, it indicates that data has been loaded into latches, i.e. it works as an acknowledgement. IBF is set by a low on STB and is reset by the rising edge of RD input.

- INTR (Interrupt Request): This active high output signal can be used to interrupt the CPU whenever an input device requests the service. INTR is set by a high STB pin and a high at IBF pin. INTE is an internal flag that can be controlled by the bit set/reset mode of either PC4 (INTEA) or PC2 (INTEB) as shown in figure.

- INTR is reset by a falling edge of RD input. Thus an external input device can be request the service of the processor by putting the data on the bus and sending the strobe signal.

Output Control Signal (Mode 1)

- OBF (Output Buffer Full): This status signal, whenever falls to low, indicates that CPU has written data to the specified output port. The OBF flip flop will beset by a rising edge of WR signal and reset by a low going edge at the ACK input.

- ACK (Acknowledge Input): ACK signal acts as an acknowledgement to be given by an output device. ACK signal, whenever low, informs the CPU that the data transferred by the CPU to the output device through the port is received by the output device.

- INTR (Interrupt Request): Thus an output signal that can be used to interrupt the CPU when an output device acknowledges the data received from the CPU.INTR is set when ACK, OBF and INTE are 1. It is reset by a falling edge on WR input. The INTEA and INTEB flags are controlled by the bit set-reset mode of PC6 and PC2 respectively.

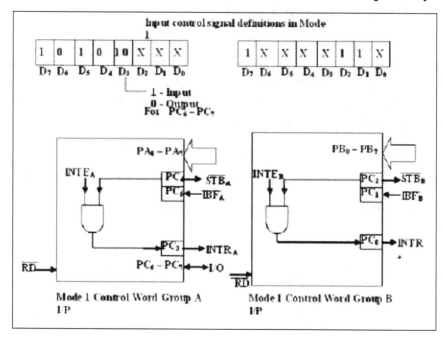

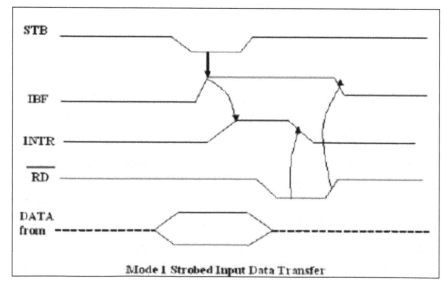

Mode 1 Strobed Input Data Transfer

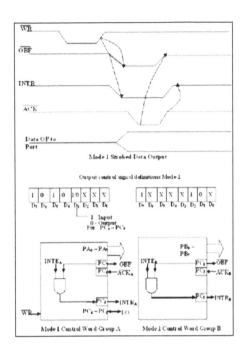

Mode 2: (Strobed Bidirectional I/O)

This mode of operation of 8255 is also called as strobed bidirectional I/O. This mode of operation provides 8255 with additional features for communicating with a peripheral device on an 8-bit data bus. Handshaking signals are provided to maintain proper data flow and synchronization between the data transmitter and receiver. The interrupt generation and other functions are similar to mode 1. In this mode, 8255 is a bidirectional 8-bit port with handshake signals. The Rd and WR signals decide whether the 8255 is going to operate as an input port or output port. The Salient features of Mode 2 of 8255 are listed as follows:

- The single 8-bit port in group A is available.

- The 8-bit port is bidirectional and additionally a 5-bit control port is available.

- Three I/O lines are available at port C.(PC2 – PC0).

- Inputs and outputs are both latched.

- The 5-bit control port C (PC3-PC7) is used for generating/accepting handshake signals for the 8-bit data transfer on port A.

Control Signal in Mode 2

- INTR: (Interrupt Request) as in mode 1, this control signal is active high and is used to interrupt the microprocessor to ask for transfer of the next data byte to/from it. This signal is used for input (read) as well as output (write) operations.

Control Signals for Output Operations

- OBF (Output Buffer Full): This signal, when falls to low level, indicates that the CPU has written data to port A. ACK (Acknowledge) This control input, when falls to logic low level,

Acknowledges that the previous data byte is received by the destination and next byte may be sent by the processor. This signal enables the internal tristate buffers to send the next data byte on port A.

- INTE1 (A flag associated with OBF): This can be controlled by bit set/reset mode with PC6.

Control Signals for Input Operations

- STB (Strobe Input): A low on this line is used to strobe in the data into the input Latches of 8255.

- IBF (Input Buffer Full): When the data is loaded into input buffer, this signal rises to logic "1". This can be used as an acknowledge that the data has been received by the receiver.

- The waveforms in figure show the operation in Mode 2 for output as well as input port.

- WR must occur before ACK and STB must be activated before RD.

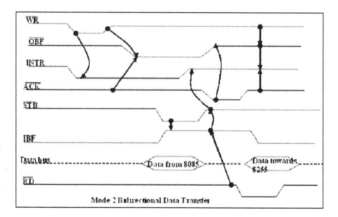

Mode 2 Bidirectional Data Transfer

The figure shows a schematic diagram containing an 8-bit bidirectional port, 5-bit control port and the relation of INTR with the control pins. Port B can either be set to Mode 0 or 1 with port A (Group A) is in Mode 2.

- Mode 2 is not available for port B.

- The INTR goes high only if IBF, INTE2, STB and RD go high or OBF.

- INTE1, ACK and WR go high. The port C can be read to know the status of the peripheral device, in terms of the control signals, using the normal I/O instructions.

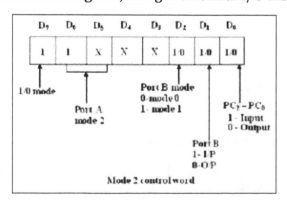

Mode 2 control word

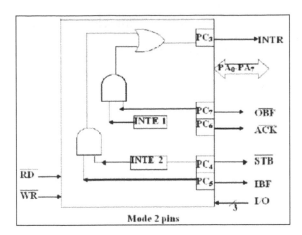

Mode 2 pins

Interfacing Analog to Digital Data Converters

- In most of the cases, the PIO 8255 is used for interfacing the analog to digital converters with microprocessor.

- We have already studied 8255 interfacing with 8086 as an I/O port. This section we will only emphasize the interfacing techniques of analog to digital converters with 8255.

- The analog to digital converters is treated as an input device by the microprocessor that sends an initializing signal to the ADC to start the analogy to digital data conversation process. The start of conversation signal is a pulse of a specific duration.

- The process of analog to digital conversion is a slow.

- Process and the microprocessor have to wait for the digital data till the conversion is over. After the conversion is over, the ADC sends end of conversion EOC signal to inform the microprocessor that the conversion is over and the result is ready at the output buffer of the ADC. These tasks of issuing an SOC pulse to ADC, reading EOC signal from the ADC and reading the digital output of the AD Care carried out by the CPU using 8255 I/O ports.

- The time taken by the ADC from the active edge of SOC pulse till the active edge of EOC signal is called as the conversion delay of the ADC.

- It may range anywhere from a few microseconds in case of fast ADC to even a few hundred milliseconds in case of slow ADCs.

- The available ADC in the market use different conversion techniques for conversion of analog signal to digitals. Successive approximation techniques and dual slope integration techniques are the most popular techniques used in the integrated ADC chip.

- General algorithm for ADC interfacing contains the following steps:

  ○ Ensure the stability of analog input, applied to the ADC.

  ○ Issue start of conversion pulse to ADC

  ○ Read end of conversion signal to mark the end of conversion processes.

○   Read digital data output of the ADC as equivalent digital output.

○   Analog input voltage must be constant at the input of the ADC right from the start of conversion till the end of the conversion to get correct results. This may be ensured by a sample and hold circuit which samples the analog signal and holds it constant for specific time duration. The microprocessor may issue a hold signal to the sample and hold circuit.

○   If the applied input changes before the complete conversion process is over, the digital equivalent of the analog input calculated by the ADC may not be correct.

Intel 8257

The Direct Memory Access or DMA mode of data transfer is the fastest amongst all the modes of data transfer. In this mode, the device may transfer data directly to/from memory without any interference from the CPU. The device requests the CPU (through a DMA controller) to hold its data, address and control bus, so that the device may transfer data directly to/from memory. The DMA data transfer is initiated only after receiving HLDA signal from the CPU. Intel's 8257 is a four channel DMA controller designed to be interfaced with their family of microprocessors. The 8257, on behalf of the devices, requests the CPU for bus access using local bus request input i.e. HOLD in minimum mode. In maximum mode of the microprocessor RQ/GT pin is used as bus request input. On receiving the HLDA signal (in minimum mode) or RQ/GT signal (in maximum mode) from the CPU, the requesting devices gets the access of the bus, and it completes the required number of DMA cycles for the data transfer and then hands over the control of the bus back to the CPU.

Internal Architecture of 8257

The internal architecture of 8257 is shown in figure. The chip support four DMA channels, i.e. four peripheral devices can independently request for DMA data transfer through these channels at a time. The DMA controller has 8-bit internal data buffer, a read/write unit, a control unit, a priority resolving unit along with a set of registers.

DMA Address Register

Each DMA channel has one DMA address register. The function of this register is to store the address of the starting memory location, which will be accessed by the DMA channel. Thus the starting address of the memory block which will be accessed by the device is first loaded in the DMA address register of the channel. The device that wants to transfer data over a DMA channel, will access the block of the memory with the starting address stored in the DMA Address Register.

Terminal Count Register

Each of the four DMA channels of 8257 has one terminal count register (TC). This 16-bit register isused for ascertaining that the data transfer through a DMA channel ceases or stops after the required number of DMA cycles. The low order 14-bits of the terminal count register are initialised with the binary equivalent of the number of required DMA cycles minus one. After each DMA cycle, the terminal count register content will be decremented by one and finally it becomes zero after the required number of DMA cycles are over. The bits 14 and 15 of this register indicate the type of the DMA operation (transfer). If the device wants to write data into the memory, the DMA operation is called DMA write operation. Bit 14 of the register in this case will be set to one and bit 15 will be set to zero. Table gives detail of DMA operation selection and corresponding bit configuration of bits 14 and 15 of the TC register.

Table: DMA Operation Selection Using A_{15}/RD and A_{14}/WR.

Bit 15	Bit 14	Type of DMA Operation
0	0	Verify DMA Cycle
0	1	Write DMA Cycle
1	0	Read DMA Cycle
1	1	(Illegal)

Mode Set Register

The mode set register is used for programming the 8257 as per the requirements of the system. The function of the mode set register is to enable the DMA channels individually and also to set the various modes of operation. The DMA channel should not be enabled till the DMA address register and the terminal count register contain valid information; otherwise, an unwanted DMA request may initiate a DMA cycle, probably destroying the valid memory data. The bits Do-D3 enable one of the four DMA channels of 8257. For example, if Do is '1', channel 0 is enabled. If bit 4 is set, rotating priority is enabled, otherwise, the normal, i.e. fixed priority is enabled.

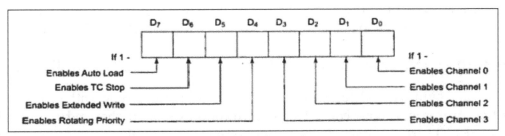

Figure: Bit Definitions of the Mode Set Register.

If the TC STOP bit is set, the selected channel is disabled after the terminal count condition is reached, and it further prevents any DMA cycle on the channel. To enable the channel again, this bit must be reprogrammed. If the TC STOP bit is programmed to be zero, the channel is not disabled, even after the count reaches zero and further request are allowed on the same channel. The auto load bit, if set, enables channel 2 for the repeat block chaining operations, without immediate software intervention between the two successive blocks. The channel 2 registers are used as usual, while the channel 3 registers are used to store the block reinitialisation parameters, i.e. the DMA starting address and terminal count. After the first block is transferred using DMA, the channel 2 registers are reloaded with the corresponding channel 3 registers for the next block transfer, if the update flag is set. The extended write bit, if set to '1', extends the duration of MEMW and IOW signals by activating them earlier, this is useful in interfacing the peripherals with different access times. If the peripheral is not accessed within the stipulated time, it is expected to give the 'NOT

READY' indication to 8257, to request it to add one or more wait states in the DMA CYCLE. The mode set register can only be written into.

Status Register

The status register of 8257 is shown in figure. The lower order 4-bits of this register contain the terminal count status for the four individual channels. If any of these bits is set, it indicates that the specific channel has reached the terminal count condition.

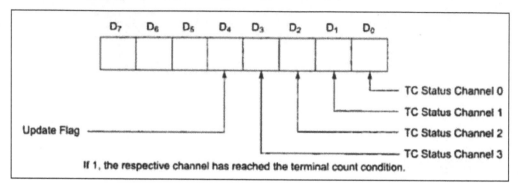

These bits remain set till either the status is read by the CPU or the 8257 is reset. The update flag is not affected by the read operation. This flag can only be cleared by resetting 8257 or by resetting the auto load bit of the mode set register. If the update flag is set, the contents of the channel 3 registers are reloaded to the corresponding registers of channel 2 whenever the channel 2 reaches a terminal count condition, after transferring one block and the next block is to be transferred using the autoload feature of 8257.

The update flag is set every time, the channel 2 registers are loaded with contents of the channel 3 registers. It is cleared by the completion of the first DMA cycle of the new block. This register can only read.

Data Bus Buffer, Read/Write Logic, Control Unit and Priority Resolver

The 8-bit. Tristate, bidirectional buffer interfaces the internal bus of 8257 with the external system bus under the control of various control signals. In the slave mode, the read/write logic accepts the I/O Read or I/O Write signals, decodes the Ao-A3 lines and either writes the contents of the data bus to the addressed internal register or reads the contents of the selected register depending upon whether IOW or IOR signal is activated. In master mode, the read/write logic generates the IOR and IOW signals to control the data flow to or from the selected peripheral. The control logic controls the sequences of operations and generates the required control signals like AEN, ADSTB, MEMR, MEMW, TC and MARK along with the address lines A4-A7, in master mode. The priority resolver resolves the priority of the four DMA channels depending upon whether normal priority or rotating priority is programmed.

Signal Description of 8257

1. DRQo-DRQ3: These are the four individual channel DMA request inputs, used by the peripheral devices for requesting the DMA services. The DRQo has the highest priority while DRQ3 has the lowest one, if the fixed priority mode is selected.

2. DACK0-DACK3: These are the active-low DMA acknowledge output lines which inform the requesting peripheral that the request has been honoured and the bus is relinquished by the CPU. These lines may act as strobe lines for the requesting devices.

3. D0-D7: These are bidirectional, data lines used to interface the system bus with the internal data bus of 8257. These lines carry command words to 8257 and status word from 8257, in slave mode, i.e. under the control of CPU. The data over these lines may be transferred in both the directions. When the 8257 is the bus master (master mode, i.e. not under CPU control), it uses D0-D7 lines to send higher byte of the generated address to the latch. This address is further latched using ADSTB signal. The address is transferred over D0-D7 during the first clock cycle of the DMA cycle. During the rest of the period, data is available on the data bus.

4. IOR: This is an active-low bidirectional tristate input line that acts as an input in the slave mode. In slave mode, this input signal is used by the CPU to read internal registers of 8257.this line acts output in master mode. In master mode, this signal is used to read data from a peripheral during a memory write cycle.

5. IOW: This is an active low bidirection tristate line that acts as input in slave mode to load the contents of the data bus to the 8-bit mode register or upper/lower byte of a 16-bit DMA address register or terminal count register. In the master mode, it is a control output that loads the data to a peripheral during DMA memory read cycle (write to peripheral).

6. CLK: This is a clock frequency input required to derive basic system timings for the internal operation of 8257.

7. RESET: This active-high asynchronous input disables all the DMA channels by clearing the mode register and tristates all the control lines.

8. A0-A3: These are the four least significant address lines. In slave mode, they act as input which select one of the registers to be read or written. In the master mode, they are the four least significant memory address output lines generated by 8257.

9. CS: This is an active-low chip select line that enables the read/write operations from/to 8257, in slave mode. In the master mode, it is automatically disabled to prevent the chip from getting selected (by CPU) while performing the DMA operation.

10. A4-A7: This is the higher nibble of the lower byte address generated by 8257 during the master mode of DMA operation.

11. READY: This is an active-high asynchronous input used to stretch memory read and write cycles of 8257 by inserting wait states. This is used while interfacing slower peripherals.

12. HRQ: The hold request output requests the access of the system bus. In the non-cascaded 8257 systems, this is connected with HOLD pin of CPU. In the cascade mode, this pin of a slave is connected with a DRQ input line of the master 8257, while that of the master is connected with HOLD input of the CPU.

13. HLDA: The CPU drives this input to the DMA controller high, while granting the bus to the device. This pin is connected to the HLDA output of the CPU. This input, if high, indicates to the DMA controller that the bus has been granted to the requesting peripheral by the CPU.

14. MEMR: This active –low memory read output is used to read data from the addressed memory locations during DMA read cycles.

15. MEMW: This active-low three state output is used to write data to the addressed memory location during DMA write operation.

16. ADST: This output from 8257 strobes the higher byte of the memory address generated by the DMA controller into the latches.

17. AEN: This output is used to disable the system data bus and the control the bus driven by the CPU, this may be used to disable the system address and data bus by using the enable input of the bus drivers to inhibit the non-DMA devices from responding during DMA operations. If the 8257 is I/O mapped, this should be used to disable the other I/O devices, when the DMA controller addresses is on the address bus.

```
            ┌─────────────────────────┐
   IOR ─┤ 1                      40 ├─ A₇
   IOW ─┤ 2                      39 ├─ A₆
  MEMR ─┤ 3                      38 ├─ A₅
  MEMW ─┤ 4                      37 ├─ A₄
  MARK ─┤ 5                      36 ├─ TC
 READY ─┤ 6                      35 ├─ A₃
  HLDA ─┤ 7                      34 ├─ A₂
 ADSTB ─┤ 8                      33 ├─ A₁
   AEN ─┤ 9                      32 ├─ A₀
   HRQ ─┤ 10        8257         31 ├─ Vcc
    CS ─┤ 11                     30 ├─ D₀
   CLK ─┤ 12                     29 ├─ D₁
 RESET ─┤ 13                     28 ├─ D₂
 DACK2 ─┤ 14                     27 ├─ D₃
 DACK3 ─┤ 15                     26 ├─ D₄
  DRQ₃ ─┤ 16                     25 ├─ DACK0
  DRQ₂ ─┤ 17                     24 ├─ DACK1
  DRQ₁ ─┤ 18                     23 ├─ D₅
  DRQ₀ ─┤ 19                     22 ├─ D₆
   GND ─┤ 20                     21 ├─ D₇
            └─────────────────────────┘
         Pin diagram of 8257
```

18. TC: Terminal count output indicates to the currently selected peripherals that the present DMA cycle is the last for the previously programmed data block. If the TC STOP bit in the mode set register is set, the selected channel will be disabled at the end of the DMA cycle. The TC pin is activated when the 14-bit content of the terminal count register of the selected channel becomes equal to zero. The lower order 14 bits of the terminal count register are to be programmed with a 14-bit equivalent of (n-1), if n is the desired number of DMA cycles.

19. MARK: The modulo 128 mark output indicates to the selected peripheral that the current DMA cycle is the 128th cycle since the previous MARK output. The mark will be activated after each 128 cycles or integral multiples of it from the beginning if the data block (the first DMA cycle), if the total number of the required DMA cycles (n) is completely divisible by 128.

20. Vcc: This is a +5v supply pin required for operation of the circuit.

21. GND: This is a return line for the supply (ground pin of the IC).

Interfacing 8257 with 8086

Once a DMA controller is initialised by a CPU property, it is ready to take control of the system bus on a DMA request, either from a peripheral or itself (in case of memory-to-memory transfer). The DMA controller sends a HOLD request to the CPU and waits for the CPU to assert the HLDA signal. The CPU relinquishes the control of the bus before asserting the HLDA signal.

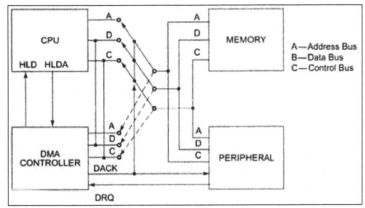

Figure: A Conceptual Implementation of the System.

Once the HLDA signal goes high, the DMA controller activates the DACK signal to the requesting peripheral and gains the control of the system bus. The DMA controller is the sole master of the bus, till the DMA operation is over. The CPU remains in the HOLD status (all of its signals are tristate except HOLD and HLDA), till the DMA controller is the master of the bus. In other words, the DMA controller interfacing circuit implements a switching arrangement for the address, data and control busses of the memory and peripheral subsystem from/to the CPU to/from the DMA controller.

Real Time Operating System

An operating system that is made to serve real-time applications, and which processes data without any buffer delays is defined as a real time operating system. This chapter discusses in detail the concepts related to real time operating system such as RTOS design, scheduling and multi-tasking in RTOS, and Windows as RTOS.

A Real Time Operating System (RTOS) is an operating system developed for real-time embedded applications evolved around processors or controllers. It allows priorities to be changed instantly and data to be processed rapidly enough that the results may be used in response to another process taking place at the same time, as in transaction processing. It has the ability to immediately respond in a predetermined and predictable way to external events. Overall a mode of action and reaction by RTOS and application software handles the entire embedded application. Let us consider the role of RTOS in the mobile phone. A cell phone has several features like call processing, notifying a waiting call, maintain a phone directory, messages and other utilities like web browsers, calculator, games, apps etc. RTOS handles each of these features as a separate task. Suppose a user is playing game on his cell phone and a call arrives, immediately the caller's ID starts flashing on the screen. After completion of the call, the user can resume the game from the level/ point it has got suspended. It is observed that in this case RTOS handled the tasks using priorities and performed multitasking using context switching and scheduler.

RTOS Design

To develop an RTOS for a particular application, one has to consider the hardware architecture available, the resources to be handled, the available memory etc. to decide for the various aspects of the Real Time Operating System.

- Task: A task also called a thread is a simple program that thinks it has the CPU all to itself. The design process for a real time application involves splitting the work to be done in different tasks. Each task is assigned a priority, its own set of CPU registers and its own stack area. Each task is typically in an infinite loop that can be in any of the five states: Dormant, Ready, Running, Waiting and Interrupted. The first step in designing of the RTOS is to decide on the number of tasks that the CPU of the embedded application can handle.

- Multitasking: It is the process of scheduling and switching the CPU between the several tasks. It maximizes the CPU utilization and makes programming efficient for designing and debugging. Processors and Controllers with inbuilt pipe lining architecture and can further increase the speed of the execution of a particular task.

- Context Switch: When a multitasking kernel decides to run different tasks, it simply saves the current task's context storage area (Task Stack). Once this operation is performed, new task's context is restored from its storage area (Stack) and execution of new task's code is resumed.

- Task Priority: Priority is assigned to a task depending on its importance such as static priority. Static priority means priority of the task does not change during run time. Dynamic priority means the priority of the task can change during run time.

- Kernel: In multitasking system, kernel is responsible for management of tasks and context switching. A kernel program will require its own code space (ROM area) and data structure space (RAM area) which will increase the system overhead. So, kernel should be designed strictly to consume 2% to 5% of overall CPU time. Kernel can provide indispensable service such as semaphore management, mailboxes, queues, time delays etc. Kernel can be Preemptive or non-preemptive.

- Resource: It is any entity used by the task. A resource can thus be an input or output device, a variable, a structure or a set of registers etc. A shared resource can be accessed by more than one task. However, each task should gain exclusive access to the shared resource to prevent data corruption. This is called Mutual Exclusion. Most common methods to obtain exclusive access to shared resources are disabling interrupts, test and set, disabling scheduling and using semaphores.

- Inter Task Communication: It is sometimes necessary for a task or an interrupt service routine has to communicate to another task. It can be done using global data under mutual exclusion. The other option available for Inter task communication is to send messages using either message mailbox or message queue.

- Interrupts: Interrupts allows controller or processor to process events when they occur. In RTOS, interrupt service routine processes the events and upon completion returns to background for a foreground/ background system, interrupted task for a non-preemptive kernel and highest priority task to run a Preemptive kernel.

- Clock Tick: It is a special interrupt that occur periodically, generally in microseconds. It is a system's heart beat and provides time outs when tasks are waiting for event to occur. The faster the tick rate, higher the overhead imposed on the system. All kernels allow tasks to be delayed for certain number of clock ticks.

Scheduling in RTOS

Each task in an embedded application has an infinite loop from start to finish. To achieve efficient CPU utilization a multitasking RTOS uses an orderly transfer of control from one code entity to another. To accomplish this RTOS must monitor the system resources and the execution state of each code entity, and it must ensure that each entity receives the control of the CPU in a timely manner. The key word here is work in a timely manner. A real-time system that does not perform a required operation at the correct time is said to have failed. That failure can have consequences that range from benign to catastrophic. The response time for a request of kernel services and the execution time of these services must be fast and predictable. In an RTOS, the application program code has to be designed to ensure that all its needs are detected and processed. Real-time applications usually consist of several tasks (also can be called processes or threads) that require control of system resources at varying times due to external or internal events. Each task must compete with all other tasks for control of system resources such as memory, execution time, or peripheral devices. The developer uses the scheduling models in the RTOS to manage this "competition" between the tasks. The program code can be compute-bound (heavily dependent on CPU resources) or I/O-bound (heavily dependent on access to external devices). Program code that is I/O bound or compute bound is not allowed to monopolize a system resource if more important tasks requires the same resource. Scheduling policies determine how the processes are selected for execution. Scheduling policies can also deliver higher CPU utilization. Right scheduling policies meet all the timing requirements and also properly utilize the CPU. Some of the scheduling policies are discussed in detail.

Simple Scheduling

A very simple scheduling policy is known as cyclo static scheduling or sometimes as Time Division Multiple Access Scheduling. Time Division Multiple Access divides the time into equal-sized time slots over an interval equal to the length of the hyper-period H. Processes always run in the same time slot. It is depending on the deadlines for some of the processes. Some time slots will be empty. Since the time slots are of equal size, some short processes may have time left over in their time slot. Utilization is used as a schedule ability measure. The total CPU time of all the processes must be less than the hyper-period. An example of Time division multiple access is shown in Figure. It shows three processes scheduled using TDMA.

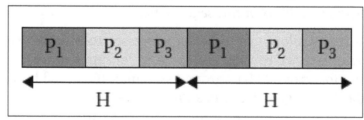

Figure: Time Division Multiple Access.

Another scheduling policy that is slightly more sophisticated is round robin. Round robin uses the same hyperperiod as cyclostatic.

Round Robin

Here also, the processes are scheduled in a cyclic fashion. However, if a process does not have any useful work to do, the round-robin scheduler moves on to the next process in order to fill the time slot with useful work. Example: All three processes execute during the first hyper-period, but during the second one, P1 has no useful work and is skipped. The processes are always executed in the same order and are shown in figure.

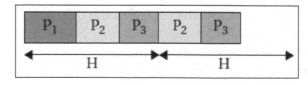

Pre-emptive Scheduling

Pre-emption is a mechanism to stop a current process and provide service to another process. In a Preemptive model, the tasks can be forcibly suspended. This is initiated by an interrupt on the CPU. OS schedules such that the higher priority task, when ready, preempts a lower priority by blocking the current running task. It solves the problem of large worst case latency for higher priority tasks. In the Preemptive scheduling model, a task must be in one of four states:

- Running: In this state, the task is in control of the CPU.

- Ready: In this state, the task is not blocked and is ready to receive control of the CPU when the scheduling policy indicates it is the highest priority task in the system that is not blocked.

- Inactive: In Inactive state, the task is blocked and requires initialization in order to become ready. Inactive is a waiting state.

- Blocked: In blocked state, the task is waiting for something to happen or for a resource to become available. Blocked is a waiting state.

There must be a way of interrupting the operation of the lesser task and granting the resource to the more important one. Then the highest-priority task ready to run is always given control of the CPU. If an ISR makes a higher-priority task ready, the higher-priority task is resumed (instead of the interrupted task). Most commercial real-time kernels are Preemptive.

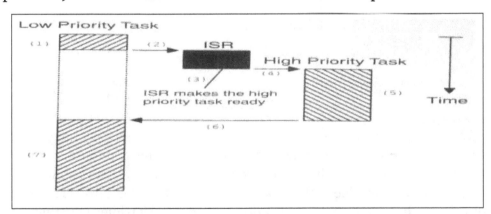

Example of Preemptive scheduling is shown in figure. In this, each task has a priority relative to all the other tasks. The most critical task is assigned the highest priority. The highest priority task that is ready to run gets control of the processor. A task runs until it yields, terminates, or blocks. Each task has its own memory stack. Before a task can run it must load its context from its memory stack (this can take many cycles). If a task is preempted it must save its current state/context; this context is restored when the task is given control of the processor. Thus context switch is an important aspect in Preemptive scheduling.

- Uses of Preemptive Scheduling: The reason for the use of Preemptive scheduling is to reduce the limitations in cooperative and cyclic scheduling of tasks.

  - Cooperative Scheduling: It waits for the running task to get finished and then schedules each ready task. A long execution time of a low- priority task lets a high priority task wait until the low-priority task finishes.

○ Cyclic Scheduling: Assume that the cooperative scheduler is cyclic, without having a predefined time slice. Consider that an interrupt for service occurs from the first task, just at the beginning of the second task. Then the first task service waits till all other remaining listed or queued tasks finish. Worst case latency equals the sum of execution times of all tasks.

• Advantage of Preemptive Scheduler: The advantage of Preemptive scheduler is that, the execution of the highest-priority task is deterministic and the task-level response time will be minimized.

• Disadvantage of Preemptive Scheduler: It should not use non-reentrant functions unless exclusive access to these functions is ensured.

Context Switch

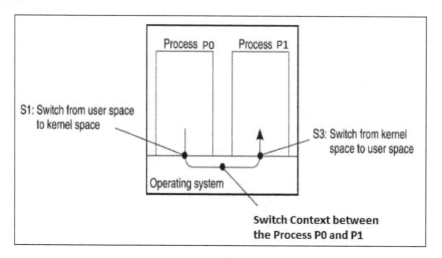

The set of registers that define a process is known as its context. The switching from one process register set to another register set is known as context switching. The data structure that holds the state of the process is known as the process control block (PCB). That is, the context of a process is represented in the PCB. The time it takes is dependent on the hardware support. The context-switch time is overhead, the system won't do any useful work while switching.

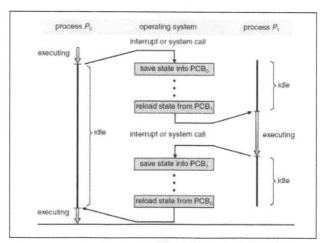

Figure: Context Switch between Processes P0 and P1.

- Context Switch between Processes: Context switch between two processes is shown in figure given below. Here the process is first switched from the user space to kernel space while switching between two processes P0 and P1.

Context switch between the processes are shown in figure. For switching, first the process P_0 gives interrupt or system call to save the state into process control Block PCB_0. At that time the process P_1 is in the idle state. Then the process P_0 will enter into reload state of PCB_1. Then the process P_0 enters into idle state, P_1 enters into executing state. After that it transfers the control to process P_0 then it goes to save state into PCB_1. Then the control is transferred to the reload state of PCB_0. Next, the process P_0 starts executing.

- Time Slice Mechanism for Multitasking: On each context switch, a task is selected by the kernel's scheduler from the 'ready' list and is put into the run state. It is then executed until another context switch occurs. This is normally signalled by a periodic interrupt from a timer. In such cases the task is simply switched out and put back on the 'ready' list, awaiting its next slot. Alternatively, the execution can be stopped by the task executing certain kernel commands. It could suspend itself, where it remains present in the system but no further execution occurs. It could become dormant, awaiting a start command from another task, or even simply waiting for a server task within the operating system to perform a special function for it. The time slice mechanism for multitasking operating system is shown in figure below:

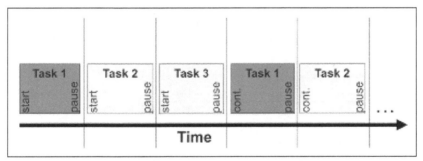

Figure: Time slice mechanism for multitasking OS.

The diagram shown gives a simplified state diagram for a typical real-time operating system which uses this time slice mechanism.

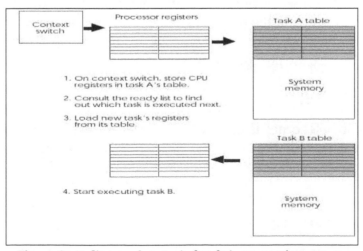

Figure: State diagram for a typical real-time operating system.

When the context switching occurs, the CPU register contents are stored in task A's table. Then the next task (task B) is identified and task B's register contents are loaded into the processor registers. Now the processor starts executing task B. This sequence of operations is illustrated in figure.

- Steps in Context Switch:

  ○ First save context of the processor including program counter and other registers.

  ○ Update the PCB of the running process with its new state and other associate information.

  ○ Move PCB to appropriate queue – ready, blocked.

  ○ Select another process for execution.

  ○ Update PCB of the selected process.

  ○ Restore CPU context from that of the selected process.

- Example of Context Switch: Figure shows the situation when context switch occurs in the system during I/O request.

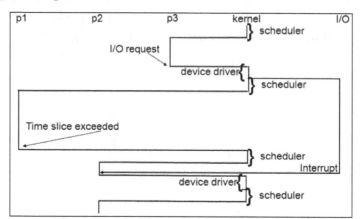

Consider that there are three processes P1, P2 and P3. Assume that the process P3 is in running state. Suddenly when an I/O request is received, the scheduler loads the corresponding device driver, and then switches to process P1. When the time slice of P1 is exceeded, it schedules P2. While P2 is executing, an interrupt (corresponding to the previous I/O request) occurs. Hence, a context switch occurs and interrupts service routine for I/O request is executed. After finishing the interrupt service, context switch again occurs to resume the previous process P2.

Priorities in Scheduling

In priority scheduling, an OS kernel determines which process is to be executed next. For each task a numerical priority is assigned. The kernel can simply look at the processes and their priorities. It sees which one actually wants to execute and selects the highest priority process that is ready to run.This mechanism is flexible and fast.

Priority-Driven Scheduling

Priority-driven scheduling is easy to implement. It does not require the prior information on the release times and execution times of the jobs. Each process has a fixed priority that does not vary during the course of execution. The ready process with the highest priority is selected for execution. A process continues execution until it completes or it is pre-empted by a higher-priority process. Table shows an example for priority process. Consider there are three processes P1, P2 and P3 with the execution time of 10, 20 and 30 time units respectively. In this example, P1 is the highest priority; P2 is having the middle priority and P3 is the lower priority process in order.

Table: Priority of Processes.

Process	Priority	Execution time
P1	1	10
P2	2	30
P3	3	20

An example of Priority scheduling for this set of processes is shown in Figure. Assume that P2 is ready to run. When the system is started, P1 is released at time 15, and P3 is released at time 18. P2 is the only ready process, so it is selected for execution. At time 15, P1 becomes ready; it pre-empts P2 and begins execution since it has a higher priority. Since P1 is the highest-priority process in the system, it is guaranteed to execute until it finishes. P3's data arrives at time 18, but it cannot pre-empt P1. Even when P1 finishes, P3 is not allowed to run. P2 is still ready and has higher priority than P3. P3 starts only when both the process P1 and P2 are finished. Priority inversion problem may occur if priority scheduling is used.

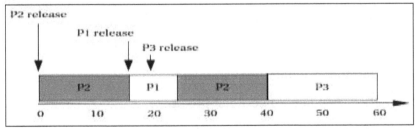

Figure: Priority Scheduling.

Priority Inversion Problem

Scheduling the processes without considering the resources those processes require, can cause priority inversion, in which a low-priority process blocks execution of a higher priority process by keeping hold of its resources. Priority inversion problem occurs commonly in real time kernels. Example: Consider task 1 has a higher priority than task 2 and task 2 has a higher priority than task 3. Assume task 1 and task 3 share a resource through mutual exclusion. While task 3 is executing and holding the resource if task 2 is ready, it is scheduled because it has higher priority. At this time, even though task 1 has higher priority it cannot execute because the blocked task 3 is holding the shared resource. That is, a lower priority process is blocking a higher priority process. This is the priority inversion problem.

A Solution to priority inversion problem is we can correct the problem by raising the priority of task 3, just for the time when it accesses the shared resource. After that, the task 3 returns to its original priority. If task 3 finishes the access before being preempted by task 1 then it incurs overhead for nothing. A better solution to priority inversion problem is priority inheritance.

Priority Inheritance

It automatically changes the task priority when needed. That is, the task that holds the resource will inherit the priority of the task that waits for that resource until it releases the resources. Once the priorities are assigned, the OS takes care of the rest by choosing the highest-priority ready process.

Assigning Task Priorities

There are two major ways to assign priorities as explained below:

- Static priorities: The priorities of the task that do not change during execution are called as static priorities. Once the Priority of the task is assigned, its value is retained till the end or completion of task. Example: Rate Monotonic Scheduling (RMS).

- Dynamic priorities: The priorities of the task that are dynamically changing during the execution are called as dynamic priorities. These priorities will change at each and every instant of time based on the current scenario. Example: Earliest Deadline First (EDF).

Rate Monotonic Scheduling (RMS)

RMS is one of the first scheduling policies developed for real-time systems and is still widely used. It is a static scheduling policy where only the fixed priorities are sufficient to efficiently schedule the processes in many situations.

The theory underlying RMS is known as rate-monotonic analysis (RMA). This theory summarized below uses a relatively simple model of the system.

- All processes run periodically on a single CPU.

- Context switching time is ignored.

- There are no data dependencies between processes.

- The execution time for a process is constant.

- All deadlines are at the ends of their periods.

- The highest-priority ready process is always selected for execution.

The major result of RMA is that a relatively simple scheduling policy is optimal under certain conditions. Priorities are assigned by rank order of period, i.e. process with the shortest period is assigned the highest priority. It provides the highest CPU utilization while ensuring that all processes meet their deadlines.

Example of Rate Monotonic Scheduling

Suppose P1 has the highest priority, P2 the middle priority, and P3 the lowest priority. Then all periods start at time zero, as per RMS execution. This is explained below:

Process	Execution time	Period
P1	1	4

| P2 | 2 | 6 |
| P3 | 3 | 12 |

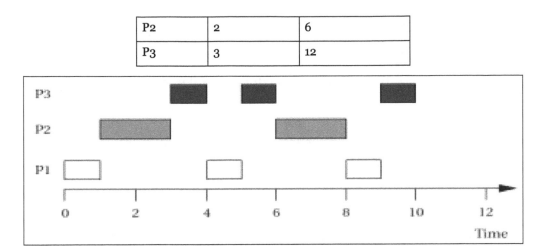

All three periods starts at time zero. P1's data arrives first. Since P1 is the highest priority process, it can start to execute immediately. After one-time unit, P1 finishes and goes out of the ready state until the start of its next period. At time 1, P2 starts executing as the highest-priority ready process. At time 3, P2 finishes and P3 starts executing. P1's next iteration starts at time 4, at which point it interrupts P3. P3 gets one more time unit of execution between the second iterations of P1 and P2, but P3 does not get to finish until after the third iteration of P1.

Consider a different set of execution times for the three processes, keeping the same deadlines as shown in figure. Each process alone has an execution time significantly less than its period. The combinations of processes can require more than 100% of the available CPU cycles. For example, during one 12 time-unit interval, we must execute P1 three times, requiring 6 units of CPU time; P2 twice, costing 6 units of CPU time; and P3 one time, requiring 3 units of CPU time. The total of 6 + 6 + 3 = 15 units of CPU time which is more than the 12 time units available, clearly exceeding the available CPU capacity.

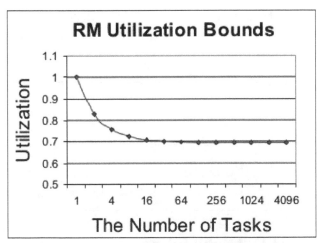

Figure: Calculation of RM Utilization Bounds.

Table: RMS with different execution times.

Process	Execution time	Period
P1	2	4

P2	3	6
P3	3	12

RM – Utilization Bound: Real-time system is schedulable under RM if

$$\sum U_i \leq n\,(2^{1/n} - 1),$$

where U is the utilization and n refers to the total number of tasks.

Example: Consider there are three tasks $T_1(1,4)$, $T_2(1,5)$, $T_3(1,10)$. The calculation of RM Utilization is as follows:

The task is represented by T (e,p) where p is the inter release time and e is the maximum execution time. The utilization is given by U = e/p.

$$\sum U_i = 1/4 + 1/5 + 1/10 = 0.55$$

Real-time system is schedulable under RM if

$$\sum U_i <= n(2^{1/n} - 1),\ \text{where n is the number of task.}$$

$$3\,(2^{1/3} - 1) \approx 0.78$$

Thus, $\{T_1, T_2, T_3\}$ is schedulable under RM. Example of RM utilization bound is shown in Figure.

Deadline Miss with RM

Consider scheduling the following task set $T_1 = (1,4)$, $T_2 = (2,6)$ and $T_4 = (3,8)$.

Utilization bound (U) = ¼ + 2/6 + ⅜ = 23/24.

The utilization is greater than the bound. Hence there is a deadline miss. Observe that at time 6, even if the deadline of task T_3 is very close, the scheduler decides to schedule task T_2. This is the main reason why T_3 misses its deadline.

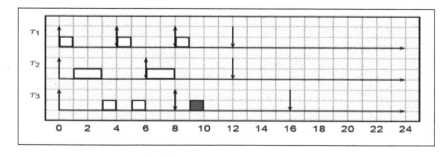

Earliest Deadline First (EDF) Scheduling

An important class of scheduling algorithms is the class of dynamic priority algorithms. In dynamic priority algorithms, the priority of a task can change during its execution based on the initiation times. Fixed priority algorithms are a subclass of the more general class of dynamic priority algorithms, the priority of a task does not change. The most important (and analyzed) dynamic priority algorithm is Earliest Deadline First (EDF). The priority of a job (instance) is inversely proportional to its absolute deadline. In other words, the highest priority job is the one with the earliest deadline. If two tasks have the same absolute deadlines, chose one of the two at random (ties can be broken arbitrarily).The priority is dynamic since it changes for different jobs of the same task. It achieves higher CPU utilizations than RMS. The highest-priority process is the one whose deadline is nearest in time, and the lowest priority process is the one whose deadline is farthest away. Priorities must be recalculated at the completion of every process. Final procedure is same as RM. Example: Scheduling with EDF, now we schedule the same task with EDF.

$T_1 = (1,4)$, $T_2 = (2,6)$ and $T_3 = (3,8)$

$U = \frac{1}{4} + 2/6 + \frac{3}{8} = 23/24$

Again the Utilization is very high. However, there is no deadline miss in the hyperperiod. (The hyperperiod is the smallest interval of time after which the periodic patterns of all the tasks is repeated). Observe that at time 6, the problem does not appear, as the earliest deadline job (the one of T_3) is executed as shown in figure. It demonstrates how the deadline miss is avoided in EDF scheduling in the above example.

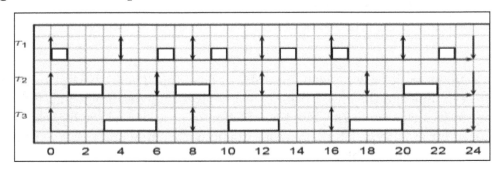

Example: Optimal dynamic priority scheduling. A task with a shorter deadline has a higher priority, i.e., it executes a job with the earliest deadline. It is an optimal scheduling algorithm. If there is a schedule for a set of real-time tasks, EDF can schedule it. This is explained in Figure shown below. It demonstrates how three tasks $T_1(1,4)$,$T_2(2,5)$ and $T_3(2,7)$ scheduled for 15 periods efficiently using earliest deadline first scheduling. There is no deadline miss and it effectively utilizes the time periods.

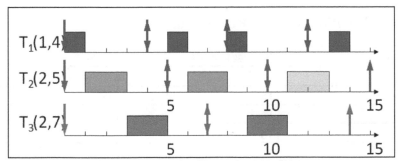

Figure: Earliest Deadline First Scheduling.

EDF Overload Conditions

A disadvantage of EDF is that Domino effect occurs during overload conditions. This is explained below in the figure with the example: $T_1(3,4)$, $T_2(3,5)$, $T_3(3,6)$, $T_4(3,7)$. The hyperperiod given is 7, but actually 12 (3+3+3+3) time slots are needed to complete all processes at least once. Hence deadline miss occurs. This overload condition is known as the domino effect. In Figure, first the three tasks T_2, T_3 and T_4 are having deadline miss. If we schedule T_3 after T_1 or T_4 after T_1, only 2 tasks will get deadline miss. When compared to the first schedule, these two are better schedules even though they have deadline miss.

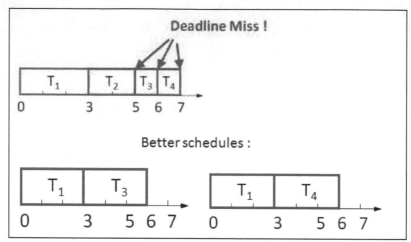

Figure: EDF overloading.

Example: In EDF, priorities are assigned in order of deadline. The highest priority process has deadline nearest in time and the lowest priority process is having deadline which is farthest away. The priorities are recalculated during every completion of process and the highest priority ready process is chosen for execution. This is another example to demonstrate EDF Scheduling for 60 time slots, which is shown in Table.

Process	Execution time	Period
P1	1	3
P2	1	4
P3	3	5

Table: Hyper Period calculation using EDF algorithm.

Time	Running progress	Deadlines
0	P1	
1	P2	
2	P3	P1
3	P3	P2
4	P1	P3
5	P2	P1
6	P1	
7	P3	P2
8	P3	P1

9	P1	P3
10	P2	
11	P3	P1,P2
12	P2	
13	P3	
14	P2	P1,P2
15	P1	P2
16	P2	
17	P3	P1
18	P1	
19	P3	P2,P3
20	P2	P1
21	P1	
22	P3	P1,P2
23	P3	P3
24	P1	
25	P2	P1
26	P3	P2
27	P1	
28	P3	P1,P3
29	P2	
30	Idle	P2
31	P1	P1
32	P3	
33	P3	P3
34	P1	P1,P2
35	P2	
36	P1	
37	P2	P1
38	P3	P2,P3
39	P3	
40	P1	
41	P2	P1
42	P1	
43	P3	P2
44	P3	P1,P3
45	P1	
46	P2	
47	P3	P1,P2
48	P3	
49	P1	P3
50	P2	P1
51	P1	P2

52	P3	
53	P3	P1
54	P2	P3
55	P1	P2
56	P2	P1
57	P1	
58	P3	
59	P3	P1,P2,P3

There is one time slot left at t =30, giving a CPU utilization of 59/60.

RMS VS. EDF

The following are some of the differences between RMS and EDF priority scheduling algorithms.

Rate Monotonic

- Simpler implementation, even in systems without explicit support for timing constraints (periods, deadlines).

- Predictability for the highest priority tasks.

EDF

- Full processor utilization.

- Misbehavior during overload conditions.

Interprocess Communication Mechanisms

Processes need communication; this is done by using Inter-process communication. This mechanism is provided by the operating system. The processes can communicate in two ways. They are blocking and non-blocking methods and are explained as follows:

- Blocking: Process enters waiting state until it gets response for a communication it has sent.

- Non-blocking: Continues execution after sending communication.

Two major styles of Inter process communications are shared memory and message passing which are discussed in detail below:

- Shared memory: Two components, such as a CPU and an I/O device, communicate through a shared memory location. The software on the CPU is designed to know the address of the shared location; the shared location is also loaded into the proper register of the I/O device. This is shown in figure. If the CPU wants to send data to the device, it writes to the shared location. The I/O device then reads the data from that location.

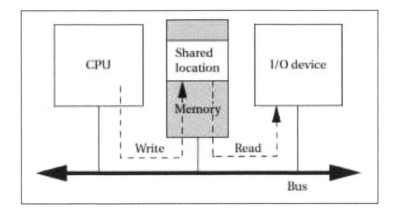

- Message Passing: Each communicating entity has its own message send/receive unit. The message is not stored on the communications link, but rather at the senders/ receivers at the end points. In contrast, shared memory communication can be seen as a memory block used as a communication device, in which all the data are stored in the communication link/memory. A message passing example is shown in Figure.

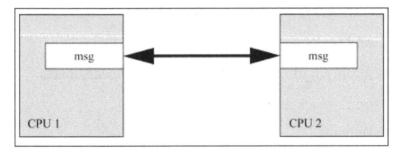

Signalling

An UNIX inter-process communication is done through the signal. A signal is a one bit output from a process for Inter Process Communication. It is generated by a process and transmitted to another process by the OS. An advantage of using signal is that it uses the shortest possible CPU time. It is the software equivalent of the flag at a register that is set on a hardware interrupt.

Multitasking in RTOS

A multitasking environment allows applications to be constructed as a set of independent tasks, each with a separate thread of execution and its own set of system resources. The inter-task communication facilities allow these tasks to synchronize and coordinate their activity. Multitasking provides the fundamental mechanism for an application to control and react to multiple, discrete real-world events and is therefore essential for many real-time applications. Multitasking creates the appearance of many threads of execution running concurrently when, in fact, the kernel interleaves their execution on the basis of a scheduling algorithm. This also leads to efficient utilisation of the CPU time and is essential for many embedded applications where processors are limited in computing speed due to cost, power, silicon area and other constraints. In a multi-tasking operating system it is assumed that the various tasks are to cooperate to serve the requirements of the overall system. Co-operation will require that the tasks communicate with each other and share common data in an orderly an disciplined manner, without creating undue contention and deadlocks. The way in which tasks communicate and share data is to be regulated such that communication or shared data access error is prevented and data, which is private to a task, is protected. Further, tasks may be dynamically created and terminated by other tasks, as and when needed. The following major functions are to be carried out:

- Process Management:

  ○ Interrupt handling.

  ○ Task scheduling and dispatch.

  ○ Create/delete, suspend/resume task.

  ○ Manage scheduling information such as priority, scheduling policy, etc.

- Interprocess Communication and Synchronization:

  ○ Code, data and device sharing.

  ○ Synchronization, coordination and data exchange mechanisms.

  ○ Deadlock and Livelock detection.

- Memory Management:

  ○ Dynamic memory allocation.

  ○ Memory locking.

  ○ Services for file creation, deletion, reposition and protection.

- Input/output Management:

  ○ Handles request and release functions and read, write functions for a variety of peripherals.

The following are important requirements that an OS must meet to be considered an RTOS in the contemporary sense:

- The operating system must be multithreaded and Preemptive. E.g. handle multiple threads and be able to preempt tasks if necessary.

- The OS must support priority of tasks and threads.

- A system of priority inheritance must exist. Priority inheritance is a mechanism to ensure that lower priority tasks cannot obstruct the execution of higher priority tasks.

- The OS must support various types of thread/task synchronization mechanisms.

- For predictable response:

    ○ The time for every system function call to execute should be predictable and independent of the number of objects in the system.

    ○ Non preemptable portions of kernel functions necessary for interprocess synchronization and communication are highly optimized, short and deterministic.

    ○ Non-preemptable portions of the interrupt handler routines are kept small and deterministic.

    ○ Interrupt handlers are scheduled and executed at appropriate priority.

    ○ The maximum time during which interrupts are masked by the OS and by device drivers must be known.

    ○ The maximum time that device drivers use to process an interrupt, and specific IRQ information relating to those device drivers, must be known.

    ○ The interrupt latency (the time from interrupt to task run) must be predictable and compatible with application requirements.

- For fast response:

    ○ Run-time overhead is decreased by reducing the unnecessary context switch.

    ○ Important timings such as context switch time, interrupt latency, semaphore get/release latency must be minimum.

Process Management

On a computer system with only one processor, only one task can run at any given time, hence the other tasks must be in some state other than running. The number of other states, the names given to those states and the transition paths between the different states vary with the operating system. A typical state diagram is given in figure and the various states are:

Task States

- Running: This is the task which has control of the CPU. It will normally be the task which has the highest current priority of the tasks which are ready to run.

- Ready: There may be several tasks in this state. The attributes of the task and the resources required to run it must be available for it to be placed in the 'ready' state.

- Waiting: The execution of tasks placed in this state has been suspended because the task requires some resources which is not available or because the task is waiting for some signal from the plant, e.g., input from the analog-to-digital converter, or the task is waiting for the elapse of time.

- New: The operating system is aware of the existence of this task, but the task has not been allocated a priority and a context and has not been included into the list of schedulable tasks.

- Terminated: The operating system has not as yet been made aware of the existence of this task, although it may be resident in the memory of the computer.

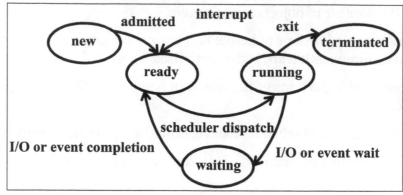

Figure: The various states a task can be in during its execution life cycle under an RTOS Task State Transitions.

When a task is "spawned", either by the operating system, or another task, it is to be created, which involves loading it into the memory, creating and updating certain OS data structures such as the Task Control Block, necessary for running the task within the multi-tasking environment. During such times the task is in the new state. Once these are over, it enters the ready state where it waits. At this time it is within the view of the scheduler and is considered for execution according to the scheduling policy. A task is made to enter the running state from the ready state by the operating system dispatcher when the scheduler determines the task to be the one to be run according to its scheduling policy. While the task is running, it may execute a normal or abnormal exit according to the program logic, in which case it enters the terminated state and then removed from the view of the OS. Software or hardware interrupts may also occur while the task is running. In such a case, depending on the priority of the interrupt, the current task may be transferred to the ready state and wait for its next time allocation by the scheduler. Finally, a task may need to wait at times during its course of execution, either due to requirements of synchronization with other tasks or for completion of some service such as I/O that it has requested for. During such a time it is in the waiting state. Once the synchronization requirement is fulfilled, or the requested service is completed, it is returned to the ready state to again wait its turn to be scheduled.

Task Control Functions

RTOSs provide functions to spawn initialise and activate new tasks. They provide functions to gather information on existing tasks in the system, for task naming, checking of the state of a given task, setting options for task execution such as use of co-processor, specific memory models, as well as task deletion. Deletion often requires special precautions, especially with respect to semaphores, for shared memory tasks.

Task Context

Whenever a task is switched its execution context, represented by the contents of the program counter, stack and registers, is saved by the operating system into a special data structure called a task control block so that the task can be resumed the next time it is scheduled. Similarly the context has to be restored from the task control block when the task state is set to running.

Task Scheduling and Dispatch

The basic purpose of task scheduling and dispatch in a real-time multi-tasking OS is to ensure that each task gets access to the CPU and other system resources in a manner that is necessary for successful and timely completion of all computation in the system. Secondly, it is desired that this is done efficiently from the point of view of resource utilisation as well as with correct synchronisation and protection of data and code for individual tasks against incorrect interference. Various task scheduling and dispatch models are in use to achieve the above. The appropriateness of a particular model depends on the application features.

Cyclic Executive

This is the simplest of the models in which all the computing tasks are required to be run periodically in cycles. The computing sequence is static and therefore, a monolithic program called the Cyclic Executive runs the tasks in the required order in a loop. At times the execution sequence may also be determined in accordance with models such as an FSM. The execution sequences and the times allocated to each task are determined a priori and are not expected to vary significantly at run time. Such systems are often employed for controllers of industrial machines such as Programmable Logic Controllers that perform fixed set of tasks in fixed orders defined by the user. These systems have the advantage of being simple to develop and configure as well as faster than some of the more complex systems since task context switching is faster and less frequent. They are however suitable for static computing environments only and are custom developed using low level programming languages for specific hardware platforms.

Coroutines

In this model of cooperative multitasking the set of tasks are distributed over a set of processes, called coroutines. These tasks mutually exchange program control rather than relinquish it to the operating system. Thus each task transfers control to one of the others after saving its data and control state. Note that the responsibility of scheduling, that is deciding which task gets control of the processor at a given time is left to the programmer, rather than the operating system. The task which is transferring control is often left in the waiting or blocked state. This model has now been adapted to a different form in multithreading.

Interrupts

In many cases task scheduling and dispatch needs to be made responsive to external signals or timing signals. In other cases running tasks may not be assumed to be transferring control to the dispatcher on their own. In such cases the facility of interrupts provided on all processors can be used for task switching. The various tasks in the system can be switched either by hardware or software interrupts. The interrupt handling routine would then transfer control to the task dispatcher. Interrupts through hardware may occur periodically, such as from a clock, or asynchronously by external devices. Interrupts can also occur by execution of special software instructions written in the code, or due to processing exceptions such as divide by zero errors. Interrupt-only systems are special case of foreground/background systems, which are widely used in embedded systems.

Foreground/Background

Typically, embedded and real-time applications involve a set of tasks, some of which are periodic and must be finished within deadlines. Others may be sporadic and may not have such deadlines associated with them. Foreground/background systems are common and simple solutions for such applications. Such systems involve a set of interrupt driven or real-time tasks called the foreground and a collection of non-interrupt driven tasks called the background. The foreground tasks run according to some real-time priority scheduling policy. The background tasks are preemptable by any foreground task.

Real Time Operating Systems

This is the most complex model for real-time multi-tasking. The major features that distinguish it from the other ones described above are the following:

1. The explicit implementation of a scheduling policy in the form of a scheduler module. The scheduler is itself a task which executes every time an internal or external interrupt occurs and computes the decision on making state transitions for every application task in the system that has been spawned and has not yet been terminated. It computes this decision based on the current priority level of the tasks, the availability of the various resources of the system etc. The scheduler also computes the current priority levels of the tasks based on various factors such as deadlines, computational dependencies, waiting times etc.

2. Based on the decisions of the scheduler, the dispatcher actually effects the state transition of the tasks by:

- Saving the computational state or context of the currently executing task from the hardware environment.

- Enabling the next task to run by loading the process context into the hardware environment.

It is also the responsibility of the dispatcher to make the short-term decisions in response to, e.g., interrupts from an input/output device or from the real-time clock. The dispatcher/scheduler has two entry conditions:

- The real-time clock interrupt and any interrupt which signals the completion of an input/output request.

- A task suspension due to a task delaying, completing or requesting an input/output transfer.

In response to the first condition the scheduler searches for work starting with the highest priority task and checking each task in priority order. Thus if tasks with a high repetition rate are given a high priority they will be treated as if they were clock-level tasks, i.e., they will be run first during each system clock period. In response to the second condition a search for work is started at the task with the next lowest priority to the task which has just been running. There cannot be another higher priority task ready to run since a higher priority task becoming ready always preempts a lower priority running task.

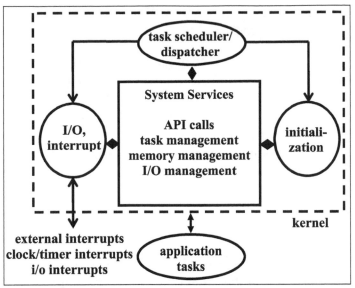

Figure: Structure of an RTOS Kernel. The typical structure of an RTOS kernel showing the interaction between the System and the Application tasks.

Windows as RTOS

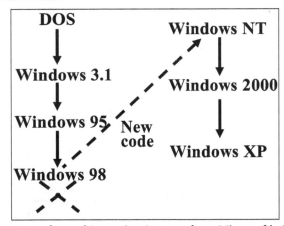

Figure: Genealogy of Operating Systems from Microsoft's Stable.

Microsoft's Windows operating systems are extremely popular in desktop computers. Windows operating systems have evolved over the years last twenty five years from the naive DOS (Disk Operating System). Microsoft developed DOS in the early eighties. Microsoft kept on announcing new versions of DOS almost every year and kept on adding new features to DOS in the successive versions. DOS evolved to the Windows operating systems, whose main distinguishing feature was a graphical front-end. As several new versions of Windows kept on appearing by way of upgrades, the Windows code was completely rewritten in 1998 to develop the Windows NT system. Since the code was completely rewritten, Windows NT system was much more stable (does not crash) than the earlier DOS-based systems. The later versions of Microsoft's operating systems were descendants of the Windows NT; the DOS-based systems were scrapped. Figure shows the genealogy of the various operating systems from the Microsoft stable. Because stability is a major requirement for hard real-time applications, we consider only the Windows NT and its descendants in our study and do not include the DOS line of products.

An organization owning Windows NT systems might be interested to use it for its real-time applications on account of either cost saving or convenience. This is especially true in prototype application development and also when only a limited number of deployments are required. In the following, we critically analyze the suitability of Windows NT for real-time application development. First, we highlight some features of Windows NT that are very relevant and useful to a real-time application developer. In the subsequent subsection, we point out some of the lacuna of Windows NT when used in real-time application development.

Features of Windows NT

Windows NT has several features which are very desirable for real-time applications such as support for multithreading, real-time priority levels, and timer. Moreover, the clock resolutions are sufficiently fine for most real-time applications. Windows NT supports 32 priority levels. Each process belongs to one of the following priority classes: idle, normal, high, real-time. By default, the priority class at which an application runs is normal. Both normal and high are variable type where the priority is recomputed periodically. NT uses priority-driven Preemptive scheduling and threads of real-time priorities have precedence over all other threads including kernel threads. Processes such as screen saver use priority class idle. NT lowers the priority of a task (belonging to variable type) if it used all of its last time slice. It raises the priority of a task if it blocked for I/O and could not use its last time slice in full. However, the change of a task from its base priority is restricted to ± 2.

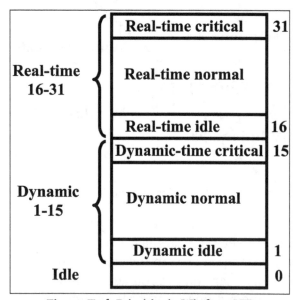

Figure: Task Priorities in Windows NT.

Shortcomings of Windows NT

In spite of the impressive support that Windows provides for real-time program development, a programmer trying to use Windows in real-time system development has to cope up with several problems. Of these, the following two main problems are the most troublesome.

1. Interrupt Processing: Priority level of interrupts is always higher than that of the user level threads; including the threads of real-time class. When an interrupt occurs, the handler routine saves the machine's state and makes the system execute an Interrupt Service Routine (ISR). Only critical processing is performed in ISR and the bulk of the processing is done as a Deferred Procedure Call (DPC). DPCs for various interrupts are queued in the DPC queue in a FIFO manner. While this separation of ISR and DPC has the advantage of providing quick response to further interrupts, it has the disadvantage of maintaining the all DPCs at the same priorities. A DPC cannot be preempted by another DPC but by an interrupt. DPCs are executed in FIFO order at a priority lower than the hardware interrupt priorities but higher than the priority of the scheduler/dispatcher. Further, it is not possible for a user-level thread to execute at a priority higher than that of ISRs or DPCs. Therefore, even ISRs and DPCs corresponding to very low priority tasks can preempt real-time processes. Therefore, the potential blocking of real-time tasks due to DPCs can be large. For example, interrupts due to page faults generated by low priority tasks would get processed faster than real-time processes. Also, ISRs and DPCs generated due to key board and mouse interactions would operate at higher priority levels compared to real-time tasks. If there are processes doing network or disk I/O, the effect of system-wide FIFO queues may lead to unbounded response times for even real-time threads. These problems have been avoided by Windows CE operating system through a priority inheritance mechanism.

2. Support for Resource Sharing Protocols: That unless appropriate resource sharing protocols are used, tasks while accessing shared resources may suffer unbounded priority inversions leading to deadline misses and even system failure. Windows NT does not provide any support (such as priority inheritance, etc.) to support real-time tasks to share critical resource among themselves. This is a major shortcoming of Windows NT when used in real-time applications. Since most real-time applications do involve resource sharing among tasks we outline below the possible ways in which user-level functionalities can be added to the Windows NT system. The simplest approach to let real-time tasks share critical resources without unbounded priority inversions is as follows. As soon as a task is successful in locking a non-preemptable resource, its priority can be raised to the highest priority (31). As soon as a task releases the required resource, its priority is restored. However, we know that this arrangement would lead to large inheritance-related inversions. Another possibility is to implement the priority ceiling protocol (PCP). To implement this protocol, we need to restrict the real-time tasks to have even priorities (i.e. 16, 18, ..., 30). The reason for this restriction is that NT does not support FIFO scheduling among equal priority tasks. If the highest priority among all tasks needing a resource is $2*n$, then the ceiling priority of the resource is $2*n+1$. In Unix, FIFO option among equal priority tasks is available; therefore all available priority levels can be used.

Windows Vs. Unix

Table: Windows NT versus Unix.

Real-Time Feature	Windows NT Unix V	Unix V
DPCs	Yes	No
Real-Time priorities	Yes	No
Locking virtual memory	Yes	Yes
Timer precision	1 msec	10 msec
Asynchronous I/O	Yes	No

Though Windows NT has many of the features desired of a real-time operating system, its implementation of DPCs together its lack of protocol support for resource sharing among equal priority tasks makes it unsuitable for use in safety-critical real-time applications. A comparison of the extent to which some of the basic features required for real-time programming are provided by Windows NT and Unix V is indicated in Table. With careful programming, Windows NT may be useful for applications that can tolerate occasional deadline misses, and have deadlines of the order of hundreds of milliseconds than microseconds. Of course, to be used in such applications, the processor utilization must be kept sufficiently low and priority inversion control must be provided at the user level.

Embedded Systems in C

The set of language extensions for the C programming language for addressing the commonality issues between different embedded systems is termed as embedded C. All the diverse concepts of embedded systems in C have been carefully discussed in this chapter.

Need for Programming 8051 in Embedded C

There are several reasons for using a high-level language such as C to program the 8051 microcontroller. It is easier and less time consuming to write programs in Embedded C than Assembly. C is easier to modify and update. We can also use code available in function libraries. Also, C code is portable to other microcontrollers with little or no modification.

Flow of Execution

We will first look at a few common structures available in Embedded C. Figure shows the flow for sequential execution, selection procedure, and looping structure.

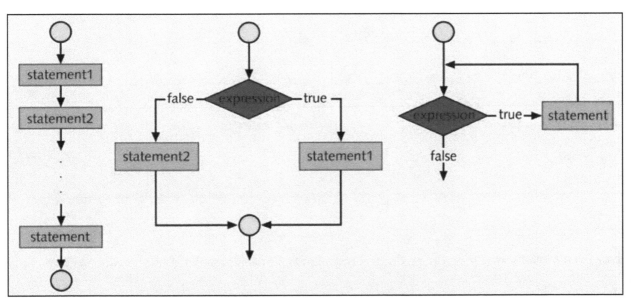

Figure: (a) Sequential, (b) Selection, (c) Repetition structure.

If and Switch Statement (Selection) Structure

Figure shows the If -then-else and switch - case statement. Like normal C programming in embedded C also programmers will use if statements and switch case statements.

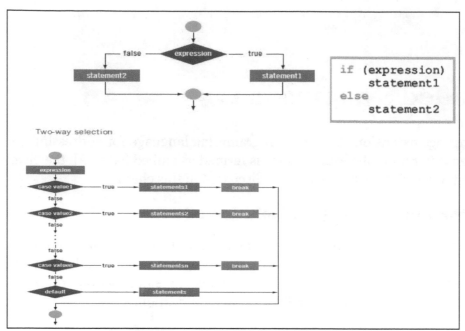

Figure: If-then else and Switch-case Statement.

```
switch (expression)

{

case valuel:

        statements1

                break;

case value2:

        statements2

        break;
        .
        .
        .

case valuen:

        statementsn

        break;

default:

        statements

}
```

While and for Looping (Repetition) Structure

For looping figure shows the structure of while loop and for looping structure.

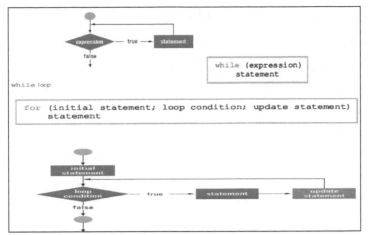

Figure: Looping Structure.

Translation between C and Assembly Code

Following is the example on how an assembly program loop will be written in embedded "c" code.

A Loop in Assembly

```
        MOV R2, #255

ABC: MOV P1, R2

        DJNZ R2, ABC
```

A For-Loop in C

```
for (int z = 255; z > 0; z--)
P1 = z;
```

Data Type and Time Delay in 8051 C

Specific C data types for 8051 can help programmers to create smaller hex files. They are:

- Unsigned char
- Signed char
- Unsigned int
- Signed int
- Sbit (single bit)
- Bit and sfr

Table shows the number of bits needed by each data type. The character data type is the most natural data choice because 8051 is an 8-bit microcontroller. The C compiler will allocate RAM space for the variables based on their data type - char, int, bit etc.

Table: Some widely used Data Types for 8051 C.

Data Type	Size in Bits	Data Range/Usage
unsigned char	8-bit	0 to 255
(signed) char	8-bit	− 128 to 127
unsigned int	16-bit	0 to 65535
(signd) int	16-bit	− 32,768 to + 32,767
Sbit	1-bit	SFR bit-addressable only
bit	1-bit	RAM bit-addressable only
sfr	8-bit	RAM addresses 80-FFH only

Unsigned and Signed Char

- Unsigned Char: The most widely used data type for the 8051 is unsigned char. It uses 8-bits. The range of values taken by unsigned char is 0-255(00-FFH). In a microcontroller setup, we use unsigned char for the following:

  ◦ To set counter value.

  ◦ To handle a string of ASCII characters.

  ◦ For toggling ports.

- Signed Char: Signed char is an 8-bit data type. It uses a 2's complement representation. The range of unsigned char is -128 to +127 (00-FFH). It is used for the following purposes:

  ◦ To present a given quantity such as temperature which can take both positive and negative values.

Following are examples of programs using unsigned and signed char.

Example: Write an 8051 C program to send values 00 − FF to port P1.

Solution:

```
#include <reg51.h> // library code for changing the following code to 8051 as-
sembly code void main(void)

{

unsigned char z;

for (z=0;z<=255;z++)

P1=z;

}
```

Example: Write an 8051 C program to send hex values for ASCII characters of 0, 1, 2, 3, 4, 5, A, B, C, and D to port P1.

Solution:

```
#include <reg51.h>
void main(void)
{
unsigned char mynum[]="012345ABCD";
unsigned char z;
for (z=0;z<=10;z++)
P1=mynum[z];
}
```

Example: Write an 8051 C program to send values of −4 to +4 to port P1.

Solution:

```
//Signed numbers
#include <reg51.h>
void main(void)
{
char mynum[]={+1,-1,+2,-2,+3,-3,+4,-4};
signed char z;
for (z=0;z<=8;z++)
P1=mynum[z];
}
```

Integer

The unsigned int is a 16-bit data type. It takes a value in the range of 0 to 65535 (0000 − FFFFH). It is used to:

- Define 16-bit variables such as memory addresses.
- Set counter values of more than 256.

Since registers and memory accesses are in 8-bit chunks, the misuse of int variables will result in a larger hex file. Signed int is a 16-bit data type. It uses the most significant bit D_{15} to represent the sign, − or + . We have 15 bits for the magnitude of the number, giving a range from −32768 to +32767.

Following code shows examples for using unsigned bit and sbit.

Example: Write an 8051 C program to toggle bit D0 of the port P1 (P1.0) 50,000 times.

Solution:

```
#include <reg51.h>
sbit MYBIT=P1^0;
void main(void)
{
unsigned int z;
for (z=0;z<=50000;z++)
{
MYBIT=0;
MYBIT=1;
}
}
```

Time Delay

There are two ways to create a time delay in 8051 C: (i) using the 8051 timer and (ii) using a simple for loop. When using a loop to create the time delay, there are three factors that can affect the accuracy of the time delay. They are: (i) Crystal frequency of the 8051 system, (ii) 8051 machine cycle timing and (iii) Compiler used for 8051 C. Following are example programs for creating time delay:

Example: Write an 8051 C program to toggle bits of P1 continuously forever with some delay.

Solution:

```
//Toggle P1 forever with some delay in between "on" and "off"
#include <reg51.h>
void main(void)
{
unsigned int x;
for (;;) //repeat forever
    {
    p1=0x55;
    for (x=0;x<40000;x++); //delay size unknown
    p1=0xAA;
    for (x=0;x<40000;x++);
    }
}
```

Example: Write an 8051 C program to toggle bits of P1 ports continuously with a 250 ms delay.

Solution:

```c
#include <reg51.h>
void MSDelay(unsigned int);
void main(void)
{
while (1) //repeat forever
{
p1=0x55;
MSDelay(250);
p1=0xAA;
MSDelay(250);
}
}
void MSDelay(unsigned int itime)
{
unsigned int i, j;
for (i=0;i<itime;i++)
for (j=0;j<1275;j++);
}
```

The operating modes of the 8051 can be changed by manipulating the values of the 8051's Special Function Registers (SFRs). SFRs are accessed as if they were normal Internal RAM. The only difference is that Internal RAM is from address 00h through 7Fh whereas SFR registers exist in the address range of 80h through FFh. Each SFR has an address (80h through FFh) and a name.

Example: Write an 8051 C program to toggle all the bits of P0, P1, and P2 continuously with a 250 ms delay. Use the sfr keyword to declare the port addresses.

Solution:

```c
//Accessing Ports as SFRs using sfr data type
sfr P0=0x80;
sfr P1=0x90;
sfr P2=0xA0;
```

```
void MSDelay(unsigned int);

void main(void)

{

while (1)

    {

    P0=0x55;

    P1=0x55;

    P2=0x55;

    MSDelay(250);

    P0=0xAA;

    P1=0xAA;

    P2=0xAA;

    MSDelay(250);

    }

}
```

I/O Programming in 8051 C

The figure shows the address for the SFR registers. Through which you can access individual bit of SFR also.

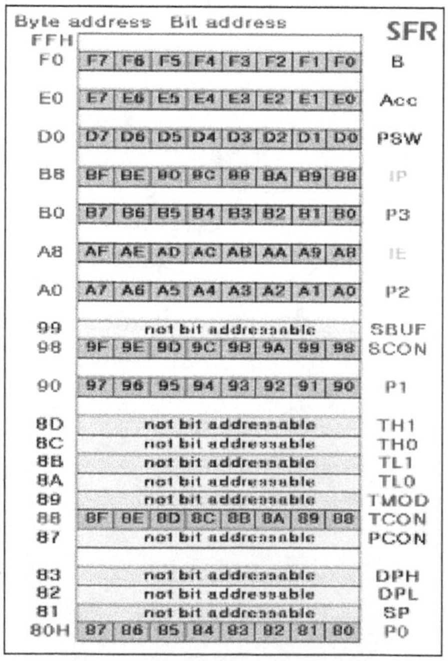

Figure: Special Function Register.

Following program is an example for the use of sbit and name of SFR:

```
#include <reg51.h>

Sbit MYBIT = P1^5; //D5 of P1

Use sbit to declare the bit of SFR and declare

Sbit MYBIT = 0x95; //D5 of P1

*reg51. h is not necessary.
```

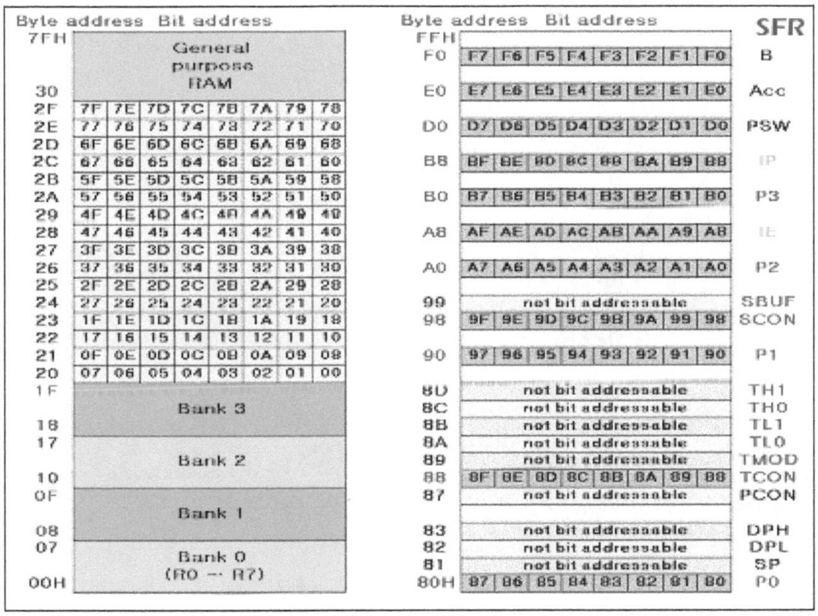

Figure: 8051 256 byte RAM.

Example: Write an 8051 C program to toggle all the bits of P0, P1, and P2 continuously with a 250 ms delay. Use the sfr keyword to declare the port addresses.

Solution:

```
//Accessing Ports as SFRs using sfr data type

sfr P0=0x80;

sfr P1=0x90;

sfr P2=0xA0;

void MSDelay(unsigned int);

void main(void)

{

while (1)

{

P0=0x55;
```

```
P1=0x55;

P2=0x55;

MSDelay(250);

P0=0xAA;

P1=0xAA;

P2=0xAA;

MSDelay(250);

}

}
```

Access Single Bit of SFR

Way to Access a Single Bit of SFR:

- Use sbit and name of SFR:

```
#include <reg51.h>

Sbit MYBIT = P1^5; //D5 of P1
```

- Use sbit to declare the bit of SFR and declare by yourself:

```
Sbit MYBIT = 0x95; //D5 of P1
```

- reg51. h is not necessary.

Example: Write an 8051 C program to turn bit P1.5 on and off 50,000 times.

Solution:

```
Sbit MYBIT = 0x95;// P1^5

void main(void)

{

unsigned intz;

for (z=0;z<50000;z++)

    {

    MYBIT=1;

    MYBIT=0;

    }

}
```

This program is similar to Example for unsigned int.

Access Bit-Addressable RAM

You can use bit to access one bit of bit-addressable section of the data RAM space 20H-2FH.

```
#include <reg51.h>

Sbit inbit= P1^0;

bit membit;//C compiler assign a RAM

        space for mybit

membit= inbit; //Read P1^0 to RAM
```

Example: Write an 8051 C program to get the status of bit P1.0, save it, and send it to P2.7 continuously.

Solution:

```
#include <reg51.h>

sbit inbit= P1^0;

sbit outbit= P2^7;

bit membit;

void main(void)

{

while(1) { //repeat forever

membit= inbit;

outbit= membit

}

}
```

Arithmetic and Logical Processing

Bitwise Operations in C

One of the most important and powerful features of the C language is its ability to perform bit wise manipulation. This section describes the action of bitwise logic operators. Table shows the bitwise logical operators.

		AND	OR	EX-OR	Inverter
A	B	A & B	A|B	A ^ B	Y = ~B
0	0	0	0	0	1

0	1	0	1	1	0
1	0	0	1	1	
1	1	1	1	0	

Using these bit wise operators embedded C will perform the logical operations bit wise on binary numbers. Following are some examples which show how they are used.

- AND &

  $0 \times 35 \ \& \ 0 \times 0F = 0 \times 05$

- OR |

  $0 \times 04 \ | \ 0 \times 68 = 0 \times 68 = 0 \times 6C$

- Exclusive – OR ^

- Inverter ~

  $\sim 0 \times 55 = 0 \times AA$

```
                0011  0101
AND             0000  1111
                ----------
                0000  0101


                0011  0100
OR              0110  1000
                ----------
                0110  1100


                0101  0100
XOR             0111  1000
                ----------
                0010  1100
```

```
NOT  0101  0101
     ----------
     0000  0101
```

Bit-Wise Shift Operation in C

There are two bit-wise shift operators in C:

- Shift right (»).
- Shift left («).

Their format in C is as follows:

- Data » number of bits to be shifted right.
- Data « number of bits to be shifted left.

Some examples are:

- Shift Right >>

  $0 \times 9A >> 3 = 0 \times 13$ 1010 1010 → 0001

                                    0011

  shift right 3 times

  $0 \times 77 >> 4 = 0 \times 07$ 0111 0111 → 0000

                                    0111

  shift right 4 times

- Shift Left <<
  $0 \times 96 << 4 = 0 \times 60$ 1001   0110 ← 0110
  shift left 4 times   0000

Following program will show the demo of the logical operations. Run the following program on your simulator and examine the results.

```c
#include <reg51.h>

void main(void)

{

P0=0x35 & 0x0F; //ANDing

P1=0x04 | 0x68; //ORing

P2=0x54 ^ 0x78; //XORing

P0=~0x55; //inverting

P1=0x9A >> 3; //shifting right 3

P2=0x77 >> 4; //shifting right 4

P0=0x6 << 4; //shifting left 4

}
```

Example: Write an 8051 C program to get bit P1.0 and send it to P2.7 after inverting it.

Solution:

```c
#include <reg51.h>
sbit inbit=P1^0;
sbit outbit=P2^7;
bit membit;
void main(void)
{
while (1)
{
membit=inbit; //get a bit from P1.0
outbit=~membit; //invert it and send
                //it to P2.7
}
}
```

Data Conversion

Many newer microcontrollers have a real-time clock (RTC) where the time and date are kept, even when the power is off. Very often the RTC provides the time and date in packed BCD. However, to display them they must be converted to ASCII. Like this example, we need to convert the data from one form to another form. In this section we show some example programs to demo how Embedded C helps for data conversions. Some data conversions needed are:

- Packed BCD to ASCII conversion.

- ASCII to packed BCD conversion.

- Checksum byte in ROM.

- Binary to decimal and ASCII conversion in C.

Table shows the ASCII, binary and BCD codes for the digits 0 to 9.

Key	ASCII (hex)	Binary	BCD (unpacked)
0	30	011 0000	0000 0000
1	31	011 0001	0000 0001
2	32	011 0010	0000 0010
3	33	011 0011	0000 0011
4	34	011 0100	0000 0100
5	35	011 0101	0000 0101
6	36	011 0110	0000 0110
7	37	011 0111	0000 0111
8	38	011 1000	0000 1000
9	39	011 1001	0000 1001

Example: Write an 8051 C program to convert packed BCD 0x29 to ASCII and display the bytes on P1 and P2.

Solution:

```
#include <reg51.h>

void main(void)

{

unsigned char x,y,z;

unsigned char mybyte=0x29;

x=mybyte&0x0F;

P1=x|0x30;

y=mybyte&0xF0;

y=y>>4;

P2=y|0x30;

}
```

Example: Write an 8051 C program to convert ASCII digits of '4' and '7' to packed BCD and display them on P1.

Solution:

```c
#include <reg51.h>

void main(void)

{

unsigned char bcdbyte;

unsigned char w='4';

unsigned char z='7';

w=w&0x0F;

w=w<<4;

z=z&0x0F;

bcdbyte=w|z;

P1=bcdbyte;

}
```

Example: Write an 8051 C program to calculate the checksum byte for the data 25H, 62H, 3FH, and 52H.

Steps to calculate Checksum byte in ROM are:

- Add the bytes together and drop carries.

- Take the 2's complement (invert and then add 1) of the total sum. This is the Checksum byte, which becomes the last byte of the series.

Solution:

```c
#include <reg51.h>

void main(void)

{

unsigned char mydata[]={0x25,0x62,0x3F,0x52};

unsigned char sum=0;

unsigned char x;

unsigned char chksumbyte;

for (x=0;x<4;x++)

{
```

```
P2=mydata[x];

sum=sum+mydata[x];

P1=sum;

}

chksumbyte=~sum+1; //logical operator used here

P1=chksumbyte;

}
```

Example: Write an 8051 C program to convert 11111101 (FD hex) to decimal and display the digits on P0, P1 and P2.

Solution:

```
#include <reg51.h>

void main(void)

{

unsigned char x,binbyte,d1,d2,d3;

binbyte=0xFD;

x=binbyte/10;

d1=binbyte%10;

d2=x%10;

d3=x/10;

P0=d1;

P1=d2;

P2=d3;

}
```

Accessing Code ROM Space in 8051 C

Using the code (program) space for predefined data is a widely used option in 8051. We saw how to use the Assembly language instruction MOVC to access the data stored in the 8051 code space. Here, we see the same concept with 8051 C. In 8051, we have three spaces to store data:

- The 128 bytes RAM space with address range 00-7FH:

    ∘ If you declare variables (e.g. char) to store data, C compiler will allocate a RAM space for these variable.

- User code space:

    ∘ External code memory (64K) + on-chip ROM (64K).

- ◦ Data is embedded to code or is separated as a data section.
- • External data memory for data:
  - ◦ RAM or ROM is used.

RAM Data Space Usage

The 8051 C compiler allocates RAM locations as follows:

- • Bank 0: Addresses 0 – 7.

- • Individual variables: Addresses 08 and beyond.

- • Array elements: Addresses right after variables:

  - ◦ Array elements need contiguous RAM locations and that limits the size of the array due to the fact that we have only 128 bytes of RAM for everything.

- • Stack: Addresses right after array elements.

Example: Write, compile and single-step the following program on your 8051 simulator. Examine the contents of the code space to locate the values.

Solution:

```
#include <reg51.h>

void main(void)

{

unsigned char mydata[100]; //RAM space

unsigned char x,z=0;

for (x=0;x<100;x++)

{

z--;

mydata[x]=z;

P1=z;

}

}
```

While running this program you can see how the data will be stored in an array and displayed in a port.

8052 RAM Space

One of the new features of the 8052 was an extra 128 bytes of RAM space.

- • The extra 128 bytes of RAM helps the 8051/52 C compiler to manage its registers and resources much more effectively.

- Based on 8052 architecture, you should use the reg52.h header file. Choose the 8052 option when compiling the program.

Using ROM to Store Data

To make C compiler use the code space (on-chip ROM) instead of RAM space, we can put the keyword "code" in front of the variable declaration.

```
unsigned char mydata[] = "HELLO"
```

- HELLO is saved in RAM.

```
code unsigned char mydata[] = "HELLO"
```

- HELLO is saved in ROM.

This is discussed in the following examples.

Let us compare and contrast the following programs and discuss the advantages and disadvantages of each one.

Example:

Solution:

```
#include <reg51.h>

void main(void)

{

P1="H";

P1="E";

P1="L";

P1="L";

P1="O";

}
```

Data is embedded into code. Simple, short, not flexible.

Example:

Solution:

```
#include <reg51.h>

void main(void)

{

unsigned char mydata[]="HELLO";

unsigned char z;
```

```
for (z=0; z<5; z++)

P1 = mydata[z];

}
```

Data is stored in RAM and does not occupy ROM.

Example:

Solution:

```
#include <reg51.h>

void main(void)

{

Code unsigned char mydata[]="HELLO";

unsigned char z;

for (z=0; z<5; z++)

P1 = mydata[z];

}
```

Data is stored in ROM. However, data and code are separate.

Data Serialization using 8051 C

Serializing data is a way of sending a byte of data one bit at a time through a single pin of micro-controller.

- Using the serial port.

- Transfer data one bit a time and control the sequence of data and spaces in between them.

In many new generations of devices such as LCD, ADC, and ROM, the serial versions are becoming popular since they take less space on a PCB.

Example: Write a C program to send out the value 44H serially one bit at a time via P1.0. The LSB should go out first.

Solution:

```
#include <reg51.h>

sbit P1b0=P1^0;

sbit regALSB=ACC^0;

void main(void)

{
```

```
unsigned char conbyte=0x44;

unsigned char x;

ACC=conbyte;

for (x=0;x<8;x++)

{

P1b0=regALSB;

ACC=ACC>>1;

}

}
```

Example: Write a C program to bring in a byte of data serially one bit at a time via P1.0. The MSB should come in first.

Solution:

```
#include <reg51.h>

sbit P1b0=P1^0;

sbit regALSB=ACC^0;

bit membit;

void main(void)

{

unsigned char x;

for (x=0;x<8;x++)

{

membit=P1b0;

ACC=ACC<<1;

regALSB=membit;

}

P2=ACC;

}
```

Timer Programming

A timer is a clock that controls the sequence of an event while counting in fixed intervals of time. It is used for producing precise time delay. Secondly, it can be used to repeat or initiate an action after/at a known period of time. This feature is very commonly used in several applications. An example could be setting up an alarm which triggers at a point of time or after a period of time.

Need of using Timers in a Controller

Most microcontrollers have built-in timers that not only generate time delays, but can also be used as counters to count an action or event. The value of a counter increases by one every time its corresponding action or event occurs. Timers in a controller are inbuilt chips that are controlled by special function registers (SFRs) assigned for Timer operations. These SFRs are used to configure Timers in different modes of operations. While working with microcontrollers, it is more than often required to generate time delays. There are two possible ways of generating time delays. First is by using the code, like using `for or while` loops in a C program. However, the delays provided by the software are not very precise. The other method is to use Timers. Timers provide time delays that are very precise and accurate.

8051 Timers and Registers

AT89C51 microcontroller has two Timers designated as Timer0 and Timer1. Each of these timers is assigned a 16-bit register. The value of a Timer register increases by one every time a timer counts. Timer takes a time period of one machine cycle to count one. (Machine cycle is a unit that refers to the time required by the microcontroller to execute instructions.) This means that the maximum number of times a timer can count without repeating is 2^{16}, i.e., 65536. So the maximum allowed counts in value of Timer registers can be from 0000H to FFFFH. Since 8051 is an 8 bit controller, the registers of 8051 Timers are accessed as two different registers; one for lower byte and other for higher byte. For example, register of Timer0 is accessed as TL0 for lower byte and TH0 for higher byte. Similarly TL1 and TH1 are registers assigned to Timer 1.

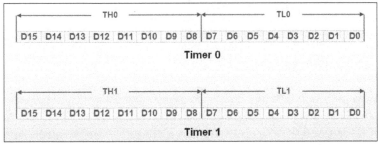

Figure: Bit Values of Timer 0 and Timer 1 of 8051 Microcontroller.

8051 Timer Issues

While using 8051 Timers certain factors need to be considered, like whether the Timer is to be used for time keeping or for counting; whether the source for time generation is external clock or the controller itself; how many bits of Timer register are to be used or left unused.

Functioning of a Timer

The registers of Timers are loaded with some initial value. The value of a Timer register increases by one after every machine cycle. One machine cycle duration is the 1/12th of the frequency of the crystal attached to the controller. For example, if the frequency of the crystal is 12 MHz, then the frequency for Timer will be 1MHz (1/12 of crystal frequency) and hence the time (T = 1/f) taken by the Timer to count by one is 1µs (1/1MHz). Similarly if an 11.0592 MHz crystal is used, operating frequency of Timer is 921.6 KHz and the time period is 1.085 µs. If no value is loaded into the Timer, it starts counting from 0000H. When the Timer reaches FFFFH, it reloads to 0000H. This roll over is communicated to the controller by raising a flag corresponding to that Timer, i.e., a flag bit is raised (set high) when the timer starts counting from 0000H again. TF0 and TF1 are the Timer flags corresponding to Timers 0 and 1. These flags must be cleared (set low) by software every time they are raised. The Timer may terminate updating register values after a roll over or continue with its operation.

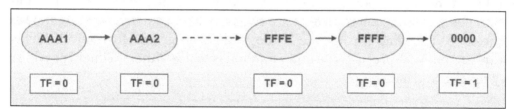

Figure: Status of Timer Flag on Roll Over.

Starting or Stopping a Timer

For every Timer, there is a corresponding Timer control bit which can be set or cleared by the program to start or stop the Timer. TR0 and TR1 are the control bits for Timers 0 and 1 respectively. Setting the control bit would start the Timer.

>TR0 = 1;   starts Timer 0

>TR1 = 1;   starts Timer 1

Clearing the control bit would stop the Timer.

>TR0 = 0;   stops Timer 0

>TR1 = 0;   stops Timer1

Configuring a Timer

A register called TMOD is used for configuring the Timers for the desired operation. TMOD is an 8-bit register with following bit configuration:

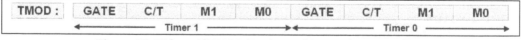

Figure: Bit Values of TMOD Register of 8051 Microcontroller.

The lower four bits (TMOD.0 – TMOD.3) are used to configure Timer 0 while the higher four bits (TMOD.4 – TMOD.7) are for Timer 1. When GATE is high, the corresponding Timer is enabled only when there is an interrupt at corresponding INTx pin of AT89C51 controller and Timer control bit is high. Otherwise only setting Timer control bit is sufficient to start the Timer. If C/T is low, Timer is used for time keeping, i.e., Timer updates its value automatically corresponding to 8051 clock source. When C/T is high, Timer is used as counter, i.e., it updates its value when it receives pulse from outside the 8051 controller. M1 and M0 bits decide the Timer modes. There are four Timer modes designated as Modes 0, 1, 2 and 3. Modes 1 and 2 are most commonly used while working with Timers.

TMOD = 0x01;   sets the mode1 of Timer0 used for timing

TMOD = 0x20;   sets the mode2 of Timer1 used for timing

Programming 8051 Timers

The programming of 8051 Timers can be done by using either polling method or by using interrupt. In polling, the microcontroller keeps monitoring the status of Timer flag. While doing so, it does no other operation and consumes all its processing time in checking the Timer flag until it is raised on a rollover. In interrupt method controller responds to only when the Timer flag is raised. The interrupt method prevents the wastage of controller's processing time unlike polling method. Polling is mostly used for time delay generation and interrupt method is more useful when waveforms are to be generated or some action has to be repeated in fixed delays.

Polling Method

The polling method involves the following algorithm:

- Configure the Timer mode by passing a hex value into the TMOD register. This will tell the controller about which Timer is be used; the mode of Timer; operation (to be used as timer or counter); and whether external interrupt is required to start Timer.

- Load the initial values in the Timer low TLx and high THx byte (x = 0/1).

- Start the Timer by setting TRx bit.

- Wait while the Timer flag TFx is raised.

- Clear the Timer flag. The Timer flag is raised when Timer rolls over from FFFFH to 0000H. If the Timer is not stopped, it will start updating from 0000H in case of modes 0 & 1 while with initial value in case of mode 2. If TFx is not cleared, controller will not be able to detect next rollover.

- Stop the Timer by clearing TRx bit. If TRx bit is not cleared the Timer will restart updating from 0000H after the rollover in case of modes 0 and 1 while with initial value in case of mode 2.

Interrupt Method

The interrupt method makes use of a register called Interrupt Enable (IE) register. An 8051 microcontroller has 6 hardware interrupts. The interrupts refer to a notification, communicated to the controller, by a hardware device or software, on receipt of which controller skips temporarily whatsoever it was doing and responds to the interrupt. The controller starts the execution of an Interrupt Service Routine (ISR) or Interrupt Handler which is a piece of code that tells the processor or controller what to do on receipt of an interrupt. After the execution of ISR, controller returns to whatever it was doing earlier (before the interrupt was received). The Interrupt Enable register has the following bits which enable or disable the hardware interrupts of 8051 microcontroller.

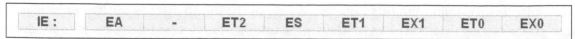

IE :	EA	-	ET2	ES	ET1	EX1	ET0	EX0

Figure: Bit Values of IE Register of 8051 Microcontroller.

When EA (IE.7) is set (=1), interrupts are enabled. When clear (EA = 0), interrupts are disabled and controller does not respond to any interrupts. ET0, ET1 & ET2 (IE.3, IE.4 & IE.5) are Timer interrupt bits. When set (high) the timer are enabled and when cleared (low) they are disabled. (8052 controllers have three Timers, so ET2 is its Timer 2 interrupt bit.) The ISR corresponding to these interrupts are executed when the TFx flags of respective Timers are raised. IE register is bit addressable. Timer programming using Timer interrupts involves following algorithm.

- Configure the Timer mode by passing a hex value to TMOD register.

- Load the initial values in the Timer low TLx and high THx byte.

- Enable the Timer interrupt by passing hex value to IE register or setting required bits of IE register. For example,

```
IE = 0x82;              enables Timer 0 interrupt
IE = 0x88;              enables Timer 1 interrupt
Or
EA = 1;
ET0 = 1;                enables Timer 0 interrupt
IE^7 = 1;
IE^3 = 1;               enables Timer 1 interrupt
```

- Start the Timer by setting TRx bit.

- Write Interrupt Service Routine (ISR) for the Timer interrupt. For example,

ISR definition for Timer 0:

```
void ISR_Timer0(void) interrupt 1
{
<Body of ISR>
}
ISR definition for Timer 1:
void ISR_Timer1(void) interrupt 3
{
<Body of ISR>
}
```

- If the Timer has to be stopped after once the interrupt has occurred, the ISR must contain the statement to stop the Timer. For example,

```
void ISR_Timer1(void) interrupt 3

{

<Body of ISR>

TR1 =0;

}
```

- If a routine written for Timer interrupt has to be repeated again and again, the Timer run bit need not be cleared. But it should be kept in mind that Timer will start updating from 0000H and not the initial values in case of mode 0 and 1. So the initial values must be re-loaded in the interrupt service routine. For example,

```
void ISR_Timer1(void) interrupt 3

{

<Body of ISR>

TH1 =0XFF;        //load with initial values if in mode 0 or 1

TL1 = 0xFC;

}
```

Different Modes of a Timer

There are four Timer modes designated as Modes 0, 1, 2 and 3. A particular mode is selected by configuring the M1 & M0 bits of TMOD register.

Mode	M1	M0	Operation
Mode 0	0	0	13-bit Timer
Mode 1	0	1	16-bit Timer
Mode 2	1	0	8-bit Auto Reload
Mode 3	1	1	Split Timer Mode

- Mode 0: 13-bit Timer - Mode 0 is a 13 bit Timer mode and uses 8 bits of high byte and 5 bit prescaler of low byte. The value that the Timer can update in mode0 is from 0000H to 1FFFH. The 5 bits of lower byte append with the bits of higher byte. The Timer rolls over from 1FFFH to 0000H to raise the Timer flag.

- Mode 1: 16-bit Timer - Mode1 is one of the most commonly used Timer modes. It allows all 16 bits to be used for the Timer and so it allows values to vary from 0000H to FFFFH. If a value, say YYXXH, is loaded into the Timer bytes, then the delay produced by the Timer will be equal to the product.

[(FFFFH – YYXXH +1) x (period of one timer clock)].

It can also be considered as follows: convert YYXXH into decimal, say NNNNN, then delay will be equal to the product:

[(65536-NNNNN) x (period of one timer clock)].

The period of one timer clock is 1.085 μs for a crystal of 11.0592 MHz frequency as discussed above. Now to produce a desired delay, divide the required delay by the Timer clock period. Assume that the division yields a number NNNNN. This is the number of times Timer must be updated before it stops. Subtract this number from 65536 (binary equivalent of FFFFH) and convert the difference into hex. This will be the initial value to be loaded into the Timer to get the desired delay.

Example code for time delay in Mode1 using polling method:

```
// Use of Timer mode 1 for blinking LED using polling method
// XTAL frequency 11.0592MHz
#include<reg51.h>
sbit led = P1^0;                        // LED connected to 1st pin of port P1
void delay();
main()
{
      unsigned int i;
      while(1)
      {
      led=~led;                         // Toggle LED
      for(i=0;i<1000;i++)
      delay();                          // Call delay
      }
}
void delay()                                    // Delay generation using Timer
0 mode 1
{
      TMOD = 0x01;                              // Mode1 of Timer0
      TH0= 0xFC;                               // FC66 evaluated hex value for
1millisecond delay
      TL0 = 0x66;
```

```
        TR0 = 1;                              // Start Timer

        while(TF0 == 0);                      // Using polling method

        TR0 = 0;                              // Stop Timer

        TF0 = 0;                              // Clear flag

    }
```

Example code for time delay in Mode1 using interrupt method:

```
    // Use of Timer mode 1 for blinking LED with interrupt method

    // XTAL frequency 11.0592MHz

    #include<reg51.h>

    sbit LED = P1^0;                          // LED connected to 1st pin of port P1

    void Timer(void) interrupt 1              // Interrupt No.1 for Timer 0

    {

        led=~led;                             // Toggle LED on interrupt

    }

    main()

    {

        TMOD = 0x01;                              // Mode1 of Timer0

        TH0=0x00;                             // Initial values loaded to Timer

        TL0=0x00;

        IE = 0x82;                            // Enable interrupt

        TR0=1;                                    // Start Timer

        while(1);                             // Do nothing

    }
```

- Mode 2: 8-bit Auto Reload - Mode 2 is an 8 bit mode. The initial value is loaded into the higher byte. A copy of the same is passed to the lower byte. The Timer can update from 00H to FFH. The Timer rolls over from FFH to initial value automatically. Mode 2 is commonly used for setting baud rates for serial communication.

Example code for time delay in Mode2 using polling method:

```
    // Use of Timer mode 2 for blinking LED with polling method

    // XTAL frequency 11.0592MHz

    #include<reg51.h>
```

```
    sbit led = P1^0;                        // LED connected to 1st pin of port
    P1void delay();

    main()

    {

        unsigned int i;

        while(1)

        {

        led=~led;                           // Toggle LED

        for(i=0;i<1000;i++)

        delay();                            // Call delay

        }

    }

    void delay()

    {

        TMOD = 0x02;                        // Mode1 of Timer0

        TH0= 0xA2;                          // Initial value loaded to Timer

        TR0 = 1;                            // Start Timer

        while(TF0 == 0);                    // Polling for flag bit

        TR0 = 0;                            // Stop Timer

        TF0 = 0;                            // Clear flag

    }
```

- Mode 3: Split Timer - In mode 3, also known as split mode, the Timer breaks into two 8-bit Timers that can count from 00H up to FFH. The initial values are loaded into the higher byte and lower byte of the Timer. In this case the start and flag bits associated with the other Timer are now associated with high byte Timer. So one cannot start or stop the other Timer. The other Timer can be used in modes 0, 1 or 2 and is updated automatically for every machine cycle. For example, if Timer0 is used in split mode, TH0 and TL0 will become separate Timers. The start and flag bits associated with Timer1 will now be associated with the TH0. Timer 1 cannot be stopped or started, but will be updated for every machine cycle. Split mode is useful when two Timers are required in addition to a baud rate generator.

Example: Write an 8051 C program to toggle all the bits of port P1 continuously with some delay in between. Use Timer 0, 16-bit mode to generate the delay.

Solution:

```
#include <reg51.h>
```

```
void T0Delay(void);

void main(void){

while (1) {

P1=0x55;

T0Delay();

P1=0xAA;

T0Delay();

} }

void T0Delay(){

TMOD=0x01;

TL0=0x00;

TH0=0x35;

TR0=1;

while (TF0==0);

TR0=0;

TF0=0;

}
```

Calculating delay:

FFFFH − 3500H = CAFFH

= 51967 + 1 = 51968

=51968 × 1.085 μs = 56.384 ms is the approximate delay.

Calculating Delay using Timer in C

The delay length depends on three factors. They are Crystal frequency, the number of clocks per machine cycle and the C compiler. To speed up the 8051, many recent versions of the 8051 have reduced the number of clocks per machine cycle from 12 to four, or even one. The frequency for the timer is always 1/12th the frequency of the crystal attached to the 8051, regardless of the 8051 version. We can also use crystal frequency as the clock source. The following are the steps to find TH, TL register values. We can assume XTAL = 11.0592 MHz for 8051 systems.

Steps for finding the TH, TL Register Values:

- Divide the desired time delay by 1.085 μs.

- Perform 65536 − n, where n is the decimal value.

- Convert the result to hex, where yyxx is the initial hex value to be loaded into the timer's register.

- Set TL = xx and TH = yy.

Times 0/1 Delay using Mode 1 (16-bit Non-auto-reload)

Example: Write an 8051 C program to toggle only bit P1.5 continuously every 50 ms. Use Timer 0, mode 1 (16-bit) to create the delay. Test the program on the (a) AT89C51 and (b) DS89C420.

Solution:

```
#include <reg51.h>

void T0M1Delay(void);

sbit mybit=P1^5;

void main(void){

while (1) {

mybit=~mybit;

T0M1Delay();

}}

void T0M1Delay(void){

TMOD=0x01;

TL0=0xFD;

TH0=0x4B;

TR0=1;

while (TF0==0);

TR0=0;

TF0=0;

}

FFFFH – 4BFDH = B402H

= 46082 + 1 = 46083

Timer delay= 46083 × 1.085 µs = 50 ms
```

Example: Write an 8051 C program to toggle all bits of P2 continuously every 500 ms. Use Timer 1, mode 1 to create the delay.

Solution:

```
//tested for DS89C420, XTAL = 11.0592 MHz
```

```
#include <reg51.h>
void T1M1Delay(void);
void main(void){
unsigned char x;
P2=0x55;
while (1) {
P2=~P2;
for (x=0;x<20;x++)
T1M1Delay();
} }
void T1M1Delay(void){
TMOD=0x10;
TL1=0xFE;
TH1=0xA5;
TR1=1;
while (TF1==0);
TR1=0;
TF1=0;}
```

Delay:

A5FEH = 42494 in decimal

65536 − 42494 = 23042

23042 × 1.085 μs = 25 ms and 20 × 25 ms = 500 ms.

Example: Write an 8051 C program to toggle only pin P1.5 continuously every 250 ms, Use Timer 0, mode 2 (8-bit auto-reload) to create the delay.

Solution:

```
#include <reg51.h>
void T0M2Delay(void);
sbit mybit=P1^5;
void main(void){
unsigned char x,y;
```

```
while (1) {

mybit=~mybit;

for (x=0;x<250;x++)

for (y=0;y<36;y++) //we put 36, not 40 due to overhead of the for loop in C

T0M2Delay();

} }

void T0M2Delay(void){

TMOD=0x02;

TH0=-23;

TR0=1;

while (TF0==0);

TR0=0;

TF0=0;}
```

Time Delay:

$$256 - 23 = 233$$

$$23 \times 1.085 \, \mu s = 25 \, \mu s$$

$$25 \, \mu s \times 250 \times 40 = 250 \, ms$$

Due to overhead of the for loop in C, we put 36 instead of 40.

Example: Write an 8051 C program to create a frequency of 2500 Hz on pin P2.7. Use Timer 1, mode 2 to create delay.

Solution:

```
#include <reg51.h>

void T1M2Delay(void);

sbit mybit=P2^7;

void main(void){

unsigned char x;

while (1) {

mybit=~mybit;

T1M2Delay();

}}
```

```
void T1M2Delay(void){

TMOD=0x20;

TH1=-184;

TR1=1;

while (TF1==0);

TR1=0;

TF1=0;}
```

Time Delay:

$$1/2500 \text{ Hz} = 400 \text{ µs}$$

$$400 \text{ µs} /2 = 200 \text{ µs}$$

$$200 \text{ µs} / 1.085 \text{ µs} = 184$$

Example: A switch is connected to pin P1.2. Write an 8051 C program to monitor SW and create the following frequencies on pin P1.7:

SW=0: 500Hz

SW=1: 750Hz, use Timer 0, mode 1 for both of them.

Solution:

```
#include <reg51.h>

sbit mybit=P1^5;

sbit SW=P1^7;

void T0M1Delay(unsigned char);

void main(void){

SW=1;

while (1) {

mybit=~mybit;

if (SW==0)

T0M1Delay(0);

else

T0M1Delay(1);

}}

void T0M1Delay(unsigned char c){
```

```
TMOD=0x01;

if (c==0) {

TL0=0x67;

TH0=0xFC;}

else {

TL0=0x9A;

TH0=0xFD;

}

TR0=1;

while (TF0==0);

TR0=0;

TF0=0;}
```

Frequency:

$$FC67H = 64615$$

$$65536 - 64615 = 921$$

$$921 \times 1.085\ \mu s = 999.285\ \mu s$$

$$1 / (999.285\ \mu s \times 2) = 500\ Hz$$

C Programming of Timers 0 and 1 as Counters

Timers can also be used as counters counting events happening outside the 8051.When it is used as a counter, it is a pulse outside of the 8051 that increments TH, TL registers. TMOD and TH, TL registers are the same as for the timer discussed previously. Programming the timer in the last section also applies to programming it as a counter, except the source of the frequency. The C/T bit in the TMOD registers decides the source of the clock for the timer. When C/T = 1, the timer is used as a counter and gets its pulses from outside the 8051, the counter counts up as pulses are fed from pins 14 and 15, these pins are called T0 (timer0 input) and T1 (timer 1 input). The following figure shows the port 3 used for Timers 0 and 1 function.

Port 3 pins used for Timers 0 and 1			
Pin	Port Pin	Function	Description
14	P3.4	T0	Timer/counter 0 external input
15	P3.5	T1	Timer/counter 1 external input

The figure shown below gives the details about functions of timers with external input in mode 1 and mode 2.

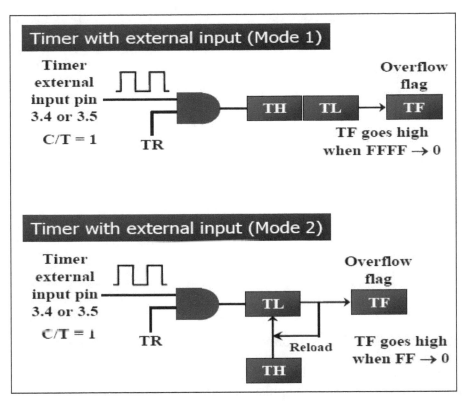

TCON register is a bit addressable register. The following is the function of TCON register for counters. The equivalent instruction for the TCON register is:

For timer 0					
	SETB	TR0	=	SETB	TCON.4
	CLR	TR0	=	CLR	TCON.4
	SETB	TF0	=	SETB	TCON.5
	CLR	TF0	=	CLR	TCON.5
For timer 1					
	SETB	TR1	=	SETB	TCON.6
	CLR	TR1	=	CLR	TCON.6
	SETB	TF1	=	SETB	TCON.7
	CLR	TF1	=	CLR	TCON.7

Example: Assume that a 1-Hz external clock is being fed into pin T1 (P3.5). Write a C program for counter 1 in mode 2 (8-bit auto reload) to count up and display the state of the TL1 count on P1. Start the count at 0H.

Solution:

```
#include <reg51.h>

sbit T1=P3^5;
```

```
void main(void){

T1=1;

TMOD=0x60;

TH1=0;

while (1) {

do {

TR1=1;

P1=TL1;

}

while (TF1==0);

TR1=0;

TF1=0;

}}
```

P1 is connected to 8 LEDs. T1 (P3.5) is connected to a 1-Hz external clock.

Example: Assume that a 1-Hz external clock is being fed into pin T0 (P3.4). Write a C program for counter 0 in mode 1 (16-bit) to count the pulses and display the state of the TH0 and TL0 registers on P2 and P1, respectively.

Solution:

```
#include <reg51.h>

void main(void){

T0=1;

TMOD=0x05;

TL0=0

TH0=0;

while (1) {

do {

TR0=1;

P1=TL0;

P2=TH0;

}

while (TF0==0);
```

```
TR0=0;

TF0=0;

} }
```

The example explained above shows the 8051 C program to count up and display it on TH0 and TL0 registers in pin P2 and P1 respectively. The External clock connected to T0 on P3.4.

Interrupts in 8051

It is a sub-routine calls that given by the microcontroller when some other program with high priority is request for acquiring the system buses than interrupt occur in current running program. Interrupts provide a method to postpone or delay the current process, performs a sub-routine task and then restart the standard program again.

Types of Interrupt in 8051 Microcontroller

- Timer 0 overflow interrupt: TF0.

- External hardware interrupt: INT0.

- Timer 1 overflow interrupt: TF1.

- External hardware interrupt: INT1.

- Scrial communication interrupt: RI/TI.

The timer and serial interrupts are internally produced by the microcontroller, whereas the external interrupts are produced by additional interfacing devices or switches that are externally connected with the microcontroller. These external interrupts can be level triggered or edge triggered. When interrupt occur then the microcontroller executes the interrupt service routine. Therefore the memory location corresponds to interrupt enables it. Consider the interrupt corresponding to the memory location is shown in the interrupt vector table.

Interrupt Number	Interrupt Description	Address
0	EXTERNAL INT 0	0003h
1	TIMER/COUNTER 0	000Bh
2	EXTERNAL INT 1	0013h
3	TIMER/COUNTER 1	001Bh
4	SERIAL PORT	0023h

Interrupt Structure of 8051 Microcontroller

After 'RESET' all the interrupts get disabled, and therefore, all the interrupts is enabled by software. From all the five interrupts, if anyone or all interrupt are activated, this will sets the corresponding interrupt flags as represent in the figure which corresponds to interrupt structure of 8051 micro-controller:

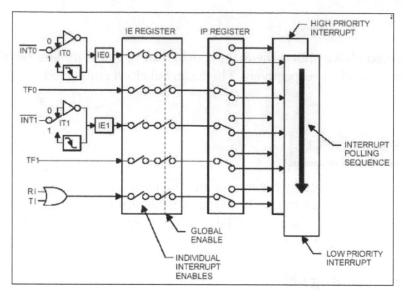

All the interrupts can be set or cleared by some special function register that is also known as interrupt enabled (IE), and it is totally depends on the priority, which is executed by using interrupt priority register.

Interrupt Enable (IE) Register

IE register is used for enabling and disabling the interrupt. This is a bit addressable register in which EA value must be set to one for enabling interrupts. The individual bits in this register enables the particular interrupt like timer, serial and external inputs. Consider in the below IE register, bit corresponds to 1 activate the interrupt and 0 disable the interrupt.

EA	--	--	ES	ET1	EX1	ET0	EX0

EA	IE.7	Disables all interrupts, If EA = 0, no interrupt will be acknowledged. If EA = 1, interrupt source is individually enable or disabled by setting or clearing its enable bit.
--	IE.6	Not implemented, reserved for future use.
--	IE.5	Not implemented, reserved for future use.
ES	IE.4	Enable or disable the Serial port interrupt.
ET1	IE.3	Enable or disable the Timer 1 overflow interrupt.
EX1	IE.2	Enable or disable External interrupt 1.
ET0	IE.1	Enable or disable the Timer 0 overflow interrupt.
EX0	IE.0	Enable or disable External interrupt 0.

Interrupt Priority Register (IP)

Using IP register it is possible to change the priority levels of an interrupts by clearing or setting the individual bit in the Interrupt priority (IP) register as shown in figure. It allows the low priority interrupt can interrupt the high-priority interrupt, but it prohibits the interruption by using another low-priority interrupt. If the priorities of interrupt are not programmed, then microcontroller executes the instruction in a predefined manner and its order are INT0, TF0, INT1, TF1, and SI.

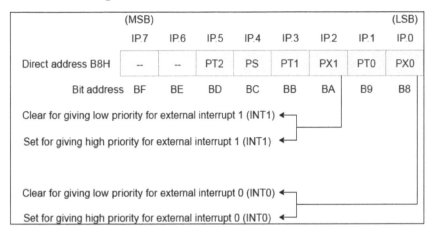

The timer flag (TF) is raised when the timer rolls over:

- In polling mode, we have to wait until the TF is raised. The microcontroller is tied down while waiting for TF to be raised, and cannot do anything else.

- If the timer interrupt in the IE register is enabled, whenever the timer rolls over, the Timer Flag is raised. After that the microcontroller is interrupted in whatever it is doing, and jumps to the interrupt vector table to service the ISR. In this way, the microcontroller can do other work until it is notified that the timer has rolled over.

The figure shown below gives the details about TF interrupt. If the timer interrupt is enabled, whenever TF=1, the microcontroller is interrupted in whatever it is doing, and jumps to the interrupt vector table to service the ISR.

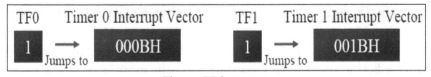

Figure: TF interrupt.

The Example gives details about generating a square wave using Timer 0 assuming that XTAL value is 11.0592 MHz.

Example: Write a C program that continuously gets a single bit of data from P1.7 and sends it to P1.0, while simultaneously creating a square wave of 200 µs period on pin P2.5. Use Timer 0 to create the square wave. Assume that XTAL = 11.0592 MHz.

Solution: We will use timer 0 in mode 2 (auto-reload). One half of the period is 100 µs. 100/1.085 µs = 92, and TH0 = 256 - 92 = 164 or A4H.

```
#include <reg51.h>

sbit SW =P1^7;

sbit IND =P1^0;

sbit WAVE =P2^5;

void timer0(void) interrupt 1

{

WAVE=~WAVE; //toggle pin

}

void main()

{

SW=1; //make switch input

TMOD=0x02;

TH0=0xA4; //TH0=-92

IE=0x82; //enable interrupt for timer 0

while (1)

{

IND=SW; //send switch to LED

}

}
```

Programming the Serial Communication Interrupt

There is only one interrupt for serial communication. It is used to both send and receive the data. If the interrupt bit in the IE register (IE.4) is enabled, when RI (Received interrupt) or TI (transfer interrupt) is raised, the 8051 gets interrupted and jumps to memory location 0023H to execute the ISR. In ISR, the programmer has to examine the TI and RI flags to see which one has caused the interrupt and take action accordingly. Serial interrupt mainly used for receiving and not for sending the data.

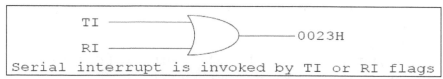

Figure: Single Interrupt for both TI and RI.

Example below is used for creating a square wave of 200 us period on pin P2.5 and sending letter 'A' to the serial port. It uses Timer0 to create the square wave.

Example: Write a C program that continuously gets a single bit of data from P1.7 and sends it to P1.0, while simultaneously (a) creating a square wave of 200 us period on pin P2.5, and (b) sending letter 'A' to the serial port. Use Timer 0 to create the square wave. Assume that XTAL = 11.0592 MHz. Use the 9600 baud rate.

Solution: We will use Time 0 in mode 2 (auto-reload). TH0 = 100/1.085 µs = −92, which is A4H.

```c
#include <reg51.h>

sbit SW     = p1 ^ 7;

sbit IND    = p1 ^ 0;

sbit WAVE   = p2 ^ 5;

void timer0 (void) interrupt 1

{

      WAVE = ~ WAVE;          //toggle pin

}

Void serial0 () interrupt 4

{

      if (TI ==1)

         {

            SBUF = 'A' ;       //send A to serial port

            TI = 0;            // clear interrupt

         }

      else

         {

      RI = 0;                  //clear interrupt

         }

}

void main ()

   {

            SW = 1;            //make switch input

            TH1 = -3;          //9600 baud

            TMOD = 0 × 22;     //mode 2 for both timers

            TH0 = 0 × A4;      //-92 = A4H for timer 0
```

```
SCON = 0 × 50;

TR0 = 1;

TR1 = 1;            //start timer

IE = 0 × 92         //enable interrupt for T0

While (1)           //stay here
{
        IND = SW;   //send switch to LED
}
}
```

Programming the External Hardware Interrupt

Two external hardware interrupts are available in 8051.They are level triggered and edge triggered interrupt. The interrupt vector table locations 0003H and 0013H are set aside for INT0 and INT1.

- Level Triggered Interrupt: The level-triggered or level-activated interrupt is the default mode upon reset of the 8051. INT0 and INT1 pins are normally high in the level trigger mode, while the low-level signal on INT0 or INT1 triggers the interrupt. Once the interrupt occurs, the microcontroller stops whatever it is doing and jumps to the interrupt vector table to service that interrupt. The low-level interrupt signal is to be removed before the execution of the last instruction of the ISR, RETI. If low level signal is not removed it results in another interrupt being generated.

- Edge Triggered Interrupt: To make INT0 and INT1 edge triggered interrupts, we must program the bits of the TCON register. The details of TCON register is given in table.

Table: TCON Register.

7	6	5	4	3	2	1	0
TF1	TR1	TF0	TR0	IE1	IT1	IE0	IT0
Bit Number	Bit Mnemonic	Description					
7	TF1	Timer 1 Overflow Flag Cleared by hardware when processor vectors to interrupt routine. Set by hardware on timer/counter overflow, when the timer 1 register overflows.					
6	TR1	Timer 1 Run Control Bit Clear to turn off timer/counter 1. Set to turn on timer/counter 1.					

5	TF0	Timer 0 overflow Flag
		Cleared by hardware when processor vectors to interrupt routine.
		Set by hardware on timer/counter overflow, when the timer 0 register overflows.
4	TR0	Timer 0 Run Control Bit
		Clear to turn off timer/counter 0.
		Set to turn on timer/counter 0.
3	IE1	Interrupt 1 Edge Flag
		Cleared by hardware when interrupt is processed if edge-triggered.
		Set by hardware when interrupt is detected on INT#1.
2	IT1	Interrupt 1 Type Control Bit
		Clear to select low level active (level triggered) for external interrupt 1 (INT1#).
		Set to select falling edge active (edge triggered) for external interrupt 1.
1	IE0	Interrupt 0 Edge Flag
		Cleared by hardware when interrupt is processed if edge-triggered.
		Set by hardware when external interrupt is detected on INT0# pin.
0	IT0	Interrupt 0 Type Control Bit
		Clear to select low level active (level triggered) for external interrupt 0 (INT0#).
		Set to select falling edge active (edge triggered) for external interrupt.

Sampling the Edge-Triggered Interrupt

The external source must be held high for at least one machine cycle, and then held low for at least one machine cycle. The falling edge of pins INT0 and INT1 are latched by the 8051 and are held by the TCON.1 and TCON.3 bits of TCON register. These function as interrupt-inservice flags. It indicates that the interrupt is being serviced now. On this INTn pin, no new interrupt will be responded to until this service is finished. When the ISRs are finished, TCON.1 and TCON.3 are cleared. The interrupt is finished and the 8051 is ready to respond to another interrupt on that pin. During the time that the interrupt service routine is being executed, the INTn pin is ignored, no matter how many times it makes a high-to-low transition. RETI clears the corresponding bit in TCON register (TCON.1 or TCON.3). There is no need for instruction CLR TCON.1 before RETI in the ISR associated with INT0.

Example below shows a C program to Light all LEDS connected to Port 0 if the switch is pressed and display "y" at port2.

Example: A switch is connected to pin P3.2. When switch is pressed the corresponding line goes low. Write a C program to Light all LEDS connected to Port 0 if the switch is pressed. Display "y" at port2.

Solution:

```
# include <reg51.h>

Sbit switch = P3^2;
```

```
void extint0() // interrupt 0

{

P0=0xFF;

}

void main()

{

    Switch=1;

    IE=0x81;

    While(1)

  {

        P2="y";

  }

}
```

Interrupt Flag Bits for 8051

The TCON register holds four of the interrupt flags in the 8051. The interrupt flag bits for 8051 are shown in table. The SCON register has the RI and TI flags.

Table: Interrupt Flag Bits for the 8051.

Interrupt	Flag	SFR Register Bit
External 0	IE0	TCON.1
External 1	IE1	TCON.3
Timer 0	TF0	TCON.5
Timer 1	TF1	TCON.7
Serial port	T1	SCON.1
Timer 2	TF2	T2CON.7 (AT89C52)
Timer 2	EXT2	T2CON.6 (AT89C52)

Example shown below gives the C program to receive data serially and send it to P0.

Example: Write a C program using interrupts to do the following: (a) Receive data serially and send it to P0 (b) Read port P1, transmit data serially, and give a copy to P2 (c) Make timer 0 generate a square wave of 5 kHz frequency on P0.1. Assume that XTAL = 11.0592 MHz. Set the baud rate at 4800.

Solution:

```
void main()

{

unsigned char x;
```

```
P1=0xFF; //make P1 an input

TMOD=0x22;

TH1=0xF6; //4800 baud rate

SCON=0x50;

TH0=0xA4; //5 kHz has T=200us

IE=0x92; //enable interrupts

TR1=1; //start timer 1

TR0=1; //start timer 0

while (1)

{

x=P1; //read value from pins

SBUF=x; //put value in buffer

P2=x; //write value to pins

}

}
```

Example given below show the details about how to write an Embedded C program to generate 10 KHz frequency wave and use timer 1 as an event counter to count up to 1-Hz pulse.

Example: Write a C program using interrupts to do the following: (a) Generate a 10 KHz frequency on P2.1 using T0 8-bit auto-reload, (b) Use timer 1 as an event counter to count up a 1-Hz pulse and display it on P0. The pulse is connected to EX1. Assume that XTAL = 11.0592 MHz. Set the baud rate at 9600.

Solution:

```
#include <reg51.h>

sbit WAVE =P2^1;

Unsigned char cnt;

void timer0() interrupt 1

{

WAVE=~WAVE; //toggle pin

}

void timer1() interrupt 3

{

cnt++; //increment counter
```

```
P0=cnt; //display value on pins

}

void main()

{

cnt=0; //set counter to 0

TMOD=0x42;

TH0=0x-46; //10 KHz

IE=0x86; //enable interrupts

TR0=1; //start timer 0

while (1); //wait until interrupted

}
```

Serial Port Programming in Embedded C

The microcontroller MCS51 has an inbuilt UART for carrying out serial communication. The serial communication is done in the asynchronous mode. A serial port, like other PC ports, is a physical interface to establish data transfer between computer and an external hardware or device. This transfer, through serial port, takes place bit by bit.

- Bit Addressable: We can assign the values bit by bit. For example for single bit we can set weather 1 or 0.

- Byte Addressable: We can't assign the values bit by bit. We can set only byte by byte. First we will see the SFRs.

Registers used for UART

- SCON (Serial Control Register) – Bit Addressable.
- SBUF (Serial Buffer Register) – Byte Addressable.
- PCON (Power Control Register) – Byte Addressable.

SCON (Serial Control Register)

This register is bit addressable:

SM0	SM1	SM2	REN	TB8	RB8	TI	RI

- SM0: Serial Port Mode Specifier 1 bit.
- SM1: Serial port Mode Specifier 2 bit.

These two bits are used to select the Mode of the UART:

SM0	SM1	Mode	Baudrate
0	0	Shift Register (Mode 0)	Fosc/12
0	1	8-bit UART (Mode 1)	Variable (Set by Timer 1)
1	0	9-bit UART (Mode 2)	Fosc/32 or Fosc/64
1	1	9-bit UART (Mode 3)	Variable (Set by Timer 1)

- SM2: Multiprocessor communications bit. Set/cleared by program to enable multiprocessor communications in modes 2 and 3. When set to 1 an interrupt is generated if bit 9 of the received data is a 1; no interrupt is generated if bit 9 is a 0. If set to 1 for mode 1, no interrupt will be generated unless a valid stop bit is received. Clear to 0 if mode 0 is in use.

- REN: Receive enable bit. Set to 1 to enable reception; cleared to 0 to disable reception.

- TB8: Transmitted bit 8. Set/cleared by program in modes 2 and 3.

- RB8: Received bit 8. Bit 8 of received data in modes 2 and 3; stop bit in mode1. Not used in mode 0.

- TI: Transmit Interrupt flag. Set to one at the end of bit 7 time in mode 0, and at the beginning of the stop bit for other modes. Must be cleared by the program.

- RI: Receive Interrupt flag. Set to one at the end of bit 7 time in mode 0, and halfway through the stop bit for other moves. Must be cleared by the program.

The first four bits (bits 4 through 7) are configuration bits. Bits SM0 and SM1 let us set the serial mode to a value between 0 and 3, inclusive. The four modes are defined in the chart immediately above. As you can see, selecting the Serial Mode selects the mode of operation (8-bit/9-bit, UART or Shift Register) and also determines how the baud rate will be calculated. In modes 0 and 2 the baud rate is fixed based on the oscillator's frequency. In modes 1 and 3 the baud rate is variable based on how often Timer 1 overflows. We'll talk more about the various Serial Modes in a moment. The next bit, SM2, is a flag for "Multiprocessor communication." Generally, whenever a byte has been received the 8051 will set the "RI" (Receive Interrupt) flag. This lets the program know that a byte has been received and that it needs to be processed. However, when SM2 is set the "RI" flag will only be triggered if the 9th bit received was a "1". That is to say, if SM2 is set and a byte is received whose 9th bit is clear, the RI flag will never be set. This can be useful in certain advanced serial applications. For now it is safe to say that you will almost always want to clear this bit so that the flag is set upon reception of any character. The next bit, REN, is "Receiver Enable." This bit is very straightforward: If you want to receive data via the serial port, set this bit. You will almost always want to set this bit. The last four bits (bits 0 through 3) are operational bits. They are used when actually sending and receiving data. They are not used to configure the serial port.

The TB8 bit is used in modes 2 and 3. In modes 2 and 3, a total of nine data bits are transmitted. The first 8 data bits are the 8 bits of the main value, and the ninth bit is taken from TB8. If TB8 is set and a value is written to the serial port, the data's bits will be written to the serial line followed by a "set" ninth bit. If TB8 is clear the ninth bit will be "clear." The RB8 also operates in modes 2 and 3 and functions essentially the same way as TB8, but on the reception side. When a byte is received in modes 2 or 3, a total of nine bits are received. In this case, the first eight bits received are the data of the serial byte received and the value of the ninth bit received will be placed in RB8. TI means "Transmit Interrupt." When a program writes a value to the serial port, a certain amount of time will pass before the individual bits of the byte are "clocked out" the serial port. If the program were to write another byte to the serial port before the first byte was completely output, the data being sent would be garbled. Thus, the 8051 lets the program know that it has "clocked out" the last byte by setting the TI bit. When the TI bit is set, the program may assume that the serial port is "free" and ready to send the next byte. Finally, the RI bit means "Receive Interrupt." It functions similarly to the "TI" bit, but it indicates that a byte has been received. That is to say, whenever the 8051 has received a complete byte it will trigger the RI bit to let the program know that it needs to read the value quickly, before another byte is read.

SBUF (Serial Buffer Register)

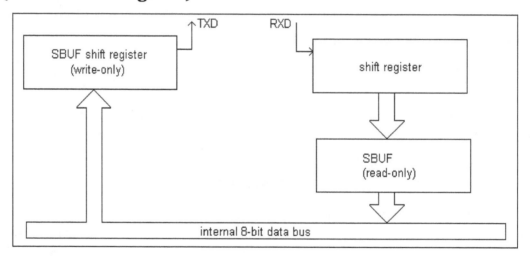

- SBUF Register: For a byte of data to be transferred via the TxD line, it must be placed in the SBUF.

- SBUF holds the byte of data when it is received by the MCS51's RxD line.

PCON (Power Control Register)

This Register is not Bit Addressable:

SMOD	–	–	–	GF1	GF0	PD	IDL

- SMOD: Double baud rate bit. If Timer 1 is used to generate baud rate and SMOD = 1, the baud rate is doubled when the serial port is used in modes 1, 2, or 3.

- GF1: General-purpose flag bit.

- GF0: General-purpose flag bit.

- PD: Power Down bit. Setting this bit activates the Power Down operation in the 8051BH. (Available only in CHMOS).

- IDL: Idle Mode bit. Setting this bit activates Idle Mode operation in the 8051BH. (Available only in CHMOS).

Initialize the UART (Configuration)

That's all about Registers. When using the integrated serial port, obviously configure it. This lets us tell the 8051 how many data bits we want, the baud rate we will be using, and how the baud rate will be determined. Here we are going to use Mode 1. Because that is 8-bit UART and we can generate baudrate using Timer 1. So, Mode 1 means we have to give 0x50 value to the SCON Register.

Generating Baudrate using Timer 1

Once the Serial Port Mode has been configured, as explained above, the program must configure the serial port's baud rate. This only applies to Serial Port modes 1 and 3. The Baud Rate is determined based on the oscillator's frequency when in mode 0 and 2. In mode 0, the baud rate is always the oscillator frequency divided by 12. This means if you're crystal is 11.0592Mhz, mode 0 baud rate will always be 921,583 baud. In mode 2 the baud rate is always the oscillator frequency divided by 64, so a 11.059Mhz crystal speed will yield a baud rate of 172,797. In modes 1 and 3, the baud rate is determined by how frequently timer 1 overflows. The more frequently timer 1 overflows, the higher the baud rate. There are many ways one can cause timer 1 to overflow at a rate that determines a baud rate, but the most common method is to put timer 1 in 8-bit auto-reload mode (timer mode 2) and set a reload value (TH1) that causes Timer 1 to overflow at a frequency appropriate to generate a baud rate. To determine the value that must be placed in TH1 to generate a given baud rate, we may use the following equation (assuming PCON.7 is clear).

Calculation:

TH1 = 256 - ((Crystal / 384) / Baud)

If PCON.7 is set then the baud rate is effectively doubled, thus the equation becomes:

TH1 = 256 - ((Crystal / 192) / Baud)

For example, if we have an 11.0592Mhz crystal and we want to configure the serial port to 19,200 baud we try plugging it in the first equation:

TH1 = 256 - ((Crystal / 384) / Baud)

TH1 = 256 - ((11059000 / 384) / 19200)

TH1 = 256 - ((28,799) / 19200)

TH1 = 256 - 1.5 = 254.5

As you can see, to obtain 19,200 baud on a 11.059Mhz crystal we'd have to set TH1 to 254.5. If we set it to 254 we will have achieved 14,400 baud and if we set it to 255 we will have achieved 28,800 baud. Thus we're stuck. But not quite to achieve 19,200 baud we simply need to set PCON.7 (SMOD). When we do this we double the baud rate and utilize the second equation mentioned above. Thus we have:

TH1 = 256 - ((Crystal / 192) / Baud)

TH1 = 256 - ((11059000 / 192) / 19200)

$$TH1 = 256 - ((57699) / 19200)$$

$$TH1 = 256 - 3 = 253$$

Here we are able to calculate a nice, even TH1 value. Therefore, to obtain 19,200 baud with an 11.059MHz crystal we must:

- Configure Serial Port mode 1 or 3.

- Configure Timer 1 to timer mode 2 (8-bit auto-reload).

- Set TH1 to 253 to reflect the correct frequency for 19,200 baud.

- Set PCON.7 (SMOD) to double the baud rate.

Code for Generating 9600 Baudrate

```
SCON=0x50;          //Mode 1, Baudrate generating using Timer 1

TMOD=0x20;          //Timer 1 Auto reload mode

TH1=TL1=0xfd;       //Values Calculated for 9600 baudrate

TR1=1;              //Run the timer
```

Programming for UART

Program: This program is used to send the data "embetronicx" via serial port to the computer.

```
#include<reg51.h>

void send(unsigned char *s)

{

    while(*s) {

        SBUF=*s++;

        while(TI==0);

        TI=0;

    }

}

void main()

{

    unsigned int i;

    SCON=0x50;

    TMOD=0x20;

    TH1=TL1=0xfd;
```

```
    TR1=1;

    while(1) {

        send("Embetronicx  ");

        for(i=0;  i<=35000;  i++);

    }

}
```

Output:

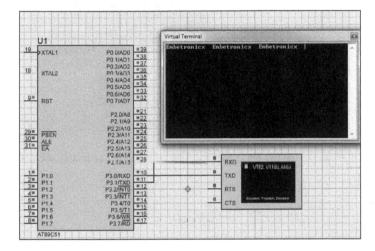

Program: In this program we have added the receiver code also. This code sends the data to 8051 microcontroller whatever we typing in the keyboard of the computer. Then microcontroller again resend the data to computer.

```
#include<reg51.h>

void main()

{

    unsigned char a;

    SCON=0x50;

    TMOD=0x20;

    TH1=TL1=0xfd;

    TR1=1;

    while(1) {

        while(RI==0);

        RI-0;

        a=SBUF;              //Received data is stored into the a variable

        SBUF=a;              //Send the character in the variable a
```

```
        while(TI==0);

        TI=0;

    }

}
```

Output:

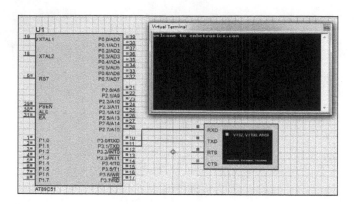

Example: Write a C program for 8051 to transfer the letter "A" serially at 4800 baud continuously. Use 8-bit data and 1 stop bit.

Solution:

```
#include <reg51.h>

void main(void){

TMOD=0x20; //use Timer 1, mode 2

TH1=0xFA; //4800 baud rate

SCON=0x50;

TR1=1;

while (1) {

SBUF='A'; //place value in buffer

while (TI==0);

TI=0;

}

}
```

Example: Write an 8051 C program to transfer the message "YES" serially at 9600 baud, 8-bit data, 1 stop bit. Do this continuously.

Solution:

```
#include <reg51.h>

void SerTx(unsigned char);
```

```c
void main(void){
TMOD=0x20; //use Timer 1, mode 2
TH1=0xFD; //9600 baud rate
SCON=0x50;
TR1=1; //start timer
while (1) {
SerTx('Y');
SerTx('E');
SerTx('S');
}
}
void SerTx(unsigned char x){
SBUF=x; //place value in buffer
while (TI==0); //wait until transmitted
TI=0;
}
```

Example below gives the details about how to receive the data serially and put in Port P1 with 4800 baud and 1 stop bit. Here, Timer 1 in mode 2 is used for stopping the bit while receiving the data. The received data stored in the SBUF is then written to port P1.

Example: Program the 8051 in C to receive bytes of data serially and put them in P1. Set the baud rate at 4800; use 8-bit data, and 1 stop bit.

```c
#include <reg51.h>
void main(void){
unsigned char mybyte;
TMOD=0x20; //use Timer 1, mode 2
TH1=0xFA; //4800 baud rate
SCON=0x50;
TR1=1; //start timer
while (1) { //repeat forever
      while (RI==0); //wait to receive
            mybyte=SBUF; //save value
P1=mybyte; //write value to port
```

```
RI=0;

}

}
```

Example described below gives the details about sending two messages to serial port with 28,800 and 56K baud. Here Timer 1 in mode 2 is used. The data is stored in the SBUF and then it waits to transmit to the corresponding destination.

Example: Write an 8051 C Program to send the two messages "Normal Speed" and "High Speed" to the serial port. Assuming that SW is connected to pin P2.0, monitor its status and set the baud rate as follows: SW = 0, 28,800 baud rate, SW = 1, 56K baud rate. Assume that XTAL = 11.0592 MHz for both cases.

Solution:

```
#include <reg51.h>

sbit MYSW=P2^0; //input switch

void main(void){

unsigned char z;

unsigned char Mess1[]="Normal Speed";

unsigned char Mess2[]="High Speed";

TMOD=0x20; //use Timer 1, mode 2

TH1=0xFF; //28800 for normal

SCON=0x50;

TR1=1; //start timer

if(MYSW==0) {

for (z=0;z<12;z++) {

      SBUF=Mess1[z]; //place value in buffer

      while(TI==0); //wait for transmit

      TI=0;

}

}

else {

PCON=PCON|0x80; //for high speed of 56K

      for (z=0;z<10;z++) {

            SBUF=Mess2[z]; //place value in buffer
```

```
                    while(TI==0); //wait for transmit

                    TI=0;

}

}

}
```

Example described below gives the details about transferring the letter A serially with 4,800 baud continuously. Here Timer 1 in mode 2 is used to set the baud rate. The data is stored in the SBUF and new addresses for DS89C4x0 chip are declared using SFR registers using sfr keyword.

Example: Write a C program for the DS89C4x0 to transfer the letter "A" serially at 4800 baud continuously. Use the second serial port with 8-bit data and 1 stop bit. (We can only use Timer 1 to set the baud rate).

Solution:

```
#include <reg51.h>

sfr SBUF1=0xC1;

sfr SCON1=0xC0;

sbit TI1=0xC1;

void main(void){

TMOD=0x20; //use Timer 1, mode 2

TH1=0xFA; //4800 baud rate

SCON1=0x50; //use 2nd serial port SCON1

TR1=1; //start timer

while (1) {

SBUF1='A'; //use 2nd serial port SBUF1

while (TI1==0); //wait for transmit

TI1=0;

}}
```

Example described below gives the details about receiving the data serially with 9,600 bauds via second serial port. Here Timer 1 in mode 2 is used to set the baud rate.

Example: Program the DS89C4x0 in C to receive bytes of data serially via the second serial port and put them in P1. Set the baud rate at 9600, 8-bit data and 1 stop bit. Use Timer 1 for baud rate generation.

Solution:

```
#include <reg51.h>
```

```
sfr SBUF1=0xC1;

sfr SCON1=0xC0;

sbit RI1=0xC0;

void main(void){

unsigned char mybyte;

TMOD=0x20; //use Timer 1, mode 2

TH1=0xFD; //9600 baud rate

SCON1=0x50; //use 2nd serial port SCON1

TR1=1; //start timer

while (1) {

    while (RI1==0); //monitor RI1

    mybyte=SBUF1; //use SBUF1

    P2=mybyte; //place value on port

    RI1=0;

}

}
```

Permissions

Index

Printed in the USA
CPSIA information can be obtained
at www.ICGtesting.com
JSHW051420221024
72173JS00006B/1383